FASHION & PERVERSITY

FASHION & PERVERSITY

A Life of
Vivienne Westwood

and the sixties laid bare

Fred Vermorel

BLOOMSBURY

First published in Great Britain 1996
Bloomsbury Publishing Plc, 2 Soho Square, London W1V 6HB
Copyright © 1996 by Fred Vermorel
The moral right of the author has been asserted

PICTURE SOURCES
Lisa Butler: page 6 *top*
Bob Gruen: page 3 *top*
Richard Lappas: page 1 *top left & right*
Laurie Lewis/*Sunday Times*: page 7 *top*
Norman Lomax: pages 6 *bottom*, 8 *inset*
Barry Plummer: page 4 *bottom*
Rex Features: page 4 *bottom*
Solo Syndication: pages 5 *top*, 8
Today/Rex Features: page 7 *bottom*
Virgin: page 3 *bottom*
Richard Young/Rex Features: page 5 *bottom*

A CIP catalogue record for this book is
available from the British Library

ISBN 0 7475 2343 6

10 9 8 7 6 5 4 3 2 1

Typeset by Hewer Text Composition Services, Edinburgh
Printed in Great Britain by Clays Ltd, St Ives plc

For my students

'Dare to do something worthy of transportation or imprisonment if you wish to be of consequence.'

Juvenal

Contents

Introduction

Vivienne's secret, as she admits, is Malcolm McLaren. Malcolm's secret is told here for the first time in Part Two.

Part One: Vivienne Westwood, An Imaginary Interview is me taking liberties with everything I can recall Vivienne saying to me over thirty years, plus what she's said in her many published interviews. Quite a lot, as you will see. Some of this is put into her mouth from other sources as well – for example, her family and Malcolm.

I also put two of my students on the case, and they extensively interviewed people from Vivienne's past. It's got that rather flat 'interview' tone, but I also think it's got a lot of her. If you think 'We've got a right one here!', then I've done the job OK. This section is in a sense 'factional', as it has some 'dramatised' sections but is based on what I know and on what has been documented by others. In other words, I didn't make any of it up, though you might be tempted to think so. I also resisted the temptation to put my own spin on events in the guise of her voice – my version comes in Part Two. Needless to say, however, this 'Imaginary Interview' doesn't claim to represent what Vivienne might say on her own account or what she might say about all this in retrospect.

Like me, Vivienne and Malcolm are sixties people. That was our formative decade. But a lot of shit has been written about the sixties. I've tried to go beyond the clichés and examine our origins more ruthlessly by interrogating my own experience along with theirs. So this section is an eyewitness account of how we grew up together in an inconspicuous corner of the sixties, roughly from 1963 to the early to mid-seventies, when the sixties finally began to peter out – or are they still with us? There's a lot about me in this, because biographies, after all, overlap, and shared circumstances and attitudes can say it all. Hence Part Two: Growing up as a Genius in the Sixties.

In this section I also reveal the strange secret of Malcolm McLaren's talent – his talent for genius. I sketch the Romantic context of this talent – where it can thrive – and show how Vivienne has absorbed and made it her own.

To bring it all up to date I wrote Part Three: Pictures from the Revolution, which traces a line of vignettes up to October 1995, when I observed the scenes behind Vivienne's Paris show at the Grand Hôtel. I've also tried here to give a sense of that curious organization, Vivienne Westwood Ltd.

PART ONE

Vivienne Westwood:
an Imaginary Interview

The funny thing was, everyone assumed that because we were at the centre of punk Malcolm and I were incredibly debauched and perverted.

There were stories, for instance, that I used to lock Malcolm up in a cupboard all day, and that our Clapham flat was the scene of wild orgies, some of them lesbian, featuring me and young punk girls. In fact we were probably the straightest couple on that scene. Though the rumours were good for business.

Of course, there's always been a dominant side to me, and Malcolm sometimes liked to enact his childhood traumas. But all that is very private to us, and I would never tell anyone anything that might hurt Malcolm. Whatever he has said about me since our break-up, I still feel very loyal to him. In any case we were usually too busy with our projects and our business to do anything very exotic. In fact, I don't recall either of us having very much sex around that period – straight or kinky.

When did Malcolm and I split up? Perhaps it really started around the time of my Pirate collection, 1979–80. Adam Ant – around then.

I had known Adam for some time as someone who used to hang around SEX, our boutique in the King's Road. I thought him a nice boy, very polite. Adam had been pestering Malcolm for ages to manage him. Eventually Malcolm gave him advice about stage presentation, like painting a big white stripe on his nose. He charged Adam £1000 for this advice. That was probably the best advice Adam ever got.

But Malcolm needed a band himself at the time, since he was thinking of starting Bow Wow Wow. So he got talking to Adam's backing band. He explained that Adam was basically a no-hoper. Malcolm suggested they should leave Adam and form another band with another lead singer, and he would then manage them as Bow Wow Wow. He was thinking they might front the pirate look I'd been designing.

That band were all such craven boys really. They had no loyalty to Adam, and caved in pretty quickly. So Malcolm put them to work, sending them to recording studios to record demos.

He'd tell them to go into a studio, work there for several days, and once the engineer's back was turned, steal the tape and do a runner. Then they would take the same tape to another studio and start all over again. That way all the demos were made for free – another kind of piracy, plus he sent a buzz of notoriety around the industry in advance of any sales pitch.

Then Malcolm came up with Annabella. She was fourteen then, with a high, shrill voice and a manic presentation. I thought she was crap to start with and the first time I heard a tape of her I smashed the cassette machine! But then Malcolm got a deal with EMI, of all companies, which was a surprise to everyone.

At the time Malcolm was also writing a film script. He wanted to fuse this with the band he was creating. The script was about the 'Mile High Club', a group of kids who meet in the ruined fuselage of a plane and use it for meetings which turn into sex orgies which get more and more elaborate and outrageous. I thought this was quite a promising idea.

You see, Malcolm thought the rock industry was really about kids having sex and wanted to rub its nose in the fact. So the idea was to get the industry involved in some aspect of supposedly underage sex, and then say innocently: 'Oh, but what's the problem with that then? It's what you do all the time! It's what makes the wheels go round!'

While this was going on, a BBC film crew headed by Alan Yentob was making a documentary about Malcolm creating this band. They were filming meetings inside EMI, with EMI people solemnly checking out pictures of kids in sexy poses, and listening to Annabella having an orgasm on 'Sexy Eiffel Towers'. They were all making judicious comments about the whole thing and acting as if it was business as usual. They didn't realize that Malcolm was setting up a crafty trap. But then everything started to go wrong.

Adam had sworn revenge on Malcolm. He'd got together with Marco Pirroni to form a rival band to Bow Wow Wow. Adam then pinched Bow Wow Wow's 'Burundi beat' (which Malcolm had pinched from Bernard Rhodes, who got it from an old sixties single). Adam even stole my eighteenth-century feel in costumes and the pirate look!

Then Adam was very successful and had big hits with all this, while Bow Wow Wow was left standing.

I remember when Malcolm told the Bow Wow Wow boys that Adam had just released 'Dog Eat Dog'. Malcolm said they looked so fed up. We thought that was funny!

But Malcolm had overstretched the kiddy sex angle – especially through a series of photo shoots in different locations across London. These were about Annabella and the band with lots of other kids, and they took place in different houses all over town during one day.

As ever, Malcolm wanted to push things as far as he could – to make it really crazy – and had these kids posing with the band erotically. This started to worry the photographer. Then, at the last place we went, Malcolm started a situation in which the photographer and a twelve-year-old girl were locked into a confrontation. The girl was supposed to take off all her clothes, but instead she held a cushion in front of herself. Malcolm was shouting: 'Take that away!' and the girl burst into tears.

Her mother, who had been watching television in the next room, was furious, and the photographer couldn't believe what he'd been involved in. That was just Malcolm getting carried away as usual.

I think it was one thing to implicate the industry in its own salacious tastes, but another to upset children like that. I didn't agree with it.

After that, things went from bad to worse. The BBC abandoned their documentary and locked the film they'd made in the vaults, like it was a deadly virus. Alan Yentob is one of those people who likes to be thrilled, but not that much.

Then Annabella's mother heard about some of what was going on and started making all sorts of mischief. She had some funny idea that Malcolm was depraving and corrupting her daughter and made a huge fuss, contacting Scotland Yard and all the papers, and ringing the record company non-stop.

Eventually Bow Wow Wow failed, and I think it was for several reasons. To start with, those boys in the band. Basically, they just wouldn't try hard enough or persist, so really they didn't deserve any success. They had an attitude problem. Then Annabella was a real problem. She just wouldn't do her bit properly and became very childish. I remember me and Malcolm endlessly trying to talk her into taking her clothes off. We wanted her in the nude and therefore in the news. But the poor silly girl couldn't see that. She was so hung up about sex. I said to her: 'You've got a beautiful body, so what's wrong with showing it?' But she was still a mummy's girl.

After that, sadly, she got raped by one of the band, or so I heard, and then hooked on drugs, and the whole thing became a complete mess. A pity really.

But I also have to say the music wasn't very good. And the fact that Malcolm wrote the lyrics perhaps didn't help. That was his megalomania. By then he had got to thinking he was an all-time, all-round genius. That everything he did had to work and everyone who disagreed was a traitor. I think he is a genius, but sometimes he won't listen to sense.

And I wonder in a way if he didn't really hijack what I was doing at that time. Because Bow Wow Wow was never as strong as my fashion.

The pirate thing took off phenomenally and in some ways was the most successful thing I've ever done. I exhibited it as a collection in the Pillar Hall at Olympia in March 1981. My slogan was 'a new age of glamorous heroes standing tall and slim and proud'. Some of those designs also featured in Bloomingdale's and Macy's and Henri Bendel. And my ideas went all round the world and popped up in other people's collections on catwalks from Milan to Tokyo. I couldn't believe how much I was copied. It was very flattering in a way as I'd not got much self-confidence at that stage. I suppose it's ironic that the one thing that really did get pirated was my pirate collection!

But it was around about then that things between me and Malcolm started to go seriously wrong.

I'd usually tolerated his affairs with other women because he'd told me he needed to do that. I tried to understand his needs as an artist to explore himself and experiment with his freedom. So when he slept with Helen Waddington-Smith (the dwarf in the film *The Great Rock and Roll Swindle*) for example, I just thought, well, if that's what turns you on! I hardly thought of her as a rival.

Then, in 1980, Malcolm got himself a flat in Paddington and took up with this horrid German girl, Andrea. I thought she was a bloodsucker and a groupie. She had a hard little face and a putty-like expression. We had quite a few rows over Andrea. Once I even hit Malcolm at a show where Bow Wow Wow were modelling my clothes. That caused a commotion backstage! Malcolm told me he was in love with this Andrea girl, but I just knew it wasn't true. I was convinced he said it simply to hurt me.

He even had the nerve to say Andrea was only his mistress and that I was his real partner – as if I wouldn't mind or would tolerate that kind of situation. When he told me that I saw red. I thought it was an insult to even compare me with someone like Andrea. I threw Malcolm out of the flat and said don't you ever come back in here. After all we'd done together! As if I was some kind of housewife! I was so angry that night. I really punched him hard. That night I really wanted to hurt him.

A few days later I went round to his flat. Like a coward, he wouldn't let me in, so I made quite a commotion in the street. Then I threw a brick through his window and went back to Clapham. I was in my pirate clothes so I don't know what the neighbours thought.

Even so, we didn't really split up then. We had too much invested in each other. We had the shop and the collection and we had all the culture we shared and all the culture we had made together. I still needed him to feed me with ideas and he still needed me to turn his ideas into clothes. So eventually he came back yet again and sheepishly admitted he'd made a mistake. And perhaps stupidly, I took him back.

It wasn't until 1983 that the final break came. Though, to tell the truth, there had been so many breaks and reconciliations already that in the end I couldn't really put an exact time or place to it. All I know is, it just started to hurt more and more as it became inevitable that we would have to part in a radical or complete way. Both emotionally and professionally.

But one good thing did come out of the split – I got closer to my mother. Malcolm had always come between us as a source of suspicion, poisoning my feelings towards my parents and my past. My mother has always disliked him. She calls him 'the interloper'.

My family had come from Tintwistle, in the Derbyshire Peak District, a grim, working-class village straggling both sides of the Manchester Road. They had lived in the village since about the year dot.

Life was settled there, and it still is. Many of the people I grew up with are still around, in Tintwistle itself, or in Glossop, the nearest town. The place was founded on the cotton trade in the industrial revolution. The Victorians built its factories, schools and chapels and people like my dad joined the village brass band, and the Odd Fellows, with their secret handshakes and ancient rituals. All of them were self-made, self-reliant and self-educated – like me.

In the 1940s my father's mother ran a grocery store. In that area this meant they were lower middle class. They were also the only family with a car, which my father drove to Manchester and back early in the morning for shop supplies.

My mother, born Dora Ball, worked in a modern cotton mill which also produced silk. She was able to buy material cheaply and she loved making dresses, especially to go out dancing in. She was a committed ballroom dancer, and started 'serious' dancing at the age of sixteen. She never lost her love of ballroom dancing, so I suppose I was brought up with bits of fabric, exotic colours, sexy slippery silks. Quite a contrast to the sensible tweeds and wellington boots of everyday life in Tintwistle.

In those days the cottages were two-up two-downs with outside lavatories. The water was heated by a log fire in a zinc tank and there was a tin bath. Immediately behind was a common area called 'the quarry'. There were no fences because the quarry was like one big back garden with a disused wash-house where everyone had a washing line and all the children from the terrace played. No one would lock their doors in those days and we would wander in and out of neighbours' cottages. People stood and gossiped at the back doors, not the front.

But in our house there was something extra: cupboards crammed with nets and silky froth. Frocks on the back of bedroom doors. Sequins that peeked out at you and suggested there was another side to life – though I never made the connection at the time.

In trying to fit in with Malcolm and his ideas I had suppressed Tintwistle and my childhood. But then it all started to flood back. In a way my Harris Tweed collection was a way of dealing with that. I showed it in March 1987 at Olympia. It was a trip to Italy which had given me a perspective on the British way of dressing. I thought about all those uniforms we developed for sports and casual wear, from the gentleman's blazer to the riding-to-hounds clothes.

I was also exploring the kind of clothes I wore as a working-class girl in Tintwistle – how they were like the kind of clothes the Queen might wear. The sort of tradition and style that surrounded me back then, and that we looked up to. I took that essential frumpiness and reworked it to subvert it with a touch of glamour: Harris tweed suits and coats with Peter Pan collars decorated with crowns, sashes and medals.

In that collection I also emphasized an hourglass shape to the body and began to develop my trade-mark platform soles.

People criticised me at the time for harping on royalty and being a so-called conservative. Well, if they couldn't see the humour in what I was doing, how could I help that? I've always taken pleasure in amusing myself and knowing that what amuses me will also amuse others.

I even did a photograph for *Tatler* disguised as Margaret Thatcher. When my mother saw that she was amazed at the resemblance. I've heard that some people seem to think this showed me up as a secret Tory. But really I am someone who always votes Labour and always will. I would never support the Tories in anything.

The only time I met Margaret Thatcher was at an event at Number Ten to promote British Fashion Week. I got this terrifically negative charge from Thatcher. I remember wondering if she was really human! We may both be the children of shopkeepers, but I think that's where the resemblance ends!

It was through my mother's passion for dancing that she met my father. That was one fateful evening, two weeks before Christmas. Dora had been in Glossop to buy herself a new ballroom dress and missed the last bus. She was forced to walk to another bus stop on the outskirts of town.

As she passed St Mary's dance hall carrying her new dress, she saw the handsome and notorious Gordon Swire, my dad. She'd known him for ages. Around there everyone knew everybody. And she knew that Gordon was the Jack-the-Lad of the district. She'd been warned about him; he had a wicked reputation with the girls as a flirt and a gadabout.

So she assumed he was waiting to see whom he could pick up. Then she heard him call across the street.

'Where are you going?'

'Home.'

Gordon asked if he could walk with her. She immediately replied: 'No, thank you!', fearful for her reputation.

But then she let him anyway. And suddenly, as they were walking together, they knew that was it.

They married in 1939, two weeks before the outbreak of World War Two, in Christ Church, the Tintwistle village church. For their honeymoon they went to Scarborough, travelling there and back in the car. Then they set up home in a terrace of twelve labourers' cottages called Millbrook. They were in number six.

On 8 April 1941 they had me, Vivienne Isabel, their first-born. When I was still quite small, my mother would often lift me over the fence at the back so I could go into the countryside and play.

All around was woodland, fields and streams. In those days you could walk for miles without seeing anyone or any traffic. Wandering freely in the countryside, daydreaming by streams, climbing trees, is where I learned the pleasures of solitude. I still love to be alone, just with myself. It often irritates me to have to go out and deal with all these people as I'm constantly doing these days. Sometimes I think I'd just like to disappear inside myself again, tucking my skirt in my knickers to hop boulder to boulder across a stream.

Only this time, perhaps, in a library. Wandering along the shelves from 'Aldous Huxley' to 'Flagellation', 'Coco Chanel' to 'Tourette's syndrome'. There's so much to find out!

Tintwistle has all changed so much now. There are fences at the back and cars parked along the road. It's turned into what my mother calls 'an eyesore'.

The war was on when I was born and my dad, being a peaceable kind, didn't fancy his chances fighting Hitler. He found himself a job in an aircraft factory as a storekeeper.

Our village was hardly affected by the war, though there was a blackout and a food shortage. But with my dad's mum being a grocer my parents didn't even need their ration book. And there was plenty of milk for a newborn baby like me. A man came round with a big container on a horse and cart and we took as much as we wanted.

Sometimes, at night, when Manchester was being bombed, the sky was all red. But apart from that I hardly remember the war. After all, I was only four when it ended.

I do remember when my sister, Olga, was born. I was three then. I hadn't realized someone else was coming into the cottage. When Olga was brought home I was peeved and jealous. She seemed like another person I didn't want in the home, cluttering it up with her crying and messes. I felt that now she was the baby I had to grow up as quickly as possible and become the capable one with clever hands who made sure everything was just right.

Olga was always very different from me. Malcolm would laugh at her for being solid and stolid, calling her 'Olga from the Volga'. Olga is methodical and rarely takes risks.

She was also unlike me in her passion for animals. As a child Olga had dogs instead of dolls. (To this day she still breeds chinchillas and iguanas in a shed at the bottom of her garden.) My parents also loved animals and bred lots of rabbits and dogs. Our house was always a lively place with plenty of creatures scampering about.

Two years after the war, Gordon, my brother, was born. Dad didn't really want to call their son Gordon, but Mum insisted. I think she loved my father so much she wanted two of him! This time I wasn't at all put out. I had been looking forward to him coming and hoping he would be like a doll I could cuddle and look after. However, I was a little cross that he didn't seem as small as he should have been. I thought him rather big for a baby.

Then our family was complete. The same pram did for all three of us.

When I was about four I had an experience which marked me for life. I saw a crucifix and asked what it was. When they told me I was completely shocked. Not being a Catholic, I had never seen any-thing like it – they didn't have that kind of savage picture in our church or Sunday school. A man twisted in agony with nails driven through his hands and feet! I couldn't believe people could do that to someone. It seemed so cruel and unnecessary.

But what really got to me was that my teachers had more or less lied. They had covered up this gruesome fact of crucifixion. They told us all about sweet baby Jesus, and 'Away in a Manger' and 'All Things Bright and Beautiful', but they hadn't let on about how he was killed in that dreadful way. It was all fairy tales and I realized there was a much grimmer world out there and this had been covered up. That shook my confidence in grown-ups. What else were they hiding?

But that image also made me determined to stick up for the underdog. At school, from then on, I was determined to protect weak people from bullies. I was always the one who stood up for people. I suppose I took the Christian message very much to heart. In fact I was a complete believer up to the age of about eleven. After that, of course, I realized it was all silly nonsense.

But that feeling of wanting to help the underdog has never left me. I've been a sort of freedom fighter all my life. An instinctive rebel.

*   *   *

So was Sid Vicious. We got Sid into the Sex Pistols when the band was going through its final phase. That was really to break it up.

Malcolm had started a row between Glen Matlock and the other members of the band, who didn't like Glen anyway because they thought he was middle-class and stuck-up. Glen had also started asking awkward questions like: 'Where is all the money going?'

At the time, Malcolm was pouring most of the Pistols' earnings into various film projects. The boys were on really quite small wages and had no idea of the business dealings going on in their name. But they would have only thrown it away on luxuries, so it was right that Malcolm was spending it to keep the ideas going. Anyway, he thought it was a good idea to get rid of Glen. In any case, Glen didn't really like the rebellious aspect of it all. With his soft face he just wanted to be a Beatle really.

We realized around that time that we had created a monster that might grow up and get out of our control. Perhaps even become established like the Rolling Stones! So really we had to destroy the band. That was the only way to snatch the initiative back from the record industry. We had to end the whole adventure in the spirit it began.

Unfortunately, in the end we couldn't trust the band to be radical. Perhaps because they didn't have our background, and were basically naïve and susceptible to congratulations and flattery from the likes of John Peel. In the end all of them just wanted to be rock and roll stars – even Sid. So I suppose we had to put a stop to that. The last thing we wanted was for the band to become everything it had set out to destroy – famous and stupid music.

So we got Sid in to replace Glen. That was enough to destroy any band!

By then Sid was on a suicide trip. He had shacked up with that awful Nancy Spungen and had his famous heroin habit. Nancy had come over with the first wave of New York punks who came to London when they heard of all the record deals being struck. And these American punks brought heroin with them, which began to replace the drink and speed of the English punks. I thought Nancy was appalling. She was a groupie and a leech. Everyone hated her.

She had a shrill, whining voice and homed in like a vulture on poor Sid's weaknesses.

Sid became a fabulous disaster, the face of the Pistols' self-destruction. I suppose he was heading for disaster all his life. That was his great attraction. Sid was always out of control. Into every kind of mayhem, he was a genuine punk. One day he got hold of the cab account number for the band's management company, Glitterbest. He went round London telling every punk he met what the number was. For a month the whole of London was full of punks on the dole riding around in cabs, even cabbing down to their benefit offices. That cost over £4000 before anyone found out.

Before killing off the band we thought we should make a celluloid version which preserved its original ethos. Malcolm wanted to implicate lots of British character actors in some outrageous porno/punk movie. He'd heard of a porn producer who had actually achieved something like this by hiring well-known actors to play scenes without realizing they were acting in a porn film. The film was then released with their names blazoned all over it. That was a very subversive idea, really clever.

The film we originally wanted to make was called *Who Killed Bambi?* The idea was to show a clash between the Sex Pistols and a hippie entrepreneur called Proby who was trying to cash in on the punk thing. Proby was supposed to be helping a thinly disguised Mick Jagger rejuvenate himself as a punk hero.

In the end a young punk girl would shoot the Jagger character dead and there would be a riot at Proby's mansion. It was a bit like the Gordon riots in the eighteenth century, when rich people were dragged off their horses and beaten to death in the streets of London, and quite a few luxurious houses were burned down. We thought that sounded like a very punk thing – something which might be going on in the King's Road in 1976.

Sid's mum was to be depicted in the film as a raddled old drug addict, who would be played by Marianne Faithfull. In one scene Sid comes home unexpectedly to his council flat to find his mother shooting up. Sid was supposedly having an incestuous relationship with his mother, and in this scene they go into the bedroom and start having sex. Then her boyfriend comes home and sees what's going on. Shouting 'That's illegal!', he attacks Sid with his belt. But like a hero – and I do think that boy was a hero in real life in so many ways – Sid fights back with a chain and then knocks the boyfriend out with a karate chop.

All this was a much better idea than the Swindle and it's such a pity everything went wrong and the film never got made. There were so many hassles about money and in the end Russ Meyer, the American soft-porn director who was supposed to make it, went back to America in a huff. Meyer was a bit of a bully, and even managed to frighten Malcolm. We were all relieved when he left.

Jamie Reid had meanwhile found a fifties magazine article about Lonnie Donegan saying: 'Rock and Roll, it's a Swindle.' So then Malcolm had the idea of announcing that the Pistols were actually a gigantic con trick. Because by then even bores like John Peel were saying: 'What a great band. They can really play. This is genuine rock and roll.' Our new idea was to say: 'No, they're just crap. It was a hoax. And you fell for it!'

But by now there had been so much trouble with scripts and finance that we were left with only Julian Temple to make the Swindle. Julian was willing, but dizzy. He was never really into the punk thing and all he wanted was a start for himself in films, which is what I blame mostly for that film being rather woolly. I personally thought that Gordon, my brother, who worked as a film editor, would have made a much better job. But by that time it had all got too complicated to change directors.

To manage the destruction of the Sex Pistols Malcolm then planned a tour of America. He realized America would not be ready for the Sex Pistols. So he booked them into venues in red-neck areas or where there would be cowboys walking around with guns who wouldn't like such spiky-haired young ruffians. Malcolm also booked them into venues which were too small, so that there would be fights as a result of people trying to squeeze in.

All this worked out very well and the band did eventually break up in America. All the members fell out with one another and Sid made a suitable disgrace of himself, slashing his chest with glass on stage, getting into fights and causing all sorts of trouble.

But I'm sure that Sid didn't mean to kill Nancy. He just wanted to hurt her. Warn her, perhaps. She was a very dishonest girl. Sometimes Sid would try to get through to her, to have an honest relationship. But he never could. I think that's why in the end he stabbed her.

After Sid was jailed I tried to stir things up in my own way. I put out a T-shirt saying: 'She's dead, I'm alive, I'm yours.' This upset quite a lot of people, but hopefully it also made them think.

It does make me smile nowadays when John Lydon says that ideas like situationism had little to do with the Sex Pistols, and that he was what counted. In fact, maybe it was John himself who had little to do with the Sex Pistols. 'Johnny Rotten' was really just a face and a mouthpiece for ideas John was often too uneducated to understand, and attitudes he was too cowardly to follow through.

Although John was a real poet, he really wanted to be a star. Then he became frightened of his own fame and became a parody of himself – which is what he is now.

The record industry ignored the punk thing at first. It was doing very nicely with all those millionaire types like Pete Townshend and Rod Stewart. Sniffing things in their mansions and going through divorce settlements. But then came a time when the panic we wanted to create really did set in. Record companies were suddenly desperate not to be left out. All you needed to get signed was green, spiky hair or a 'Destroy' T-shirt.

WEA even signed up John's little brother. I suppose they thought something 'Rotten' might rub off.

Although Virgin had wanted to sign the Pistols right from the start, we were suspicious of them. Malcolm, especially, wanted to sign to EMI. He knew we had to go to the most conservative and established record company to make the maximum impact. To cause trouble on what was then a small label would have meant nothing. But to cause trouble in Manchester Square, home of the Beatles, would be scandalous.

At one time Malcolm wanted me to go to Madame Tussaud's and

set fire to the wax effigies of the Beatles. I thought that was inspired. Only I was worried it might start a fire and someone would get hurt.

Eventually EMI signed the Sex Pistols. But then, of course, they couldn't handle all our stage-managed 'bad' publicity and sacked the band, having to pay them money in the process. All that was good for business. Then Derek Green of A&M Records signed them up. And within one week he had to ring his bosses in America and ask if they would let him drop the band. He said he couldn't handle it – it was out of control; he had miscalculated.

One week must be a record in the record business!

Derek Green thought he'd be dealing with a bunch of working-class hooligans, a bit like himself. He was a Saturday footballer, a beer-swilling sort of man who thought he recognized himself in the band. But instead of the Sex Pistols he got Glitterbest Ltd.

The way rock and roll works is that the band is supposed to behave badly and then, when things start to get difficult, the record company contacts the management and things get sorted out. Damage is paid for and the band is sent on a tour of Sweden while the fuss dies down.

But in this case the management was even worse than the band. So when the record companies complained to the management company, Glitterbest, we just rubbed our hands together. Well, we thought, if vomiting at Heathrow airport gets people interested, surely we should have more of it.

You see, we all had this art college background and knew it was just a game. That you can never go too far. We knew about avant-garde heroes like Marinetti, the crazy tactics of those Dadaist people, about situationism and the power of negative thinking, about black humour and Surrealism. We had role models like Van Gogh, Trotsky and André Breton. We knew that Lenin said: 'You can't make an omelette without breaking eggs.' We realized that when authority figures warn that you are 'going too far' you just have to be courageous and just keep on going and going. And all that ever happens is that you get rich (if you're lucky) and famous (nearly always) and end up in the history books.

It's only fools – and most of them, unfortunately, happen to be the uneducated and working-class people of this world – who get frightened and intimidated into retreating or apologizing.

And after that, they disappear.

Whatever else my parents gave me they gave me confidence in myself, something to build on. Perhaps, too, something vital to my creativity. After I was born their social life suffered. But luckily for them a neighbour from the terrace used to babysit so they could keep up their ballroom dancing. They would go dancing at the Sunday school halls at Tintwistle and Hollingworth, or at the Victoria Hall in Glossop, or in Ashton-under-Lyne, a six-mile bus ride away.

My father also loved to sing in clubs or pubs. Plus he was a great bowler and bowled in the village and all around the district. But mostly it was the dancing – foxtrot, waltz, tango – under the lights in each other's arms around the floor. They were happy to be together and to be married in an uncomplicated and devoted way, in love all their lives. They never wanted anyone but each other and they adored their children.

We didn't often see my parents dancing, but I always had in my mind their bodies moving. I sometimes went to sleep with the vision of them moving in perfect harmony. Fabric swaying and rustling. I was always fascinated by the perfection of that image.

Nowadays I am even more fascinated by the relationship of the body to clothing. This underlies all my design, and I can't stress enough how important it is in general. Self-awareness about the body separates good from mediocre design.

I once had a student from Chicago who helped me for two months doing chores and helping with pattern cutting, and towards the end I set her a project. I gave her a book on Chanel and said imagine that Vivienne Westwood has to produce a collection inspired by Chanel, and then produce some drawings. So off she went.

She showed me her drawings some time later. Not one of them was anywhere near as good as the original. She hadn't used her brain. She hadn't dealt with the most basic requirement – making the garment fit the body. She couldn't see the wood for the trees; she wasn't dealing with the most primary thing – the body.

This is what seems to happen with students – all they can see is the trees. They should stop pissing about!

At Millbrook Cottages us kids were squashed into one bedroom. I've always liked my own space and I didn't like having Olga and Gordon in there all the time. But in 1954 my mother was offered the chance to become a postmistress, so we moved to a bigger house in the village. Mr and Mrs Senior, who ran the Tintwistle post office, had become ill and had to retire. It was my father's idea. He thought there wasn't much of a future in what he and Mum were doing and wanted to move on. So we all moved about a mile up the same street, the main road to Manchester.

The village post office was, I suppose, very fifties – dark and dingy. In those days nearly everything seemed to be chocolate brown or some shade of grey. Our shop sold sweets, papers and stamps. We were there for four years.

At the age of four I'd been sent to the Hollingworth school, but then my parents decided to change me to Tintwistle – the same school my mother went to – as they thought this gave a better education.

My first memory of school is getting a good slap on my first day for going into the boys' toilets. I suppose that was typical of me. We'd been queuing up nicely in the morning but at lunchtime I thought, why should we do this? Why can't I just go into that toilet for a change? I was slapped really hard.

It was a strict school, secure in the knowledge of what was right and wrong. That did me a lot of good. It's a pity that schools aren't more like that now.

I used to take Olga and Gordon to school, which was behind the village church, and we would walk through the graveyard. We looked out of our classrooms to the hills of the Peak District, which loomed up darkly. Downwards, you could see a huge reservoir and holding tanks and weirs.

I was taught to read at this school, and how to write in a clear, round hand. My writing still goes round and round, in fact, rather like the wheels of a bicycle.

Perhaps I also learned a sort of role, of being in charge and instructing. Of being teacherly, which is what people tell me I sometimes still am. In any case I got on well with my teachers.

Since having my own sons I've realized how a child's personality is there right from the start. What they are even as babies carries right into adulthood. Whatever parents do, children are born with certain characteristics – it's their bag of tools. Yet I think that nurture also has a lot to do with it. The way I've brought up both my boys must have had an impact.

Ben is nowadays a soft-porn photographer and my other son, Joe, runs a sex boutique in Soho, Undercover, which sells high-class sex aids and underwear. I think they both got a lot out of my being their mother. But I do also wish I could have given them more of an education. In fact I would have liked to have sent them to a private tutor. Perhaps I could have isolated them in that way, and stopped their access to this non-stop distraction – protect them from bad influences. If nothing else, children should grow up with a sense of pride – even contempt. But then it didn't work out like that.

One reason why Malcolm doesn't see Joe any more is that Malcolm wanted Joe to go to college and Joe refused. I suppose Malcolm thinks Joseph ought to do something better than 'selling knickers'; that he ought to better himself. After all, education is where ideas come from, and that's how things move forward – through discipline and education.

There were only three classes in my first school – infants, juniors and seniors. In each class, whatever you did you were taught by one teacher for two years. Then you moved up one, and another teacher taught you for the next two years. That happened three times, and then you left school. All the teachers taught all subjects – reading, writing and arithmetic, plus history and geography and, of course, poetry. Poetry was quite a big thing. We'd all learn it by heart and have to stand up in class to read it out aloud.

As infants we had Miss Story. She was quite a favourite with everyone. Then, for juniors, it was Miss Leeny, a bit sterner. When

24

you got up to seniors you had Miss Wood, who was also the headmistress, and you knew she meant business.

Miss Wood was tall and straight with grey hair, a grey skirt and a short-sleeved grey jumper. She was very strict, but stricter with boys than girls. If you forgot something or talked in class you got lines. For more serious things you got the cane. It was usually the boys who got caned.

When Miss Wood caned someone it made me feel funny. I could almost imagine myself as a teacher, standing there holding the stick with my lips pursed. I felt my legs tingle and my stomach shrink.

There was no proper uniform. In summer, girls would wear plain printed summer dresses and a cardigan, and in winter, kilts. Our classes were mixed, but boys and girls played separately. So at playtime my friends and I might play rounders on the sloping tarmac, or skipping with a long rope. We'd line up and go: 'Monday, Tuesday, Wednesday, Thursday, Friday, Saturday . . .' And if you were 'Sunday' you went: 'Pitch, patch, pepper' and the rope swung faster – you had to see how many jumps you could do. What else? Monday morning was swimming lessons at Stowbridge baths, and back in time for dinner. The cook was Mrs Sharp, who used to make quite an effort with her home-made meat pies. And at Christmas the partitions dividing the school into three classes were slid back to make one big room for Father Christmas to visit.

I remember it as a happy place to be, so different from the inner-city schools I would later teach in.

We three Swire children were popular at school. I think we were all well-adjusted, intelligent and unproblematic. While our parents never pressured us – in fact, scarcely even encouraged us – we did enjoy learning.

My parents were not 'bookish'; not interested in anything 'intellectual'. I hardly like to say that, because they were both very bright people. But what we never had at home was any literature, and they never used to read to us. I remember my mother once bought a set of encyclopedias, but they weren't the right sort, where you could look things up easily. So our house was the last place you might expect to find culture. Our parents were very loving and kind to us, but theirs was very much a country attitude – rather than culture, they were more interested in dogs and rabbits and things like that.

So I had never realized the vast store of knowledge that exists. I never thought of going to the library. I didn't know what a library was even when I was at grammar school. How could I have been so stupid?

Even so, I practised the piano from about the age of eight to thirteen – 'Chopsticks', bits of Chopin and that sort of thing. My mother encouraged me. But then I stopped, finding the practice so tedious.

From my earliest youth, though, I was afraid of being stupid. I sometimes wondered whether I was. At the same time I thought that no one around me had enough information to give me, information that would help me. I would have to find it out all on my own.

Perhaps because of this I grew up very independent. For example, although I adored my mother, as I still do, I was never attached to her in the way that other girls are to their mothers. But perhaps my independence also came from the fact that I had very sane parents who both adored me. That gives you a lot of confidence.

As I was the eldest child, I was supposed to take Gordon and Olga everywhere. I took them to Saturday morning cinema in Glossop and to Sunday school. Tintwistle Sunday school was the same one my mother went to. I'm not sure if my parents really believed in religion very much but they sent us anyway. Sunday was taken very seriously in our village and respectable children like us weren't allowed to play with bikes or roller-skates. All you could do on Sunday was go for walks or visit relatives.

There were lots of interesting processions in Tintwistle. It was a ceremonial sort of place. The village brass band used to march around the village and we used to march behind it. Me in my frock and sandals, marching behind the band. Originally there were two bands, the Foresters and Tinsel Crash – what great names! – but because of rivalry they merged.

Every June, there was 'The Sermon', which was the anniversary of the Sunday school. This also involved a procession led by the vicar, the church warden and the church band. We would march all around the village and stop at certain points to sing hymns. Afterwards everyone would go back to church for a service. This was a special event. We all had to wear new clothes – either a new dress, a new coat or new shoes – and look our very best. Everyone dressed to kill! All the villagers took part in these occasions. What with my parents dancing and me parading, maybe it brought out the exhibitionist in me.

There was still more dressing up at the July carnival. People in fancy dress would parade all round the village. That was brilliant. And then they'd have races. The band would march us around the village and then they would go for tea to the Sunday school, where a special tea was put on for them Then the band would take chairs on to the green and sit there and play during all the flat races, the egg-and-spoon race, the 'slow bicycle' and the three-legged race. A vanished world!

It all seems so English – or what English means to me. Our post office might be in an Ealing comedy, ripe for Miss Marple or Alastair Sim to walk in and begin a dotty adventure with Mr and Mrs Swire and their three charming children in the potty village of Tintwistle. In the film, we Swires are constantly steaming open the villagers' letters. And perhaps the actors are dressed in a Westwood Harris tweed collection – woolly pullies and the Queen's way of dressing up.

I remember the Coronation, which was a big event in our village. That was in June 1953. It was raining. The Tintwistle Sunday school had a tea party and all the village streets were festooned with banners and rosettes. We Swires went to one of the other Millbrook cottages to watch it. I think there were twelve households from the Millbrook terrace all crammed into that one sitting room!

But after a while most of us kids got bored. It was all so grey and flickery and there was this pompous voice-over saying obvious things like: 'Now the Queen is having the crown put on her head.' We could see that. But this was history supposedly, and it was important, so we thought we ought to watch.

In those days the Queen was such a big thing. (Have you noticed, by the way, how when Tories say 'Queen' they draw back the sides of their mouth to make the 'ween' sound cute and delicate? It's as if they're worried that saying the word roughly might drop Her Majesty on the floor like a precious porcelain vase.)

In the fifties royalty was respected. All church services began with 'God Save the Queen'. At the end of every film performance everyone stood up with their hat off while it was played. No one dared do otherwise, though some who didn't mind catching the odd glare would nip out before it began.

I did wonder – as everybody did, I suppose – whether I'd ever get to meet the Queen, and I did!

When in 1991 I won the Designer of the Year award for the second time running, Princess Michael of Kent presented it. 'Congratulations,' she said, and I replied: 'How lovely you look!' She was wearing such a beautiful dress and looked brilliant – very fashionable. I understand there were some bitter things said about me by other contestants. But I just quoted Elvis Presley. 'Don't you ever kiss me once, kiss me twice – treat me nice!'

I was delighted. And very surprised too. I had no inkling it was going to happen, as the result is kept a secret. Also, it was by a landslide – I got sixty per cent of the votes. I thought it was amazing how popular I was and I was ever so pleased about that. I felt I'd given a lot to British fashion and now it was nice to get something back. Not that I'm too impressed by such awards. But it was especially nice for the people I work with.

Needless to say, my mother was ecstatic about all this acclaim.

Then, in 1992, I was given the OBE. I hadn't decided on purpose not to wear knickers for that ceremony. In fact I hardly ever wear knickers. I find them constricting, and even when riding my bike I am generally knickerless.

So when I came out after the ceremony into the courtyard of Buckingham Palace wearing a long skirt and all the photographers shouted 'Give us a twirl, Vivienne,' I didn't really think about it. I twirled round and my skirts lifted and of course I revealed all as everyone could see all over the front pages of the tabloids next day.

I hadn't meant to insult the Queen. I really thought she was sweet, a very interesting person I could have stayed chatting to for ages. In fact, my whole notion of royalty has changed completely since the days of punk and the Sex Pistols' anti-anthem, 'God Save the Queen'. I now prefer the real anthem. I've got over all that revolution, and anti-monarchy, anti-establishment stuff. I'm still just as radical but in a more thoughtful way, and about different issues.

Nowadays I'm all for elitism.

I really despise this democratic envy which is promoted by Hollywood. Where no one is supposed to stand out any more and everyone is supposed to be no better than anyone else. For the same reasons I also hate magazines and I hate television. Both are filled with non-stop rubbish. People who watch television or read magazines – their minds are like dustbins and it's just frightening. It doesn't seem to worry them that they just clog their minds up with unending distraction. It's impossible to think in that state, or to have any fresh ideas.

I've never had a television in my home and I never will. Come to think of it, maybe I started to give up television in 1953 while watching the Coronation!

Nineteen fifty-three was also the year I took my Eleven-plus. I got a good grade and won a place at Glossop Grammar School, in Talbot Street in the town centre. Inside it was dark and severe with an entrance hall with wood panelling and a black and white tiled floor, and that school smell! The school motto was 'Virtus, Veritas, Libertas' – 'Honour, Truth and Liberty'. This stood over the school entrance and also on the badges on our blazers – over our hearts, in fact.

Funnily enough, someone else who made his name from sex – like I suppose I did – went to this school, although a few years before I got there. That was Paul Raymond, now one of the very richest men in England. In those days he was called Geoffrey Quinn.

Our school uniform was stripes of maroon and navy blue. In summer we wore blue and white flowery A-line dresses and in winter we wore a short fitted grey gym slip, a white blouse and a striped tie.

In the third year it was a navy skirt, a white blouse and a striped tie, and you had to wear a beret. You had to wear that even on the way home. If you were seen without it you were reported.

We all had to wear this uniform, and they were very strict about that. If you didn't wear the proper uniform, you'd get lines – 'I must wear my school uniform' 500 times. We used to write 'I,I,I . . .' in columns. So many lines. You even got lines if you lost something. Then, if you went to Lost Property to get it back, you got yet more lines!

Our uniforms were very uncomfortable, especially the knickers. We had to wear big bloomer-type things. Perhaps that's why I don't wear knickers now! One of the teachers would stand at the bottom of the stairs as we were going up – always in single file at a ladylike pace – and she would look up to see if anyone was wearing a white underskirt or the wrong knickers.

(But what a lovely word that is: 'knickers'. It sounds like something light and airy that ought to be thrown on to the back of a chair. Knick-knacks, knickerbockers, knicker-knackers . . . 'Oh, knickers!')

And they were very particular about our hair. It had to be tied back – and washed! The teachers used to tell pupils if their hair needed washing. Once I turned up to school with the front of mine dyed in a red rinse. I wasn't sent home but was told to rinse it out that night. That also happened when I came in one Monday after a weekend at Butlins with my hair dyed green!

Our headmaster was Mr Lord, and that was a good name for this stern and strict man. He used to overpower a lot of the children and his eyebrows would quiver ominously whenever he was cross with someone.

Like Tintwistle, it was a strict school, and the cane was often used, but only on the boys. We often had to stay behind for detention, though. I once rebelled at that. I've had enough of this, I said, and climbed out the window and went home!

One teacher I remember was George Donaldson. We called him 'Penguin' because he walked like one, and he had a tight white collar and red hair. Then there was Fanny Cuthbert, a rather plump lady who took us for needlework and cookery. 'Spell' Brown was our English master. Then there was Miss Greenwood, who later became the headmistress. We nicknamed her 'Dolly Greenwood' because she was so small.

My favourite class was the art class. I chose art instead of domestic science. The art teacher was Gordon Bell. We used to call him 'Arty', or sometimes 'Clanger', from his surname Bell. He was very relaxed and friendly but he hated chewing gum. If he caught someone with gum he made them stay for detention. For Mr Bell mastication was even worse than masturbation!

But he was dedicated as an art teacher. He gave me the only training I've ever really had in drawing, sketching and colouring. Sometimes I'd visit his house in the holidays with my portfolio, asking for advice. I don't know what his wife thought. She gave me a funny look sometimes. It was well known that Mr Bell appreciated a good-looking girl and that some of the girls fancied him.

In fact, I had quite a reputation. I was always the one who kissed teacher under the mistletoe. And once I made a dive for the French teacher and landed on top of him, so that we both fell to the floor.

We were allowed free rein in our art classes. Sometimes we did poster work or art work to advertise school plays. Sometimes we painted still lifes. But although I loved it, my only prize was a commendation in March 1956 for my poster for the school play, *She Stoops to Conquer*.

Although I didn't like games much I was quite good at them. In 1957, for example, I came third in the long jump on sports day, and I was in the school hockey team. I had long legs! When the weather was too bad for hockey, we used to have dancing in the school gym. Foxtrots and waltzes, just like my parents, but also jive and all the rock and roll dances. That was better than the country dancing we did at Tintwistle. Here it was boys dancing with girls. And picking a boy to dance with was a good way to show you fancied him.

We were taught the facts of life in segregated classrooms. The girls were told by Dolly Greenwood and she was quite straightforward about it, though it was difficult to really work out what it all meant, and what went where or did what exactly. The boys were told by a teacher named Charlie Magnet who got it all muddled up. He told them that masturbation gave you bad eyesight. It's never done that to me!

After the upset of splitting up with Malcolm I stayed more or less alone from the late eighties into the nineties. I felt better that way. I found I didn't need a partner – a man would just get in the way. Besides, I've always liked to be private. I like to have my own space.

I sometimes get up in the middle of the night, having dreamed an idea, say, and then spend the rest of the night sketching and working it out. Or I might stay awake all night because of the full moon – it has that effect on me! Sometimes too I just like to get into bed at any time to think or read. Those are my favourite moments. You can't do all that comfortably with someone else around.

I think it's fine to live alone. I like isolation. You don't think properly if you're with other people; you have conversations instead. And conversations are only experiments about what you've been thinking.

In any case, I didn't particularly go for sex at that time. Though I did masturbate a lot. I would imagine I was being carried away by hard-faced men with strong, rippling backs. I've always been attracted to such male-chauvinist types. Once a bloke bent down to fix my bike and all the muscles in his back looked brilliant under his suit jacket!

Incidentally, I don't think masturbation is anything to be ashamed of. I've even designed a 'masturbation skirt' to make it easier.

I'm very hard to please as far as men go. Perhaps I'm also a bit of a Victorian – I don't think I've ever had a one-night stand. Not that I'm against them. But intellectual things are often more interesting than sex. My relationship with Malcolm, for example, was much more about ideas and working together than sex. He was never my ideal of a sexy man anyway.

Art and creativity are supposed to be sublimations of the sexual drive, so perhaps that satisfies me.

I've always felt good inside my own body and taken pleasure in it. I like myself physically and I probably see things in my face that others don't. I think it's a nice face with all kinds of secrets and depth. Nowadays I've got these horribly saggy folds under my chin, but I'd never have a face-lift because it just wouldn't look like me.

When I was young I often used to look at Brigitte Bardot, thinking I would never be as pretty as her. But nowadays I look much better! I deplore the idea of plastic surgery, and I also think aerobics is a waste of time. Jane Fonda would be better off using her time reading a good book!

I suppose I have amazing confidence in my looks. I really do think that any man would be mad or idiotic if he didn't choose me out of a roomful of women.

Eventually at school we had mixed biology classes and learned more technical facts about sex. Ivan Bell, the son of the art teacher, used to sit over the aisle from me during these classes. He'd start sniggering and sometimes I couldn't help joining in.

In general there wasn't a lot of knowledge about and several girls in our school became pregnant. There was one who just disappeared from school one day. We all knew why. We didn't know anything about contraception. In any case, in those days you could only get condoms from the barber's shop. 'Something to go with the Brylcreem, sir?' So if you had sex the chances were you'd get caught out.

I started to wear a bra when I was fourteen. Not that I particularly needed one then – or later. I've always had small breasts, and I've often wished they were bigger. It wasn't hard to see big breasts were what boys liked. They used to chase us round the playground, teasing us and twanging our bra straps.

The first menstrual period for most of us girls was quite a shock and not something we were prepared for. And sanitary towels in those days were big things, not at all discreet. No nice convenient wings. They were just towels attached by hooks to a belt round the waist. So all the boys knew when you were wearing one. They used to pull them up as you went past, and sometimes when you walked down the class, which was extremely embarrassing.

After school I'd catch the bus back to Tintwistle. My bus wasn't until quarter past five, so sometimes I'd hang around in Woolworths. Sometimes I'd meet boys in there and chat. Then there were the bus shelters in Howard Road. Otherwise we might mooch around the town centre. There weren't a lot of cafés in Glossop in those days, though we sometimes spent an hour or so in Brockshaw's café.

Sometimes I'd visit my best friend, Maureen Purcell, whose family had a hardware shop in the Sheffield Road. This was like my second home. We spent many of our lunch hours in the back room of the store, looking at sheet music and singing along to popular records on Maureen's Mum's record player. Sometimes I used to do my homework at Maureen's. I'd lie with her on the rug in front of the coal fire.

I used to love staying at the Purcells' because it meant I could stay out later with my friends and I couldn't do that at Tintwistle. My mother used to make me be in by 10 p.m.

Maureen was a rebel, like me. I suppose we were a bit wild. We were boy-mad and dancing-mad and loved clothes. Above all, I loved shoes. Sometimes when I stopped over at the Purcells' I would bring a collection of shoes and line them all up along the skirting board just to admire them.

Maureen was the first of our crowd to wear a bra. But she was Jewish, so there came a time when her mother wouldn't let her go out in Glossop any more. She was sent to places in Manchester – Jewish events and so on. This was because there were no Jewish boys in Glossop and Maureen was expected to marry a Jew.

As a teenager I began making my own dresses. I made quite a few for special occasions such as dances. I'd cut out bits of material all over the floor, then survey them, then run them up. I've always been good at three-dimensional things like that, planning and making things.

School dances were on a Friday night, upstairs at the Fitzwilliam Hall. These dances were just for people at our school. We'd dance and chat up boys, or we'd get chatted up. It was all the expected rituals.

There was no alcohol but some of the boys used to swig illegal lager. We'd also smoke lots of cigarettes. I've always been quite a puffer and liked to see myself at the end of a long trail of blue smoke, appearing elegantly through the clouds it formed.

School dances ended at 11.30 p.m. Everyone would then walk home in groups or in couples. Sometimes at the bus stop I'd snog a boy. I knew what French kissing was all about and I was an expert in long, deep and passionate kisses with my back pressed against a wall, my tongue searching and searching.

But for what? Sometimes it all seemed quite pointless. The kisses were as damp and overcast as the skies around Tintwistle. Was that all there was to life, twisting your tongue around in a boy's mouth?

None of these boys seemed really worth the effort. I had so many boyfriends – sometimes one a week, though none really serious. So I didn't lose my virginity until I was in my late teens.

There were also Saturday night dances at the Victoria Hall. It used to be packed. Mostly there were people of our age, with a sprinkling of older ones. We'd go with our girlfriends and it was boys on one side of the hall and girls on the other. Then the boys used to come over and ask us to dance. Some of them could dance quite well, but others just used to shuffle around.

We never went into pubs. In those days girls didn't.

Later on, when some people got more daring, they'd go down to Ashton-under-Lyne, to the 'Pally', or to Manchester. They'd go on the train and nobody had any qualms about it. You could get the last train from Manchester, which would get to Hadfield about midnight. There used to be one bus that came from Glossop and went round all the villages – Tintwistle, Hollingworth and so on. It was called the 'ghost bus'. Nobody in those days was frightened about being out late.

Then there was the Empire cinema. Sunday was a good time to go, even though some of us were supposed to be in church then. People would sneak in, dreading anyone seeing them, and then sit at the back.

As a child my mother bought my clothes in C&A in Manchester. The first thing I ever chose for myself was a really sexy and tight pencil skirt, and after that a pair of high-heeled shoes.

I always felt as a child that I was in waiting. I thought I wasn't pretty, but I always had the idea I would be pretty one day. And I knew the key to that was through clothes. Clothes could transform me – I could be anyone I fancied. Whenever I dressed up and went out I just knew I looked better than anyone else.

A lot of my friends used to get clothes from C&A. Flock nylon dresses, for example, which they used to starch with sugar. We also went in for seamless skirts, pullovers and gingham dresses.

My dresses could be a bit different since I sometimes made them myself. Once I made a Suzy Wong dress in one day and wore it that same night. I loved the way it felt on my body and how my leg showed bare through the split.

In those days the boys often wore Teddy-boy suits. In fact Glossop became quite a centre for Teds. Rock and roll came in about that time and soon the traditional dances were replaced by the jive and then the twist. Manchester was a much bigger scene, of course, but this led to coffee and expresso bars in Glossop.

I enjoyed being a teenager in the rock and roll fifties. In fact, being sixteen was the most wonderful time of my life, just dressing up and going to dances with my girlfriends.

Up north around then you always knew exactly which street corner to hang about on and which café to go in in any of the local towns. You could link up with people easily through your tastes and friendships.

Around that time there were lots of American singers with crew cuts. And, of course, Tommy Steele. I decided to modernize my brother Gordon by giving him a crew cut. He was dead against this but I talked him into it. He got into trouble at school for that. I was quite strong-willed even then. I knew how to get people to do things; I was persuasive.

Living in the heart of the Peak District, I'd often go for walks over the local hills, especially in summertime, from Tintwistle to Oldham or Greenfields. There would be family hikes with my parents and brother and sister, just us walking in the countryside together. Other times I'd go rambling with four or five of my friends.

We'd also organize more strenuous hikes for Easter and sometimes on Sundays. Then everyone would go up on the hills in their white dresses and straw hats, dotted all over the landscape, and we'd be out all day picking flowers and watching out for rare birds.

Later, as a teacher in inner-city schools, I thought it scandalous that some of my pupils had never seen the countryside. I would organize expeditions and take them on plant and tree-spotting walks. But nowhere as beautiful as the Peak District.

On some of the more demanding walks Ivan Bell was our guide. We'd go up over the moors to Little Hayfield and over Kinder Scout. I loved these longer walks, as the views were spectacular and there was an undercurrent of danger. Kinder Scout, for example, can be risky, with treacherous peat bogs and mists that come up all of a sudden and trap you.

Some of these walks were really hard work. We would get soaking wet and so hungry. One Easter I went out with a group including Maureen Purcell, and because she was Jewish the only food she had was water and special kosher bread. We loved this bread and ate it all, but Maureen didn't dare touch our sandwiches. I suppose she thought God would appear there in the hills and denounce her.

At that time I had very little idea of what you might call culture. I'd never been to the theatre and I had been only once to an art gallery, in Manchester. Before that I'd never seen a real painting. And I never dreamed of going to college or university. It just never entered my head. There was a little clique at grammar school – the snobby gang, who were all going to university. The boys in that set carried umbrellas and we thought that was so very effeminate! As for me, I just wanted to leave and earn my living.

The biggest thing that transformed my life was my family moving down to London. That was in the late fifties. My parents had found a sub post office in South Harrow. They wanted to get on and move up the social scale and there was no future in Tintwistle. They thought that moving would give their children a better start.

We all drove down in the family car. I was astonished at the size of London – the spread of the city, sprawling and rolling in front of us as our car went through streets and streets of houses and shops. Until eventually we arrived at the junction of Field End Road and

Eastcote Lane. We drove into the car park behind the flats and unloaded, puffing upstairs with our luggage.

Our post office was next to a roundabout in a fairly modern building. We lived upstairs. In the front of the shop my parents sold children's clothes. They did quite well and it was not long before they got another post office, in Stanmore, which my dad ran on his own. Every Saturday night they'd be up late adding up all the money. There were no calculators in those days and they were always panicking in case they were short.

For a time I went to the local grammar school. But I was unhappy and uneasy. My northern accent marked me out and I missed the Peak District. I used to go to dances on my own. I can remember that, after having one dance, no one asked me again because I didn't dance in the way they did. That would never have happened up north; it was far less cliquey there.

But this didn't dent my confidence in myself. If you're born in the north, it does give you confidence. You're in a small spot and the world is your horizon. In London you feel your back's to the wall from the very beginning.

By now I realized I wanted more from life. And yet I could hardly say what. It certainly never entered my head that one day I would be famous, let alone a fashion designer! In lots of ways I was an innocent Tintwistle girl who thought it was a real treat to go to Butlins for a holiday with my girl friends, or to the Isle of Man, where I went with them when I was fifteen. And I'd only been abroad once, to Switzerland on a school trip with some other girls. (We sent a postcard of the hotel to the ones left behind with 'Will this do?' on the back.)

And once, when I was invited out to dinner, I thought my hosts were unbelievably sophisticated when they offered me spaghetti! I'd never seen spaghetti before and it seemed so suave and continental. Meanwhile I had heard of art school. This appealed to me. So at seventeen I enrolled on a silversmithing course. But when I got there it seemed I'd aimed too high. The people were cultured and knowledgeable. I'll never know all that! I thought.

I was in the silversmithing studio, scraping and tapping away at my jewellery, but I felt out of place – an upstart. I did one term there and then left. How could this ever earn me a living? I asked myself. I wanted to be a painter, but, being working-class, I thought I should go out to work and earn some money. Then maybe I could be artistic in the margins with something to fall back on. I didn't know you could get a grant. That's how working-class I was!

Then I saw an advert on the tube for a secretarial college. I thought I'd better save some money to go there. So I went to work in the Kodak factory just opposite our post office. I was in the colour printing room and quite enjoyed it – especially the company of the other girls. But while I was there I realized I could never do a job like secretarial work that didn't stimulate me mentally.

I then decided to go to teacher training college. I would specialize in art and in that way I could hedge my bets. If I didn't make it as a painter I could fall back on school teaching. That seemed a secure thing to do. Mum and Dad were delighted. A teacher in the family! That seemed like a big thing for people like us.

My time at teacher training college was quite an eye-opener. They taught quite a lot about how you should allow children freedom to become creative. Nowadays I know it was crap. All that self-expression has just created a generation of morons, hooked on an endless appetite for rubbish.

I really do wish young people today would read and study! I think reading is so important. There are so many books dealing with human experience and they go back thousands of years. I can't have a conversation with someone who doesn't read. I can never have enough reading inside me.

I wanted my sons Joseph and Benjamin to be readers; to be scholarly and intellectually inquisitive. But as far as I know Joseph has only read things like books about the Great Train Robbers or the ex-gangster Jimmy Boyle's autobiography.

Perhaps it's not surprising that my sons are not academic, given their background. So many changes and moves, so much excitement. After all, they had a mother who would walk around the streets in rubber gear causing a commotion. Whenever I passed a building site the workmen would shout: 'Look at the state of her!'

And then, when they were at boarding school, instead of sending them Action Man kits, I would send my boys boxes of pineapples and oranges, and bin liners full of pirate clothes and leather jackets with 'Rock' studded on the back. When everyone else was wearing flares they had drainpipes. I even used to have things they liked from SEX made up in their sizes. They would turn up to school in leather trousers and earrings long before such things were acceptable.

On top of all this they had the Sex Pistols occasionally turning up at the school gate to meet them. John, for example, once took them to hold his hand when he went to the dentist, because he was terrified of being injected.

So perhaps it's hardly surprising they are more interested in style and clothes than books.

But without books where will they get any new ideas? I love books. There is nothing I like better than to sit at home reading. My idea of paradise is a well-stocked library.

I did enjoy teaching at first. It was a treat to see all those little faces in the morning, and to deal with their scrapes. I especially liked the slower children, ones with learning difficulties. It was a challenge to show them they could also read and write, and to see their little smudges turn into real words and proper sentences.

By then I had met Derek Westwood. He was a working-class boy, handsome and friendly – just the job for the girl I thought I still was.

Derek was a tool-shop apprentice at a Hoover factory, but he had dreams. I think that's one reason I took to him. He was always trying to better himself. He worked at odd jobs like the bingo hall and in hotels, or helping to manage local clubs. Best of all, Derek longed to fly! He had an ambition to become a pilot and soar through the clouds. I thought that was exciting.

My parents loved him. He was just the son-in-law they'd always wanted. And then, before I knew it, I'd gone through all these stages and was on the other side of a commitment. We were getting married.

It all happened so fast really, too fast to slow down or think, now look here, what am I doing? I was only twenty.

I made my own wedding dress. And then it was the morning of 21 July 1962 and I was on my way to Sopers department store in Harrow to get my hair fixed and everything seemed to go wrong.

When I came out my hair was stiff and lacquered, all sticky. I remember furiously combing it out. I was in tears and so angry. There was Derek smiling and me smiling and all our parents smiling. We were posing outside St John's Church in Greenhill, near Harrow, and I had only wanted a register office wedding. It was my parents who had insisted that only a church affair would do for their eldest daughter, and at the last moment I had given in.

For our honeymoon we went to North Devon. I liked the sense of isolation you can get there. After that, everything seemed to settle down for a while and I soon became pregnant with Ben.

Right from the start Ben was always such a cheeky monkey. He never liked to be cuddled and would wriggle away, trying to walk on his own. We lived just round the corner from my parents' post office on the main road to Harrow. Sometimes I would leave Ben with my Mum and he would climb all over the parcels and scribble over the money order forms.

At times I wondered where all my girlhood dreams had vanished. Was I a ballerina or an ice-skater? Was I an inventor or an airline stewardess? I had to admit I was none of these. In fact, I was Mrs Westwood.

I knew I had brains and ability. And looks too. Julie Christie looks, people said. Quite hard and chiselled. I was quite a striking blonde in those days. Once I was stopped near Olympia by a TV crew who asked me to pose near a fruit stall. I suppose that was my first-ever media appearance.

Several times I escaped – back up to Tintwistle or to my Auntie Ethel's holiday caravan in Wales. This caravan became a sort of staging-post for my thoughts and then my rebellion.

I started to take more of an interest in my brother's goings-on around then. Unlike me, Gordon had persisted with grammar school. He was a nonchalant but efficient worker. But he often complained about how boring school was and about the stupid restrictions. In fact he was expelled temporarily for refusing to be caned. Then, because of the greater freedom there, he decided to finish his A levels at Harrow Technical College.

At this college he got in with a crowd of cosmopolitan boys who went around together as a gang. Some of these seemed more interesting than the people I was going around with.

Gordon was the only one who had a car, so he was quite in demand. He was a good-looking boy and had lots of girlfriends, au pairs and student types, and the car came in handy here.

It also came in handy for putting up a homeless art student. This was Malcolm McLaren, then known as Malcolm Edwards, the man who was to transform my life.

Malcolm was the strangest of Gordon's crowd. I can't quite recall when I first saw him, whether it was in the car or not. But I remember talking to him alone for the first time in my parents' living room. My first thought was that he was crazy. He had a strange look and acted very oddly, sort of uncoordinated and jerky. And he would be talking quite normally and then suddenly open his mouth really wide and laugh and you could see the insides of his mouth like an explosion of pink gums. It would scare the life out of you.

I thought that was quite horrible.

What's more, I usually like people with hard faces. I suppose you like people who look a bit like yourself. Malcolm has a soft face, with very gentle bone structure and lovely curling red hair. So I wasn't attracted to him at first.

Malcolm had these awful parents who objected to him carrying on like any art student and going to all-night parties. They'd thrown him out and he'd been living for a while in Harrow on the Hill cemetery.

Gordon asked our parents if Malcolm could stay in the flat, but they were horrified by the way he looked. They also thought Malcolm very rude. Which he was. (Malcolm was even ruder than Fred Vermorel, who, when he used to come round, would knock on the door and then just push past my mother without a word and go up to Gordon's bedroom.)

42

My mother hated Malcolm; she still does. I think she blames him for 'corrupting' me in some way. Which, I suppose, he did. But then again, that's what I wanted.

Sometimes I would listen to the conversations of Gordon, Malcolm and Fred. I felt this strange attraction to all three of them. They talked so intensely about things I wanted to hear about, that were important to me, like ideas and art. And they did it without any phoney artiness or posh accents. They were ordinary-sounding people arguing about paintings and books and films I'd never heard of, but wanted desperately to know about.

They swore and laughed about the action painting of Jackson Pollock or Orson Welles's new film of Kafka's novel The Trial. Malcolm said the film made him depressed for days afterwards. Fred shouted that, according to Jean-Paul Sartre, depression was all a matter of will-power!

I had never known people who could talk about such things in that way. I used to think culture was for Tories, that you couldn't say things like that without a plum or a silver spoon in your mouth.

So I went back for more. Every time I went round to see my parents I was hoping that Malcolm in particular would be there. But although I wanted to very much, I didn't dare join in their conversations. I've always been very shy. I was afraid I'd make a fool of myself. But I'd stay as long as I could – until Ben started tugging at my sleeve and it was time to go home to Derek.

Sometimes I used to look at Derek and wonder whether he really wanted as much from life as myself. I wasn't sure if I was still in love. Or if I was, was love only this? I was looking at him and feeling empty inside.

I think the problem was that romantic ideal of expecting your partner to be almost everything, to fulfil every need. Of course, Derek couldn't do that. Nowadays I have got over that and I'd be very happy with a man like Derek. After all, he was so nice. But in those days I thought that because we had different interests it would never work.

I decided I had to leave him. But sometimes it's hard to leave someone. I think it's sometimes harder to do the leaving than be left

43

behind. And then where would I fit in? Because, next to Gordon and his friends, I felt quite old. I had a marriage and a son, chores and a home, and they had so much freedom.

But I wanted their life. And bit by bit I realized I sort of wanted Malcolm as well. But soon Malcolm was gone – he'd found digs elsewhere. And I only heard about him from Gordon and Fred.

Gordon eventually passed his A levels in Physics, Maths and Chemistry, all with A grades. He was a bright boy. But he had been bitten by the creativity bug. So instead of going to university he got a place in a film school in Covent Garden. He was thinking of becoming a director. The Polanski of Tintwistle. In fact, he has done very well and is now a respected film editor.

So Gordon moved out of Harrow into a flat with some other film students in West London. And then I heard that Malcolm had moved in with them. By now it seemed like a plot was unfolding in my life. But even then I wasn't too sure what it was, and what all these coincidences might mean. Although, to tell the truth, I don't really believe in coincidences. I suppose I just knew very strongly what I wanted and I went for it.

By now I had told Derek I no longer loved him. Poor man, he was so heartbroken. I felt like a rat, for he'd never done me any harm. He cried and asked me why. But how could I tell him he was just boring? I wished I could just fly away and leave all this mess my life had become. I was so unhappy.

I left Derek several times and then went back. He pleaded and I gave in and then we argued again and then I would leave again. I would stay with my parents. They were worried but tried to be understanding, thinking it would all blow over.

Just before I left Derek for good I spent some more time in Wales in Auntie Ethel's caravan to think things out. When I came back, out of the blue, Gordon suggested Ben and me could stay in his flat. Or was it, I wonder, so out of the blue? Blue, in any case, is a rather mysterious colour. I love that blue flush in Watteau and Fragonard skies, over a picnic – or is it an orgy? – in Arcadia.

Malcolm was as pale and crazy as ever, but now more manic and busy at his work. His room was an amazing pigsty, with piles of half-finished or abandoned sketches and gouache paintings, wood debris from efforts at sculpture, and furious drawings he did on rolls of wallpaper he used to unroll and tear bits from.

He was like that – working on throwaway stuff as if he didn't care or was in too much of a hurry, leaving the edges of everything all ragged. That was his whole style then and for all our years together – desperate to make his mark, running away from his past, burning all his bridges in madcap bonfires.

He was homeless and rootless and proud of it. In fact he's never been able to make a home, and no matter where he stays it's as if he's camping for the night or he's in a hotel. I liked that; it had a kind of existential soundness. After all, everyone is homeless really. So why erect all those knick-knacks and ornaments on a mantelpiece in face of the coming void? Home is where your work is.

He was also anti-social and I found that very appealing. In those days I thought our society was repulsive and dangerous and that anybody who was anti-social had the interests of society at heart. Up till then, the most anti-social thing I'd done was to give away all my savings to Oxfam.

And Malcolm was certainly a one-off. He was fascinating and mad, whereas I felt I was ordinary and very sane. It was as though I was a coin and he showed the other side of me.

At first he seemed quite dismissive of me and Ben. But then I noticed a change in his attitude. When he hurried and squeezed by me in the corridor, I wondered, was there a coy appeal? I even began to think he was courting me in his clumsy sort of way. Sweetening me up for a conquest perhaps. But what a strange way to go about it. He was so awkward and harsh. And I wasn't sure I really wanted him. After all, I'd just left one man in tatters. Did I want to begin again so soon? Well, maybe I did really, but I thought I'd better play safe and hold out for a while.

That house was bohemia. A setting for genius to flower in and take over the world. Most evenings we would cluster in the living room and talk. It was Woodbines and William Morris, Nescafé and Nietzsche.

We'd sit in front of the electric fire, the twin bars glowing like orange lips and I would watch the filaments until sometimes they burst and snapped and then Gordon would wait for the bar to cool down and twist the filament together for a repair. Sometimes the talking would go on until dawn.

Malcolm was at home more often than the others. The others all studied in central London but at the time his art college was in nearby Chiswick. Maybe it was that proximity, with us alone in the house, apart from Ben. I know that Malcolm has since claimed that it was me who seduced him. And that I would walk about scantily dressed or in the nude. To me that was normal, not a come-on. I was a freethinker, and in the sixties nudism came naturally. But I admit I was intrigued to see what effect it might have on him.

At the time I wasn't even sure if he was capable of having sex. I was fairly sure he wasn't a homosexual, but I did wonder if he'd taken some sort of chastity vow, like a monk. It was also hard somehow to imagine him making love. His body language didn't seem to fit with the act. I also wondered whether Malcolm was frightened of women. Which, as I know now, he was – terribly!

Anyway, the day came when he complained of a stomach ache. He was groaning and clutching his stomach, and the blood had gone from his face. I suddenly felt so sorry for him. I looked at him and thought he really was a rather special kind of person and that maybe I ought to take care of him. He seemed so vulnerable.

He was lying on the filthy old mattress he used to keep on the floor in his room and I told him to go and lie in my bed while I fetched him some medicine.

When I came back from the chemist's with a bottle of Milk of Magnesia he seemed a little better – and quite at home in my bed! Then, later on, when I said he should leave as I wanted to go to sleep, he refused!

He'd recently cut his hair with a razor; hacked it away down to the scalp, some bits of which were bruised and scratched with beads of dried blood. I thought in some strange way he'd done that for me. Perhaps it was a bizarre declaration. Like Van Gogh and his ear – here it is, my vulnerability, take it and love me!

As he lay there in bed with that chopped-up hair and an idiotic grin, with the sheets tucked under his softly stubbled chin, he looked quite cute, not like the raging ogre of Art. Then I slipped in beside him.

I was naked, as I have always detested pyjamas. Is this young man normal? I thought. I was curious. My hand felt under the sheets. His penis was limp. I took his hand and pressed it to my breast. He seemed puzzled. This must be his first time, I thought. Poor boy! He doesn't know what to do.

I rolled the sheets down. He lay frozen in his Marks & Spencer Y-fronts. I tugged them down to his skinny knees and caressed the soft, gingery down on his thighs, letting my fingertips barely touch his skin and watching the tiny hairs rise up. I jiggled his balls delicately, and felt them slither inside his warm hairy sack of skin. I then gathered his penis in my hand and let it lie in my palm, as if weighing it.

Then, gently, I began to knead. Little by little it came alive, began to flex and stiffen.

A puzzled look had crept into Malcolm's eyes. He had been circumcised, and this allowed me to ply my fingers around the reddishness beneath his foreskin. I tickled the ridge of his penis, and slipped my hands over his shaft, which by now stood erect and proud in its garden of ginger tufts, like a guardsman outside Buckingham Palace, or like the Monument in the City of London which commemorates the spot where the Great Fire of London started, all those years ago in Pudding Lane.

Malcolm's breathing came faster. Semen began to ooze as I smoothed up and down, my hands full of his hotness. And then his climax jolted through me and he bucked and came all over my hands and breasts.

Not long after that we created our first-ever joint design. Malcolm had the idea he wanted to dress in oversized workmen's overalls. He bought some fluorescent yellow material and I cut it out on the floor. Then I sewed it together and Malcolm went out into the street. People stared! He even got comments from art students who should have known better. Somehow, on him, that outfit had a mad swagger and dash.

And wearing it was heroic. That was his first real foray into dressing as confrontation. Before that he'd done things like wearing a thick overcoat in all weathers – even indoors – when everyone else was in shirtsleeves.

Malcolm always had an instinctive flair about how to make a statement through clothes – and especially how to make other people uncomfortable and uncertain about what they were wearing. But before he met me he had to combine and customize off-the-peg clothes.

After a while I taught him intercourse. Soon our lovemaking was almost regular, although with Malcolm nothing was that regular. He was so temperamental and explosive! The slightest thing might set him off. I never knew what he was thinking or might do next.

And sometimes our nights together were far from peaceful. He would have terrible nightmares and roll around in bed and scream about what he thought people were doing to him – especially his mother!

Malcolm said he was worried about me getting pregnant. He thought he couldn't afford that. Being an artist, his art came first. I said not to worry, I was on the pill. Only I was lying. I used to pretend I took them. Because I'd now decided I wanted to get pregnant by him. I wanted Malcolm and I wanted his child. I thought the two would go together.

About two months later I did become pregnant, with Joe. Malcolm ranted and raved. He was so horrible, saying I was a whore and ruining his life and his chances of being an artist. He even said it wasn't his child. I was so hurt. How could he think that? I loved him so much!

He persuaded me to have an abortion and borrowed the money from his grandmother. But when we got to the door of the clinic I rebelled. I said: 'Look, Malcolm, I want this child. We can have it. It will be all right.' He calmed down then. We spent the money on a blue cashmere suit for me.

During that period I was educating myself politically and absorbing the influence of other people. Like Lesley, the great love of Gordon's life. Lesley was an American whose father was a scientist. She was brought up in this town – in Tennessee, I think – which is just for scientists. Lesley was so fierce and clear about everything. She told me about Vietnam, and got me thinking a lot about politics in general and how we needed a revolution to sweep away old ideas.

When she went back to America, Gordon missed her very much. He wrote asking to meet again, but never got a reply. I don't know what became of her.

Lesley politicized Gordon too. He decided the world was such a shitty place, so unsafe, that he'd never ever bring a child into it. He's stuck to that pledge all his life.

Poor Ben thought Malcolm was horrible; that Mum had taken up with a madman. He missed his real father. And on top of that Malcolm could be wicked to him. He sometimes acted as if he was jealous of Ben. Once he even deliberately stood on Ben's foot to test him. Ben stood there in pain but too proud to cry.

I was too weak to intervene. Vivienne Weakwood, that's me! Especially when I'm in love.

Malcolm was at Croydon Art College by now and that was how I first met Jamie Reid. I felt less outside of their talk by now and I was gradually collecting my own ideas. I had a good idea of what was radical. I would sometimes criticize Malcolm's friends for not being revolutionary enough. Like Robin Scott, for example, who lived with us for a while. I thought him so complacent I asked him to leave.

I was still teaching to make ends meet. But I was also making jewellery. I'd learned the rudiments of this at Harrow. I found I had quite a knack for 3D design – I've got that kind of brain – and I enjoyed having ideas and making up brooches and earrings. I got a stall on the Portobello Road and sold my stuff on Saturdays. It was useful extra money, and untaxed.

Sometimes too, Malcolm would help with designs. I realized how genuinely strange some of his ideas were. I couldn't work out how he got them.

I was so busy with my jewellery I almost forgot I was pregnant. Joe

49

was overdue by a whole month and I kept thinking: Oh God, I hope this baby doesn't come today. I was working right up to the day I delivered him. I had to have him induced, and that was painful.

I went into hospital around 2 p.m. and my last meeting about the jewellery had been about midday. Joseph was born around teatime. I'd been hoping for a girl, but Joseph was so lovely! Delightful right from the start. A great big baby with a strong, straight back and a peaches-and-cream face framed with honey-coloured curls.

I think the happiest time of my life was in bed just lying there and playing with my new baby.

But Malcolm acted as if he couldn't have cared less. It took him six days before he visited Joe. The ward sister even asked him if he was a long-distance lorry driver. Even so, I was overjoyed when he finally turned up, in his big overcoat with snowflakes on his hair.

Now, as a couple, we moved into a flat near the Oval in South London. We were desperately poor. But we had just enough to scrape by on. Malcolm would often spend his entire grant on himself and expect me to feed him as well as Joe and Ben. But Malcolm's grandmother, Rose, did sometimes help out with money from her pension. I did like Rose a lot. She was a shrill, crazy cockney, as thin as a stick and all shrivelled, with a laugh like a hyena. She doted on Malcolm.

At the time I was still married to Derek, and I couldn't claim social security. So when Joe was six weeks old I put him in a nursery and went back to teaching.

That was in 1968. The year with all the excitement about student rebellions all over the world. Colleges were being occupied, and everywhere there were riots. It seemed as if our generation, the baby-boomers, had gone completely mad and were trying to take over everything.

That same summer Malcolm and I went on holiday in the South of France. I left Joe with my mother. We had a wonderful and interesting time and I really thought that holiday put us back together after the upset about Joe being born.

But when we got back I was really horrified. I collected Joseph from his nursery on Friday afternoon and discovered he'd gone into a catatonic trance. I don't think I've ever been so worried about anything. I told Malcolm and we took Joe to the park and this tiny boy just sat there on the swings. He was inert, with his head bowed, not making a sound. We tried to coax him and trick him into speaking but he just sat there. In the end, he didn't respond to me but to Malcolm.

I believe he thought I'd really let him down badly.

I spent that weekend cuddling and reassuring him and then, on Monday morning, I went off to my school clutching him close and handed in my notice. I was determined I would never leave him alone, ever again.

In those days Malcolm was my teacher. I hung on every word he said. I was looking for a political direction and he had a strong, radical outlook. I needed to find clues, a formula to understand life. Malcolm was something like a God with a pot of gold at the end of the rainbow. He seemed so clever and to know so many things. He had so much culture.

We called our son 'Joseph Ferdinand' after a painting by Velázquez in the National Gallery. Malcolm also gave him the surname Corré, after his grandmother, Rose Corré. Malcolm hated his mother and stepfather so much he didn't want Joe to have their surname, Edwards.

Meanwhile Rose had moved to Clapham. She'd found a flat in a block near Clapham Common over Clapham South tube station. We wanted to move from the Oval and she found us a cheap flat on an estate nearby. This meant I could sometimes leave the boys with Rose while I was working.

Malcolm was never in. He was at art college all day and then out all night with his friends and only came back early in the morning when I was asleep.

The Clapham flat was tiny. We put our double bed in the living room and the boys had bunk beds in the one bedroom. That flat was our base for the next fourteen years. It was from that flat that we launched all our shops and collections, and it was that flat which was really the headquarters for the whole punk thing. And not to mention all my collections. I still live there, cycling to and from my workshops every day.

I have to admit I was a hopeless mother. I couldn't get meals on time or organize a thing. My cooking was all over the place. The flat was always in a mess and the washing-up never got done. Malcolm used to complain that the place was a pigsty.

And I found my boys a lot to cope with. After all, by the time I was in my mid-twenties I already had two babies under four and that is quite a responsibility. It probably would have been better to have had them when I was older and more experienced. It's such a big strain for mothers to have to earn a living and bring up children. Especially when you don't know how to do it.

And yet I must say that my boys were rarely troublesome and were often protective of me. Even as a young boy Joe always acted like a little husband. I think that came as a reaction to Malcolm and the way he was to everyone. Joe wanted to protect me from him. Joe never ever called Malcolm 'Daddy'. But then I don't think it's that important for a boy to have his father around all the time. The mother is the more important influence.

And it's from the mother that boys learn about women. I've always thought that women have a lot of strength while men have force. If you go past an old building with its windows smashed, or a cherry tree with its branches snapped, you can be sure that boys did it. Never a girl.

Not that I've particularly treated my boys as boys. I always treated them as people and gave them lots of freedom. But as a working mother I brought them up to respect my time and space. We never had a lot of house rules. I did expect them to be home at a certain hour of the day and they were always good about that. My attitude was that I knew my boys and would be the first to know if they were in trouble.

I suppose in some ways I've been a bad parent in not imposing rules. Children are often happier with rules. But then, although my mother laid down rules and tried to impose her morals, I do think my boys have respected me more than I did her. I've never imposed any puritan codes of behaviour on my children. I always accepted what they did as long as they told me the truth. But children are never easy. And then I had to cope with Malcolm too – he was like ten children all by himself.

In the end we sent both boys to boarding school. It seemed the only way to have the time to be creative and for me to keep up with Malcolm. I also thought state schools were terrible, the classes too big and the teaching disgraceful. Ben was coming home at nine years old and I could see he had been doing what I used to teach five-year-olds! From my own experience as a teacher I could also understand why the kids wanted to misbehave.

Malcolm was against sending the boys to progressive schools as he thought they would end up as dope dealers. So we chose conservative schools.

Joe was only four when he first went to boarding school. I had forebodings from the start. Taking him up there was like something out of *Jane Eyre*. On the train he joined a party of schoolchildren escorted by teachers. Joe started singing 'Rudolf the Red-nosed Reindeer'. But none of the other children responded. They were all completely silent and stared at him. I started to feel something was a bit weird.

Later on, when we visited him at school, I thought he looked lost, like a little pink pig in his blazer, navy raincoat and peaked cap. And the only thing he'd say in answer to any question was: 'I suppose so.' He'd say this in a tiny voice right at the back of his throat with his head bowed down. So we found Joe another school and this time he went there with Ben.

To be truthful, neither Ben or Joe liked going to boarding schools. I got these pathetic letters pleading for them to be let home. At one school Joe was even terrorized by teachers who used to spank him with a coat-hanger for talking after lights out in the dormitory. But Malcolm was very robust about all this. He said it would all be all right in the end and it would just make them independent.

Sometimes, as well, we couldn't afford the fees. More than once we had to creep into schools and virtually kidnap them towards the end of term as we had failed to pay. The boys quite enjoyed that. It was very cloak and dagger.

Later on I sent Joe to a dance school. I thought it would do him good as he was very self-expressive. But he didn't like it. He was self-conscious about being fat – like Malcolm, he was tubby as a child but grew into a slim adult.

In between spells at various boarding schools and short stays with us, Ben and Joe would stay with my parents. They had retired to a thatched cottage near Daventry, and after that they moved to Devon.

Malcolm was keen on anything that kept the boys away from our busy life. He wanted them to grow up as quickly as possible and not be a burden. He used to say that children are never really yours. They belong to themselves. I agree with that in some ways. I'm very proud of my boys and always have been. But, although maybe this sounds ridiculous, I judge them as if they are not my own. As children, they loved and trusted me, but still I could never put them first, as my parents did with me.

In truth, Malcolm hated the idea of children and the idea of childish dependency. He refused to accept that children were any different from adults. He used to say he agreed with Victorians that they should be put to work as soon as possible. What rot all this childhood stuff was.

From an early age my sons had to take their own clothes to the laundrette. And though we sometimes gave them pocket money they had to work for most of it, doing the housework or shining Malcolm's shoes.

One day Malcolm had a great idea to teach them independence. He decided they should cycle all the way from Clapham to Devon to stay with my parents. This was when Joe was nine and Ben was thirteen. I packed them sandwiches and soft drinks and they set off on their 200-odd-mile ride.

In the early hours of next morning they got stopped by the police, who thought they'd absconded. The police rang us and we told them it was OK for our boys to be cycling around in the countryside in the dark. The police gave them a letter of authority in case they got stopped again.

The journey took them four and a half days, and when they

finally got to my parents' house my father had put a Union Jack over the veranda to welcome them. It had been probably quite a dangerous thing to do, but I had been brought up in the country-side and I didn't think of all the risks. And it must have taught them some initiative.

By this time we had become even poorer and I was sometimes on social security. But I used to get all my food virtually free. I'd cook economically in the macrobiotic way with rice, vegetables and just a few nuts. And I'd creep around deserted gardens in Clapham to dig up dandelion roots, or I would make a dandelion salad from flowers I'd picked on Clapham Common. Sometimes I'd offer these to the boys, but they would make faces and go off to the chip shop.

I'd also go down to the local market with the pushchair and load up with bruised fruit and vegetables thrown away by stall-holders. Sometimes I retrieved perfectly good food from bins. So I managed to get us by.

Malcolm was now definitely into strange dressing. He'd wear things like fluorescent green women's shoes and skin-tight leather trousers with tassels. Things that would wind people up. Most people then were into hippie clothes, loose and floppy, like bell-bottom trousers. They thought to dress like Malcolm was shocking, somehow perverse. I thought it was great. I wanted to look like that myself – sharp and provocative.

I experimented with razor-cutting my hair in a spiky way and dyeing it various shades of blonde and pink. I shaved my temples to give me a more intellectual look. I would walk around in a pink pearlized-rubber negligée and winkle-picker boots.

I was intrigued by how people would stare at us, affronted, as if we'd kidnapped their children or blown up their garden gnomes. Sometimes they'd call out insultingly. Or they'd get aggressive, as if we were threatening them – which I suppose in a way we were. It taught me the power of dressing up – the power of fashion symbols.

Our relationship was wild. Looking back, I also think it was quite unhappy in lots of ways. I never really knew what Malcolm was doing, or whether I was really the one in his life. For example, his relationships with other women. He told me he had to try these things out because he was an artist and had to be free.

We were supposed to be like Jean-Paul Sartre and Simone de Beauvoir, in an 'open relationship'. That hurt me a lot. It wasn't what I wanted. But I tried to understand. But I thought so long as he is with me, so long as I have him, it doesn't matter what he does with other women. I've got his child now, I thought. I'm part of his life.

Malcolm in those days was such a force, always the centre of things, lively and unstoppable. And sometimes he could be such fun and such wonderful company, an inspiration to lift any grey skies with a look or a remark.

By this time he was at Goldsmiths College. In his last year there he tried to make a film about the history of Oxford Street. He did this with Jamie and Fred and some others, like Helen Mininberg. They did lots of filming in Oxford Street, particularly at the Dolphinarium, and at places like the Academy Cinema, which showed art films and Eastern European cartoons.

Malcolm thought that if Karl Marx was alive now he'd be the manager of the Academy Cinema. He was trying all sorts of strange ideas out in this film – like getting his grandmother to do a voice-over. Of course, she kept getting it wrong and muddled everything up and Malcolm lost his temper when she couldn't pronounce 'Caravaggio'.

I tried to help as well, bringing to the flat a little black boy I was teaching, to read out bits of commentary.

Malcolm sometimes used to taunt me by saying he was sleeping with Helen. He said that even though she was so ugly she was still more interesting than me. I was never sure if any of this was true. Or if he just said it to hurt me. We had so many rows. He used to make me so angry I'd hit him – sometimes hard. In fact I used to punch him quite a lot. I'd pummel his arms and sometimes he'd run crying out of the flat.

The Oxford Street film didn't come to anything. But by researching it Malcolm got interested in rock and roll as a subject, because part of the film was supposed to feature Billy Fury and his fans. Malcolm and Fred had had this big debate about who was the greatest genius in Britain at that time. It came down to Norman Wisdom or Billy Fury. They couldn't decide.

Around then Malcolm also started to collect rock and roll records and to think about a fifties kind of style. What was that style? Was it still relevant?

By then it was the end of Malcolm's art student days. In fact he had spent seven years at different art colleges. He was able to manage that by fiddling grants from different authorities – it was quite easy then. And then eventually he left without any kind of qualification. I thought that was quite funny. That happened because when he was supposed to submit some of his Oxford Street film at Goldsmiths there was nothing to show.

Malcolm found some discarded 8mm footage of one of the lecturers' summer holidays, all chewed up and mangled in a college dustbin. He stuck it all together, upside down or back to front, in the order it came out of the bin. The head of film, Malcolm LeGrice, an experimental film-maker, said it was a breakthrough and brilliant. But he still wanted to see the Oxford Street stuff, which the college had paid lots of money towards.

Malcolm did a runner.

After leaving the college Malcolm was really deflated. In fact he went to pieces. I didn't know what to do with him, he was so depressed. There was a weird time when he painted the entire hall of our flat black. It was bizarre, like opening the front door and walking into a black hole instead of a home. He said it expressed his mood.

He kept on about America and put on this absurd American accent which irritated everyone. He would drawl and then laugh because he knew his imitation was no good. Come off it, Malcolm, where's the Stetson? Or the ticket to New York?

Then he was caught shoplifting in Woolworths. There was a small court case, as a result of which he got his first mention in a local paper. That was amusing, and also a bit pathetic. But it shook him up. And it shook me up too. I decided it was about time, after nearly ten years, that we did something serious together – like earning a living. After all, I'd done my bit. He should make some money too. Perhaps by opening a shop, and why not a clothes shop?

I borrowed some money from my parents to get us going. They were dubious at first. Was Malcolm really trustworthy? I reassured them. I would be in charge.

Malcolm started to redesign himself. First he changed his surname to his real father's – McLaren. This was partly because Malcolm Edwards now had a criminal record and Malcolm was still thinking of going to America. He didn't want to be banned. But Malcolm McLaren also had more of a ring to it than Malcolm Edwards. It sounded defiant, like bagpipes.

Then he began to scout around for premises. Eventually he said he'd found this shop at the wrong end of the King's Road. At that time 430 King's Road was called Paradise Garage. Owned by a hippie named Trevor Miles, it had a black floor and a jukebox, but other than that it was full of tat. No imagination! We decided we would change all that.

This was in 1971. We made an agreement to take over the back part of the shop. Well, a sort of agreement. Give them enough time, Malcolm said, and they'll go bankrupt and then we'll have the whole shop. At that time the King's Road was in decline. The sixties had fizzled out. Chelsea was full of fading old hippies selling cheap junk to feed their drug habits. No one was buying much any more and in any case there wasn't much to buy.

It was a time of overflowings and overflowerings – floral shirts, flowing skirts, soppy, floppy collars and stupid ties with psychedelic prints. And flares! Everything 'hung out', or it was 'loose'?

We wanted to tighten all that up, pull it in, stop all that hippie smirking, be direct and stern. We didn't know quite what to do with the shop at first. We began selling fifties records and secondhand fifties clothes and fifties memorabilia. By now we were definitely interested in that era and this led on to Teddy boys. I remembered back to Glossop days and the Teds there. We thought Teds might be exciting, that they were into rebellion and could stir things up.

Malcolm had been hanging around with a group of situationists in Notting Hill called King Mob. They were revolutionaries who were interested in subverting the cultural scene. We now got very busy putting together all these ideas.

This was a period when Malcolm constantly travelled around buying up materials and items for the shop: winkle-pickers, fluorescent socks and ties and drape jackets.

Soon, as predicted, the owners of Paradise Garage went bankrupt. We inherited the whole shop. We now wanted to make the place more like a happening, a continually changing event. Décor! we thought. We started to do the shop up in ever more crazy ways. The front was just corrugated iron. We sprayed it black and put up 'Let it Rock' in pink fluorescent paper shaped like musical notes. Then we made the interior into a kind of fifties lower-middle-class living room cum coffee bar. Something out of a George Orwell novel. We put in fifties-type furniture with objects like pots of Brylcreem and earrings displayed all around.

It wasn't quite a shop and it wasn't quite art, but something in between. That shop became our ideas playpen. Malcolm filled the jukebox with rare fifties music, Eddie Cochran and early rock and roll. There were also stacks of fifties porn magazines like *Photoplay* and *Spick*. Customers could just walk in and play records for free or read, and that gave the place a relaxed feel, not like a shop at all.

'Teddy Boys are forever – rock is our business,' said our brochure.

At first business was slow. We would go on the tube down to Liverpool Street, where all the Teds hung out in pubs. I would chat them up while Malcolm watched from a corner. He had to be low-key because he dressed weird and could have been beaten up. The Teds were very nice really and after I gave them our cards with the address some said they'd come down and bring their friends.

Soon, other people noticed they could get this fifties clothing from us. We'd get all sorts in – fascinated by the Teds' regalia.

We sold quite a lot of secondhand clothes at first. As these were often frayed or worn out I had to replace collars and sew buttons on. When we started to run out of items I began running them up at home on my sewing machine. I also began to turn flares into straight trousers and dye things in the bathroom.

Gradually, we started to make entire new outfits just like the secondhand ones. Towards the end, all the trousers in Let it Rock were made by me and we used to get the jackets made by an East End tailor, Sid Green, as I couldn't do tailoring in those days.

Our shop was soon full of people thumbing through old handbills for fifties films and secondhand records from that time. And trying on our dayglo jackets, fluorescent ties and socks, and special blue and silver trousers.

More and more connoisseur types and people like art directors started to come into the shop. And we started to get our first publicity, with features in magazines and the London evening papers. Rock stars began coming in, including David Bowie, Iggy Pop and Bryan Ferry.

Soon we were asked to design costumes for Ken Russell's film *Mahler* and some television dance shows. Then we made costumes for *That'll Be The Day*, which starred David Essex and Ringo Starr (two complete fools in my opinion).

We were more impressed by a band called the New York Dolls, who came in one day in November '72. Malcolm was really taken aback by the rawness of their attitude and complete lack of respect for rock and roll traditions.

There was this Irish boy, Pat Casey, whom Malcolm had known from Harrow days, who said he'd be our shop manager and help us out because I was usually at home making and mending clothes and Malcolm was out buying and hustling.

But then Pat started to live in the shop. He'd lie there in a sleeping bag till about midday and make the place smell like a doss-house. People were banging on the door trying to get in, really pissed off. When Malcolm found out about this he thought it was quite funny. So did I really. It was so absurd.

Malcolm also realized that the more people tried to get in the shop and couldn't, the more desperate they became. So this late opening, this exclusivity idea, became part of the whole experience. If you tell people they can't have something, they want it even more. Eventually we would only open after about one o'clock. And we started refusing to let people in if we didn't like the look of them. Perhaps a funny way to do business, but it worked for us.

We went to a big rock and roll concert at Wembley Stadium in 1972. By that time we were making our own T-shirts – 'Viva la Rock and Roll' and so on. I remember we sold quite a lot of stuff that day, and made over a thousand pounds. Yet in a way the scale of turnover at that place showed us we were really quite amateurish. We essentially had a small-scale attitude, and that was something it took me ages to get out of. I'm not even sure if I have yet!

Malcolm's grandmother Rose and her husband Mick were still living down the road in Clapham. In spring that year Mick suddenly died. I was surprised how upset Rose was. To see them together you'd have thought they hated each other.

I still used to take the boys round to their place, as Rose was grateful for the distraction. She was such a live wire, always cracking jokes and mischievous. Sometimes she'd get Ben and Joe to make water bombs. They'd fill up big plastic bags with water and drop them from her fifth-floor flat on to people's heads. One day an irate man came storming upstairs and banged on the door. Rose opened it and said: 'Hello, is it raining outside?' She could get away with anything .

Then, with the shop and everything, we forgot all about Rose. One day Malcolm remembered and thought he'd better go round and visit 'the old girl'. He'd forgotten his key and when she didn't answer the door he had to break it down. He found her sitting bolt upright in bed, naked and dead. Apparently she'd died from starvation.

Because of all the trouble between Rose and Malcolm's mother, neither of us went to the funeral.

By the end of the year both of us were getting bored with Teds. They weren't such rebels after all. In fact most of them wanted to live, die and be buried in their fluorescent socks and drapes. That wasn't what we wanted.

We'd already begun making clothes, and that was our way out. I rigged up several sewing machines in our tiny flat in the front room next to our double bed and found some local women to come in and run things up.

Malcolm was buying all this amazing fabric, velvets and Lurex and so on, and soon people could hardly move in our flat for rolls of fabric and piles of clothing.

It had got tedious churning out Teds' clothing. We started to experiment with a rockers' and bike boys' look and a tougher leather look. We thought bikers might have a harder edge than Teds. We began sticking studs on the back of jackets and printing glitter on to clothes, and the whole thing started to become more creative and more fun. Why don't we change that seam or this collar too? we thought. As we experimented, the Teds began to desert the shop. They didn't want anything different or strange. They would come in and say: 'What the fuck is this?'

In 1973 we renamed the shop 'Too Fast to Live, Too Young to Die'. We were thinking of images like *The Wild One*, and *Rebel Without a Cause*. Also about Kenneth Anger's *Scorpio Rising*, which Malcolm had seen at the Arts Lab. This added homosexual and pornographic undercurrents to biker imagery. As we researched into motorbike wear we also became interested in rubber and fetish clothing.

I spelt out slogans like 'Rock and Roll' in chicken bones attached to the T-shirts. I used to boil up chickens at home in the kitchen and scrape the bones clean. We wanted to cross the biker look with the feel of witch-doctors or black magic. It was all to get the effect of a voodoo spell or a curse – a sinister undercurrent.

We started to put zips in odd places – where they shouldn't logically be. We thought about the construction of clothes. What was a zip for anyway? Was it really just a functional thing? After all, there were all sort of other sexy associations to do with zips. We also experimented with T-shirts which had bicycle tyres round the armpits.

All this made our clothes surreal and it made them seem dangerous.

I would take the new designs down to the shop in plastic bin liners in my green mini, and the assistants would get them out and often exclaim with surprise.

The research we did for all this led us into an underground fetish and sadomasochistic world. In those days not many people knew about that sort of thing. Malcolm found some under-the-counter catalogues with examples of weird fetish-wear items and we started to crossbreed the biker look with this fetish wear. For example, we added multiple chains to jackets, or sadomasochistic flourishes and accessories to biker clothes.

We got criticism from feminists who said our designs were degrading to women. They never thought that in fact women might feel in control through these clothes and accessories, that they might be empowered.

In 1972 we made our first journey to New York. This was with Malcolm's old school friend Jerry Goldstein – a bit of an idiot and a chatterbox, but quite good company. We took our newest clothes, like blouses with cigarette burns in them. But the Americans couldn't understand what we were trying to do.

In New York Malcolm met up again with the New York Dolls. We realized the Dolls were part of a new scene – something that had grown out of Andy Warhol's Factory. In fact this was what later became known as New York 'punk', though nobody used that word then.

I was impressed by the energy of New York, but I could see Malcolm had fallen in love with it.

When we came back to England it seemed greyer and more depressing than ever. But the experience had shown us that we should be harder and more upfront about what we were doing. We needed to cut through all that British gloom and hypocrisy, and make a stand and a statement.

We closed down Too Fast to Live and worked out a radical transformation of the interior, of the clothes and of the attitude. We hired a builder to transform the interior, but he was hopeless and hardly ever to be seen. In the end he left the shop in chaos and we had to do the job ourselves – carpentry and fitting and painting.

We called our new shop 'SEX'. We cut the three letters out of foam and covered them with fluorescent pink plastic and hung them outside the shop.

The interior looked like a kind of womb with spongy rubber grey material spread everywhere like an evil sort of wallpaper. We wanted to cross a feeling of being inside a womb with a sort of sexual torture chamber. We put gym bars up on the walls and we had a rubber-covered sofa, and then we hung a flying trapeze in there. A haven for fantasy.

Malcolm sprayed the interior with slogans. Some were from Valerie Solanas's *Scum Manifesto*. Solanas was the woman who shot Andy Warhol. She was an early New York feminist who founded SCUM – the Society for Cutting Up Men. She thought men were the real problem in the world and that the solution was to kill all of them. She began with Andy Warhol.

Along with these slogans Malcolm found some situationist slogans and we also used erotic illustrations of Snow White and the Seven Dwarfs and experimented quite a lot with the swastika motif. Anything to shock people into thinking for themselves.

Our slogan was: 'Rubber wear for the office'. We thought that being so blatant was a challenge to the hypocrisy which surrounded these taboo subjects. And funnily enough, soon after we put up the 'SEX' sign, all those Soho shops that called themselves the some-thing or other of 'love' started calling themselves 'Porno Palaces' and 'Sex Shops'. It was as if we had released them and now they could own up.

This shop was immediately successful. We got lots of Japanese tourists, rock stars and curious passers-by coming in, as well as pinstriped businessmen who would spend a long time in the changing rooms, which were just rubber curtains really. There was lots of groaning and they would sometimes leave a mess over the changing-room curtains which the assistants complained about having to clean off.

The assistants eventually began to sort out the real punters from the people who wanted to just get off on the stuff, and sometimes they would tell people to leave. Of course, that was what some of these men wanted – to be bossed around by women!

We were ransacking all the culture we knew and putting it together in as many perverse combinations as we could. We looked at all the cults which excited us and tried to pinpoint their vitality and energy. We also sold rubber masks, whips, chains and fetishistic lace-up boots, and all kinds of sex aids.

One speciality of our shop was T-shirts. We were making them more and more 'political'. We were also experimenting with their form. One day I was playing with two squares for a T-shirt and suddenly I thought: why bother with the sleeves? So I just sewed the squares together, highlighting the seams. That became the basis of my thinking about the way garments are made, and then using this thinking as part of the garment itself.

By this time Glen Matlock was working in the shop. He was a student at St Martin's College of Art and seemed enthusiastic about what we were doing.

Jordan had turned up too. She really looked the part, with her beehive hair-do, tight bodices, suspenders and fishnets, and her outrageous make-up. She was every bit as strange and provocative as the shop and the ideas behind it.

Jordan looked like a dominatrix in a brothel, which was perfect. She was instinctively daring. She lived in Brighton and would commute by train. She attracted so many complaints that in the end British Rail had to give her her own compartment. Jordan had a brain – unlike some of the other people who worked for us. For the first time I felt I could leave someone to manage the shop and concentrate on designing.

SEX was also a kind of social scene. People could come in and hang out, play the jukebox, make themselves coffee, sit on the sofa, chat or watch the customers. I did enjoy meeting all the young people who hung out in the shop. I felt I was coaching them, being a teacher again. Leading them away from common sense and stupid assumptions about morality, and what was normal and acceptable.

All this was really exciting. Everything kept changing and we were inventing designs all the time. But Malcolm was still restless. The work of running a shop wore him out. I knew he wanted to get involved in rock and roll. He kept on talking about the people he'd met in America, like Johnny Thunders and the New York Dolls.

Big fat Tommy Roberts often came in the shop and we'd sometimes go drinking with him in the King's Road. Tommy was 'Mr Freedom', a sixties legend who introduced Malcolm to Richard O'Brien, who wrote *The Rocky Horror Show*. Malcolm wanted to do something like that. He tried to write a script with a similar flavour, about the Notting Hill riots – Teds, rock and roll, rebellion. But even better was the idea of doing *The Rocky Horror Show* for real – in the streets and in the media.

Malcolm's obsession with America now took him back to New York. He had some vague idea he would manage the New York Dolls and turn them into something special. Make their outrageous stance more pointed and political.

He left me to run the shop and went over, taking some of our new clothing – the bondage look, with chain T-shirts, and some leather and vinyl garments.

Malcolm did have good ideas for the New York Dolls. Ideas to enrage their American audiences. He sent them on stage with communist red flags and hammer-and-sickle motifs. It shocked people and made a statement about rock and roll itself. Was it really all a communist plot? You could hear Malcolm laughing behind that idea.

But the Dolls were too far gone on heroin by then. Malcolm got them gigs, and they kept falling off stage. But he stayed around as long as he could.

That's a thing I will always admire about Malcolm. It's his special trick. He never lets go. He goes into a scene, sometimes as a complete and ridiculed outsider. People scorn this strange-looking and manically energetic 'amateur'. They think they know better. They predict he'll come a cropper and say he's being ridiculous. Often, he is. But nothing will embarrass Malcolm or put him off. He stays and stays, keeps watching and learning, exhausts everyone around him – and then he comes up with a definitive idea, something radical and completely off the wall. And usually it's brilliant. It's his revenge for all the scoffing.

And in this case the idea was to be 'punk rock'. That was a phrase never used by us at first. It's what journalists started to call it.

'Punk' was a cross-fertilization of SEX clothes and what we saw in

66

New York – for example, the safety-pin look. It was partly Malcolm's association with Richard Hell that got us into that ripped and torn look. Although well before that we'd begun experimenting independently with torn and half-off clothing after seeing it in fifties pin-up magazines.

When Malcolm came back from New York the shop was going really well. And quite a scene was developing around it. It was like a microcosm of what we'd seen in New York around Andy Warhol's Factory and the New York punks. A collection of drop-outs, art students, revolutionaries, drug addicts, poets. Bohemia!

We knew that's what you had to do. Bring such people together, fire them up with a cause, and give it maximum publicity.

Malcolm taught me quite a few lessons about publicity. Like that row we had over the 'Cambridge Rapist' T-shirt. At the time there was a rapist creeping around Cambridge in a zipped-up black mask, crawling through windows and raping female students. Malcolm had a T-shirt silk-screened with an image of that mask. Then he had some of these masks replicated and sold in the shop.

Michael Collins, an assistant, became convinced that one of our clients was the actual rapist. He got very excited and frightened about this and called Scotland Yard.

Stupidly, I thought that being associated with the idea of a rapist was bad news. So I had all those T-shirts and masks removed from the shop.

When Malcolm got back from America he went completely mad. He screamed at me: 'There's no such thing as bad publicity!' He said we were wasting a potentially good opportunity. He made us put the T-shirts back, and the masks too. And of course he was right – we'd been faint-hearted. We would never win a war like that!

Likewise with the homosexual cowboys. This particular T-shirt showed two cowboys having a conversation. They had no trousers on and their dicks were almost touching. An old lady objected to one of our shop assistants, Alan Jones, wearing it in Piccadilly. He was arrested and there was a court case against us. We had a police raid and were charged with 'exposing to public view an indecent exhibition'. We had to go to Wells Street Court and were fined.

But Malcolm thought that was great. He said we were fighting our corner. We were revolutionaries in the cause of freedom.

I thought the objections to that T-shirt were ridiculous, considering what people see and think all the time! But we brought it out into the open and confronted people with it. You have only to make an explicit and overt statement about sexuality like that and all the hounds of hell are let loose. It's odd. Sexuality brings to the surface emotional prejudices so intense that people lose all sense of proportion and froth at the mouth.

We did a photo shoot inside the shop for *Forum* magazine which involved Debbie and Tracy and Chrissie Hynde, and another girl who was a part-time hooker who posed in a rubber dress. I unzipped Alan Jones's trousers and daubed lipstick erotically on everyone's bottoms.

Malcolm saw the whole thing as a war against the Establishment. He used to say we were like the French Resistance. We only needed to be courageous, and then success would surely follow – we would defeat the enemy. This was why some of the young punks started to wear berets, French style, after the Pistols visited Paris. And why one of Malcolm's favourite drinking places was the French pub in Soho, with all those pictures of the Free French Resistance on the wall, and General de Gaulle's speech to occupied France.

We used to meet a lot of interesting people in that pub. One of the regulars was an ex-Doctor Who – the one who got the sack for being an alcoholic. Another was Robert Fraser, the art dealer. Robert, who was arrested in the sixties with Mick Jagger for drugs (he is the one handcuffed to Jagger inside the police car in the famous photo), was a great fan of the shop. Immediately he saw our stuff he began collecting it. After the Sex Pistols started, he used to creep around Soho at night, peeling Sex Pistols posters off walls with a penknife. Later on, just before he died of Aids, he arranged for the V&A to buy all the Sex Pistols' artwork. It's kept to this day in a drawer in the Theatre Museum.

Around that time Sid Vicious turned up in the shop. I knew Malcolm was thinking about putting together some sort of musical event, maybe a band or a stage show, and I immediately thought Sid looked like a star – he had such a sullen and striking presence. I mentioned him to Malcolm.

Malcolm was thinking over a proposition from Glen Matlock and some other boys who hung around the shop. They had a band called the Swankers and were looking for management. They kept badgering Malcolm about this, but he played – as ever – hard to get. Also, he was not too sure whether they had what it took.

Steve Jones was the lead singer but everyone knew that would never do. Though I liked Steve very much – he had a good heart and sound judgement – he was no front man.

But after I'd suggested Sid to Malcolm, we couldn't find him; he'd disappeared.

Malcolm made the band start writing their own songs and renamed them the Sex Pistols. That was a name he pinched from an American street gang. It fitted in very well with the ideas of the shop. At first people said: 'What a stupid name for a band.' But you never forgot it. It was just so annoying and unforgettable, and irritated away at the back of your brain.

Then John Lydon turned up in the shop and soon afterwards I heard the band had auditioned him and he was now the singer.

I was dubious to start with. I never thought at first that the Sex Pistols were a viable proposition. The shop was doing well. Why risk money in a new and untested area like music?

I was also uncertain about John Lydon. I've always thought John was a sad case, a closet mummy's boy, not as good as Sid. I actually think John wanted me to mother him, but I could never be bothered. I just thought he should get out of his pram. I think John used to see me as a sort of scold.

All those Sex Pistols did, in fact. That came from Malcolm. He spread this idea that I was the one at home, always nagging and expecting them to come home for tea. Malcolm and the band were supposed to be like young boys who want to be out all the time, only there's this fearsome mother figure at home. Of course, it was all a fantasy – I never was like that.

Then Malcolm entered his finest hour. He went into overdrive. At that time he wore black leather trousers, and over our T-shirts a black leather jacket with a diamond motif. He also had a black astrakhan overcoat with silver tips on the ends of the furry bits, and short jodhpur boots with straps. Everything was black and sleek on his wiry and explosive body.

On one finger he wore a ring that was supposed to have been owned by Aleister Crowley, the black magician reputed to have been the 'wickedest man in the world'.

Malcolm went round collecting all his old art school cronies to help. Like Helen Mininberg, who devised the famous Sex Pistols blackmail letter logo by cutting letters out of the *Evening Standard*.

Jamie Reid, from Croydon Art College days, was now living with Sophie Richmond. They were trying to subvert housewives in the Croydon area by publishing a situationist magazine and sticking up situationist posters. They would put stickers in supermarkets announcing that everything was free that day. Or paste official-looking stickers on bus stops saying: 'We are sorry your bus is late. But frankly we couldn't give a shit.'

All these situationist tactics were designed to nibble away at everyday life. But it was all small-time and Jamie liked the idea of doing something bigger on a rock and roll canvas.

Sophie also got drawn in and became the Sex Pistols' office manager. A quietly spoken ex-convent school girl, she was now in charge of the paperwork and wages and fending off journalists. She also dealt with constant tantrums from Malcolm and the band. When she had a spare moment she would sit in the office writing and typing letters of complaint about the Sex Pistols to the media, supposedly from outraged members of the public. I liked Sophie a lot and we got to know each other very well.

Malcolm was so good at bullshitting. A complete catalyst. Selling an idea and getting people going. He told everyone he was going to create something really different and radical.

But what was it? Nobody had much of a clue. There was only his belief in himself and my belief in him – as well as other people's – that he really did know what he was talking about, and that something would come from all this energy and effort.

Soon it was Steve Jones on guitar, Paul Cook on drums, Glen

Matlock from the shop on bass and John Lydon – renamed 'Johnny Rotten' – as vocalist. Glen actually wrote the music; they were his rather sweet little tunes. Without him there would have been no songs to sing. And then Steve roughed them up with his drunken guitar, and Paul bashed them about with his mad drums. And finally there was John, with his strangulated and endearing anger.

Those boys also all believed in what they were doing in that way of self-expression. They thought they were 'being themselves'. But Malcolm and all the other more educated people in that mix knew you also had to have an ironic twist. You have to have a distance; you have to seduce people while you are terrifying the life out of them. To be too literal-minded is fatal – and that's where most of the other punk bands fell down.

In any case, what did 'being yourself' really mean, when we all knew anyone could be anyone? It was all a game. No one really knows who wrote the lyrics. Sometimes it was everyone, including me, in a pub, pissed. We'd come up with lines and slogans and somehow a song would emerge. Like 'Anarchy in the UK'. That was written one evening in a pub under Centre Point.

Gradually I began to take the band more seriously. Even so, I was sometimes pissed off that they took up so much of Malcolm's time, and that he kept taking money from the shop to fund them. Sometimes he would make me go down to the shop and take money from the till to fund gigs and so on. We had quite a few rows about that.

And the band's hangers-on were becoming a nuisance. They kept coming into the shop and nicking stuff like I owed them a living – and then had the cheek to complain about the prices! But then in those days it was all fairly anarchic money-wise. Whoever was working in the shop would just take their wages out of the till at the end of the day. I never kept any accounts and it was years before I found out you were supposed to pay taxes. When I did find out, I was in such a panic I rushed down to the shop and warned everyone we might be raided.

I said, if they come in just pretend you are customers!

At first hardly anyone would give the Sex Pistols gigs. Whenever they did get one it was essential to cause a commotion. We knew that publicity was the only thing that mattered. Like that early performance at an Andrew Logan party.

Logan was an arty trendsetter who made so-called sculptures. John arrived drunk and on speed. I had a row with him and he hit me, giving me a black eye. Then Malcolm tried to stir things up even more by ordering Jordan to take off her clothes. Jordan refused. But then John ripped them off on stage.

We realized there were lots of cameras around and we wanted to give them good photographs.

The SEX fashions kept developing. We created a 'which side of the bed' T-shirt. On one side was everything that was hateful in British culture: 'the Liberal Party/John Betjeman/George Melly . . . SECURICOR . . . Honey, Harpers, Vogue, in fact all magazines that treat their readers as idiots/Bryan Ferry/Salvador Dali . . . The Playboy Club . . . POP STARS who are thick and useless . . . Bernard Delfont . . . Arse lickers/John Osborne . . . Capital Radio . . . THE ARTS COUNCIL . . . Grey skies/Dirty books that aren't all that dirty . . . The rag trade . . . Antiques of any sort . . . Bianca Jagger . . . The job you hate but are too scared to pack in . . . Chinless people . . . Antonia Fraser . . . The Archers . . . All those fucking saints.'

On the other side was everything that gave us hope: 'Eddie Cochran/Christine Keeler/Susan 6022509 . . . BRAZIL . . . Coffee bars that sell whisky under the counter . . . Valerie Solanas . . . Buenaventura Durutti . . . Archie Shepp/Olympia Press/Lennie Bruce/Joe Orton . . . Zootsuits and dreadlocks . . . Simone de Beauvoir/Dashiell Hammett/Alex Trocchi/Marianne Faithfull . . . Imagination . . .' Which side of the bed was like which side of the barricade are you on? Again, we were trying to start a war.

We designed that T-shirt in bed. In fact we did a lot of our designs in bed. Come to think of it, that bed in our Clapham flat could tell a story or two!

We were both great sleepers. I still am. Malcolm would lie there for hours and hours making phone calls all over the world, trying to drum up business for the Sex Pistols. I thought it was mad how often he was on the phone.

Sometimes we would lie in very late into the mornings thinking up crazy ideas and sketching them. People would call round to discuss business and we would still be in bed. We'd sit there negotiating. Sometimes too, Malcolm would start wanking under the sheets in front of guests. He did that to get our ideas flowing.

Soon there was a whole range of punk rock clothes, and it was starting to look like a proper fashion collection. Jordan came into the shop one day with an Oxford cloth T-shirt she'd painted with stripes. I liked that and made a similar shirt. Then I bleached bits of it and sewed on a silk portrait of Karl Marx. I stencilled on a slogan: 'Dangerously close to love'. I was thinking about a Latin American guerrilla style – the kind of thing Che Guevara might wear in the jungle stalking government soldiers.

But then I hid it. I thought if Malcolm saw it we'd have a row; he'd think it was just daft and hate it. But he found it by accident and thought it was brilliant. It was a big seller too. In fact I noticed that young people preferred this sort of candidly rebellious statement to the pornographic ones Malcolm was always wanting them to wear. I could understand that. Pornography cheapened their attitude, but revolutionary and anarchistic ideas made them feel worthwhile.

This was just one instance where I was cleverer than Malcolm at understanding the mood and getting radical things across. I was also proud because I'd helped to stop 'anarchy' being a dirty word. To me, anarchy meant not needing a leader. I felt I certainly didn't need a leader.

We also did T-shirts with slogans like: 'Only anarchists are pretty' and 'Modernity kills every night'. Or: 'Be reasonable, demand the impossible', 'Cash from chaos', 'Anarchy is the melody' and 'Do it yourself is the key'. And we made T-shirts with little see-through plastic windows where you could put a photo of your favourite revolutionary or pop star or a playing card.

Then there was our famous 'Destroy' T-shirt with an upside-down crucifix and giant swastika, where, as a final *coup de grâce*, Malcolm

73

added a postage stamp with a portrait of the Queen he'd defaced. That was also designed in bed.

Another staple of the shop was our rainbow-coloured fluffy mohair sweaters. These were very popular, and I used to love wearing them – you felt so cosy inside.

But one of our most important creations was the zipped bondage trousers. These had a cloth strip connecting both legs. We copied the basic design from American pilot suits. People really used to stare when we first wore them!

Once I gave a party at the flat and someone cut their hand badly so I drove them to hospital. The nurses laughed at my bondage trousers and said they must be really constricting. To prove they weren't I did cartwheels all down the corridor of the casualty ward.

At last the Sex Pistols were getting noticed and written up even in the hippie music press. Even so, it was still touch and go. The only way we could break through was to create a panic.

I remember a gig at the Nashville, a pub-rock place. When the band started playing I suddenly thought, Oh, this is going to be boring! We couldn't afford an anticlimax as there were so many photographers and press people there.

There was a girl standing next to me, and I just slapped her – really quite hard. She was amazed. Then her boyfriend started hitting me. Then Malcolm joined in and John dived off the stage into the fight with a crazed look in his eye. Someone caught that on camera and the photo went round the world. It said: Watch out! this is the Sex Pistols, and they are mad, bad and on their way!

Although Sid was not in the band then, he was always hanging around. I thought him such a sweet boy. But sometimes he behaved badly. Especially when drugged or drunk. At the 100 Club he threw a glass and a girl's eye got cut. We told the police it wasn't Sid but they arrested him anyway. He had to go to a remand home. While he was there I sent him a book about Charles Manson. I thought he should use his time profitably by reading.

There was also the time Sid attacked Nick Kent in the Speakeasy club with a chain. Nick Kent was a hippie journalist who used to go out with Chrissie Hynde when she was our shop assistant. He was quite badly injured by Sid and the rock press was horrified.

Instead of apologizing, Malcolm fired off telegrams to all the editors, saying Sid had been right and a revolution was coming and people like Nick Kent were in the way and they should get out – or get hurt.

To break through the wall of indifference Malcolm and Jamie and the others around us used the sort of Dadaist tactics they'd learnt about at art college. Shock and provocation and outrage. And then more of the same. Never let up, never give in. Like the situationists, they wanted to 'create a situation in which there was no going back'. Burning all bridges, going for broke.

Though Malcolm likes to claim all the credit now, the Sex Pistols' management was really that group of people focused around his Glitterbest management team, which included me, of course. Malcolm was the catalyst and the capitalist of the operation. But he could only have operated with that team of old friends who all trusted one another and shared the same outlook. In lots of ways, Malcolm is only as good as the people he works with.

Some people still think the punk thing was an eruption off the streets. Something about dole-queue rock, or working-class youngsters making a protest. But actually it was a fashion event right from the start. It was like creating one of those historical paintings of a revolution, with revolutionaries charging over a barricade. In every corner of the canvas you can see people in heroic postures, with everything in the picture meaning something revolutionary or shocking or thought-provoking.

We paid such enormous attention to detail. Malcolm and I dreamed up ideas and then I worked away to give them a focus as clothing. Then Malcolm would come in with a final twist to turn the idea on its head – make it count. All our images and slogans and clothes were so meticulously crafted and every nuance was a deliberate choice.

Some of the sources we used might surprise people. The bandage look of the muslin T-shirt sleeves and trouser flaps, for instance, came partly from Grünewald's painting of Christ Crucified, done in the sixteenth century. As a student Malcolm loved Grünewald's nightmarish images; they suited his own paranoia.

And then we thought about those Hogarth prints of the eighteenth-century mob. That was part of the leering menace of our boyish Sex Pistols in their Dickensian 'rags' – swamped in cuddly mohair jumpers or strapped up in bondage outfits.

Jamie was a help on the graphics side. But he was already drinking and sometimes needed a kick up the backside. Like when he was supposed to be designing a fanzine focused around the song 'Anarchy in the UK'. He took forever, and eventually me and Malcolm had to drive to his and Sophie's council flat near London Bridge and we stayed there all night until it was finished. In fact, one whole page was done by me.

After the Pistols got sacked from EMI and then A&M there was a point when nobody would sign them. They were the most famous band in the country, possibly in the world, and they didn't have a deal. Word had gone round: don't touch this band – there's something dodgy about the management. There were even rumours Glitterbest was funding German terrorists.

Round about this time Malcolm got a message saying that the founder of situationism, Guy Debord, would like to meet him. A meeting was arranged in a Chelsea pub. Malcolm went in great excitement, but Debord never turned up. I wonder if that was a hoax?

Now the only company that would sign the Pistols was Virgin. But Virgin were hippies. In other words, they also knew the art school games. So it was likely they wouldn't be phased by Glitterbest tactics and might worm their way out of any trouble we tried to cause them. Malcolm called this 'repressive tolerance'. Virgin would kill the thing off by kindness. He had come across this before, from liberal art college tutors.

Virgin were desperate to sign the Sex Pistols. At the time, the only thing they had ever done was Mike Oldfield's *Tubular Bells*. They had a reputation for producing double albums by long-haired people in sheepskin coats. They wanted to break into the singles market and make themselves look 'cutting edge'. So they courted Glitter-best and made all kinds of promises. They offered an amazing deal, giving Glitterbest complete control over artwork and promotion.

Eventually the Pistols signed to Virgin. At that point another game started. The game was to get off Virgin. Malcolm and Jamie started to dream up outrageous schemes to terrify them into dropping the band. But every time they went into Virgin with an idea – for example, a blow-up Sid Vicious sex doll, Virgin just laughed and rubbed their hands in glee. They said: 'Great. Let's do it!'

This, I have to admit, completely deflated and defeated Glitter-best. In order to wage war you need an enemy. Where now was the enemy?

Some people in Glitterbest even organized for people to spray-paint all over Finsbury Park that John was a queer. They thought this might damage his reputation.

Then there was the riverboat trip. This was arranged to coincide with Virgin's release of 'God Save the Queen' which came out with the Queen's Silver Jubilee. The whole country was plastered with royalist propaganda and there was media saturation about the royal family. But quite a lot of people felt resentful of the whole thing – it did seem so tawdry and insincere.

To launch 'God Save the Queen', a gig on a Thames pleasure boat was organized. The boat was decorated with a streamer saying, 'Queen Elizabeth welcomes the Sex Pistols.' Everyone got drunk and lots of speed was taken. Fights broke out and the captain radioed the police. Two police patrol boats came alongside and when the boat docked there were policemen everywhere. As we filed down the gangplank Malcolm started screaming: 'Fascist pigs!' The police dragged him off.

I shouted: 'Oh my God, they've got Malcolm.' I was terribly worried they would harm him. I tried to get into the van with him, but they charged me with assaulting the police and arrested me as well. Jamie and Sophie were also arrested.

When we all got to the police station, I did a cartwheel and everyone pissed about, laughing at the police and having a good time. The police didn't know how to take it. In fact, they were acting very stupidly. For example, they were trying to describe us on the charge sheets and they were reading out what they were typing. One policeman said I had 'four sensuous lips' because I had my lips painted in four colours.

I was locked up overnight and I was quite concerned about the boys at home, as I couldn't get a message to them.

That summer of 1976 was the hottest for about a hundred years, I believe. It really was sweltering. I think that made everyone behave more emotionally and crazily. So there were punch-ups between punks and Teds, and in fact Malcolm started some of these. He used to pay Teds to beat up punks in the King's Road – the price of a pint for a black eye.

The shop also kept getting its windows smashed in with bricks and bottles – by either passing football supporters or Teds. Or else by punks who were annoyed by how much we were charging or felt left out in some way. In the end we had metal grilles made and every time it looked like trouble was starting we rushed out to put them up.

The cast of people helping in the shop was constantly changing. There was Alan Jones and Michael Collins. And for a time, Chrissie Hynde. But Jordan stayed. As did Debbie.

Debbie was an angelic-looking girl with blonde, spiky hair, who looked like an underage tart with her smudgy make-up and naïve sensuality. Tracy was taller and darker and pretty in a classic sort of way. They were both really Sex Pistols groupies, sleeping around with the band and their entourage.

I used to go out with our assistants sometimes – most often to the Roebuck pub round the corner from the shop, or to clubs and concerts. Once we went to a Grace Jones concert and hated it so much we were shouting from the back for her to shut up. (Nowadays I never go to clubs. I find them as much fun as waiting three hours for a bus.)

As well as working in the shop, Debbie was on the game. She did the Park Lane circuit and then gravitated towards Shepherd Market. She eventually got her memoirs featured in *Men Only* – the confessions of a teenage whore.

In fact a lot of the people around that punk scene were on and off the game and involved in all kinds of strange scenes. Particularly at one brothel in a flat in Victoria just opposite New Scotland Yard. It was in a typical service flat, very big, with deep shag-pile carpets. The madam, Linda, would cook for the boys. Sometimes they would stay there for days on end and they would claim to have almost constant hard-ons. It became quite an HQ for the Sex Pistols and other punks. They got to know the girls, who became fans and gave them free blow-jobs and other treats.

Linda also had parties there. She ran the place professionally and, like a lot of other madams, would get a lot of her stuff – whips, bondage apparatus, pump-up rubber masks and so on – from the shop.

There were also a lot of homosexuals and transvestites and all sorts of 'freakish' people about on that scene, and a lot of speed was being taken. I was very interested in all this.

Debbie and others who were on the game seemed to think it was almost a noble thing – an honest way to earn money. But I sometimes wondered if I should warn some of these young punks they could get themselves in a mess with prostitution and drugs. Then I thought, it's their life so just let them get on with it.

Personally, I don't know whether drugs are bad or good. I've never taken them. Smoking and drinking is all I do.

In 1976, at the peak of all this punk madness, we changed the shop yet again. It now became 'Seditionaries', under the slogan 'Clothes for heroes'. That was my idea. I thought that to make people think you needed to hurt them emotionally. I also thought you had to be seductive at the same time. The word 'seditionaries', which I made up, was meant to suggest you needed to seduce people into revolt.

This was also yet another way to confront culture – which is what kept us going and gave us vitality. We were selling clothes for a commitment to anarchy and people were walking around on the streets in clothes you only saw before in the bedroom. But everyone dresses to attract other people. If you look like you lead an exciting life, you'll attract exciting people.

What could be more exciting than confronting apathy? It was very romantic to be in a minority, and anti-Establishment. We were not for 'pretty' ladies out to attract male chauvinist pigs.

By now the shop was definitely more my province than Malcolm's and what went into it were my designs more than his. I thought through these ideas very carefully and aimed for quality. For example, I used only the best-quality woollens and mohair and leather. These materials were warm and lively and made you feel good inside them. Most fashion items tend to be made from harsh and lifeless cloth and I believe that this has a negative effect on the people wearing it.

This philosophy did result in the clothes costing quite a lot – £150 for a tartan outfit, for example – but that was inevitable. There was no way I could have made such a sophisticated range less expensively. And after all, designing the Seditionaries range took me a year, so I was giving value for money.

These outfits were accessorized with safety-pins, razor blades and little silver phalluses.

I now began to get fashion spreads about the clothes unconnected with the Sex Pistols, and some didn't even mention Malcolm. To tell the truth, around this time I had been ready to give up on fashion. But when I saw the influence of my work on the Paris catwalks, the ripped and torn look and the safety-pins and so on, I thought I'd be crazy not to make some money out of it.

Fashion is like a baby I picked up one day and never put down.

I also started to experiment with a more high-fashion look. This was partly because I wanted to move on creatively. Before punk I'd never really thought of myself as a designer – I was just tinkering about to help Malcolm. But now I wanted to explore my potential.

Another reason for gravitating towards 'fashion' was to alienate the existing clients, who had become predictable and boring.

For Seditionaries, we redesigned the shop with a sort of high-tech look. We got in some fluorescent orange, futurist-type chairs and a charcoal-grey carpet, and made the interior clinical and cleanly lit.

On one wall we put a huge blow-up of the German city of Dresden, which had been bombed flat by the Allies during the war. A landscape of ruins which looked startling and spectral.

Opposite, we hung a blow-up of Piccadilly Circus which was upside down. Then we smashed a hole in the shop ceiling to make it look as if a bomb had recently fallen through.

The shop front was made of frosted glass so you couldn't see in from outside. Inside, you felt trapped in a milky white light. It was a bit like one of those 'surgical' shops in the fifties and early sixties which used to sell medical appliances and pornographic books.

A small brass plaque outside announced: 'Seditionaries: For soldiers, prostitutes, dykes and punks.'

We still sold bondage trousers, SEX T-shirts and quite a lot of fetish gear. But everything was much smarter now. Less underground and less provincially British.

Looking back on punk, it was the best exercise in rock and roll anyone ever attempted. It was rock and roll's last stand and I think we got it right. Punks weren't particularly trying to change anything – not like the hippies and protest singers they despised for being naïve.

Punks admitted they were victims or brain-damaged in a sense, and that was heroic in itself, and clever. They had a straightforward programme: to destroy everything. A spanner in the works and a safety-pin in the Queen's lips. In a way, though, that was attacking the Queen in quite a sweet way. Putting a safety-pin in her lips was suggesting she could be one of us!

But punk was also supposed to be the jungle beat which threatened white civilization. In the end, I realized it didn't threaten anything. And that's when I lost interest. But perhaps it never really was me, all that destruction and rebellion. Perhaps I am really a quitter and a retiring sort of person. Even so, at the time I was often the one who kept it hard and radical. Malcolm sometimes wanted to compromise, but I would tell him to pull his socks up!

After the Sex Pistols thing there was a very strange moment. For instance, Jamie went mad. During the Sex Pistols period he was almost permanently drunk. And he had papered the whole of his flat with Sex Pistols posters. This was a bit disturbing in itself – you'd think he'd need to get away from his work sometimes!

One night he was watching television while his girlfriend and her daughter were in bed. He was wearing big black boots and suddenly he stood up and kicked the television. His boot went into the screen and the TV exploded. He hurt his foot quite badly. Then he limped into the bathroom, picked up a full-length mirror and smashed it over his head.

Jamie's girlfriend was terrified. She called his father and his family came round to fetch him. He spent quite a long time in a mental hospital after that, winding down and detoxing.

Then there were those strange phone calls I kept getting. Someone on the line would whimper like a wounded animal. I was convinced it was John.

And then there was Malcolm. He went mad in his own way – he became paranoid. He thought people were after him. He was convinced John had hired Rastafarians to murder him. Everywhere he saw lies, plots and deceit. He thought he could hear Virgin employees laughing behind his back and became obsessed that Richard Branson had 'out-swindled' him. He went to Paris to escape.

While he was in Paris he got this really strange illness – he became bright yellow. He went into hospital and spent about two months recovering. I suppose after something as big as that you get these effects.

Malcolm stayed in Paris for a while and began a new music project. He wrote some lyrics and met a couple of French musicians who put tunes to them. But I persuaded him to come back to London. Paris, I said, was not the best place to start anything musical.

What I really wanted was his input on my new designs. I thought they needed Malcolm's finishing touches, to add that mad sparkle. I'd got bored with Seditionaries and bored with punk and bored with the whole anger and rebellion thing. Punk had gone stale, especially with that awful Zandra Rhodes collection and so many other things which just cashed in and made it all passé and safe.

There were imitators everywhere, like Boy. It had got mean-minded and small-time. No one was making big gestures or being provocative. I wanted to do something that was deliberately artistic, based on all those influences I'd absorbed over all those years talking with Malcolm and his art school friends. All those late-night discussions, dinner parties at the Oval flat, Sunday afternoons in the Tate Gallery.

It all seemed to come together as I began to develop my own vision of what fashion could be – a long way from anything at that time.

I revisited all the London museums and galleries, especially my favourite, the Wallace Collection. At the Victoria and Albert museum I found a collection of patterns and fabrics and decided to do some serious fashion research. I spent months in the V&A and that is where I got interested in the eighteenth century and how they used to cut clothes and the way clothes used to hang on the body.

Instead of following the lines of the body in a modern way, clothing in those days opposed the body, creating folds and sags and interesting movements as people walked or gestured. It was a very expressive sort of clothing. We tend to think that people cut clothes like that because they didn't know any better. They did. But they liked the effect.

That period of study was decisive. It confirmed my instinct for thinking through design problems in lots of different ways. Historical precedent is essential for that – to study how fashion problems have been solved in the past.

What's wrong with the British way of training fashion students is that it's mostly based on a blank as far as history goes. It's about what's in the shops at that moment. So students get stuck into a rut of doing only what is around them. Since that is mostly crap, that's what they reproduce.

It is actually very important not to keep up with the times. That's the downfall of a lot of people in design, this obsession with what's up to the minute. Karl Lagerfeld, for example. The idea of trying to capture what's happening on the street is wrong. You immediately become old-fashioned. To come up with anything original it's essential to forget what is going on at the moment. When I design my clothes I completely disregard what's around, what other designers are doing. I've got more important things to look at.

Once back in London, Malcolm saw these New Romantics in the clubs. Kids were dressing up in historical costume and fancy dress – frills and ruffs and so on. It was a reaction against the austere look of Punk.

Malcolm had also seen a bloodthirsty film about pirates. 'Why not put together a collection around the theme of pirates?' he said.

We then thought up ideas around buried treasure, looting and marauding sailors, and gold – which gave me the accessory idea of covering teeth in gold foil from cigarette packets.

I also extended my research to the Incroyables of Paris. These were dandies who flourished at the time of the French Revolution and were denounced for being outrageous and extravagant.

Malcolm was thinking about putting together a band based on the idea of pirating copyright material. This was a hot topic in the music industry at the time, because of the cheapness of blank cassettes and people making unauthorized copies of music tracks.

There was a lot of talk about how artists were being robbed of their royalties – which we thought was actually not a bad thing as some of these people earn far too much. Malcolm wanted to wind up the music industry by creating a band focused around that very idea. He said the British Empire was all based on piracy. Piracy was a key British virtue. And just as we had plundered culture to create new combinations and forms in punk, we would now extend that by pirating ideas across time and space, looting London as a cultural museum to create fresh treasures.

In 1979 we redesigned the shop once again and renamed it 'Worlds End'. The interior was now like an eighteenth-century galleon with a slanting floor made from battered pine planks. When you went in you felt disorientated, almost seasick, like setting off on an adventure with Errol Flynn on the high seas.

We put in a grey-shingled Georgian window and had crooked

steps leading from the street. On the front of the shop was a big gilt-edged clock running backwards at a mad pace.

By this time I had met Gary Ness. Gary changed my life by helping me make the intellectual transition away from Malcolm. Gary, who was then about fifty, was a Canadian artist and writer who'd come over here to study. He had white hair and a grizzled, experienced and very serious face. He'd spent the last twenty years or so in the reading room of the British Museum just reading literally everything. He was a mine of information about history, literature and art, as well as politics and economics.

Gary came from quite a wealthy background – his father, I believe, was an auctioneer in Canada. He was brilliant at school and decided to become a painter. As a student he won a scholarship to the Ecole des Beaux-Arts in Paris, which was quite a big thing in those days. After that he became a portrait painter and quite successful in America. But when he found out his agent was charging sitters $3000 and passing on only $1000, they fell out.

After that, Gary, being a hopeless businessman, couldn't find any clients, and he came to England. I met him when he was working on someone's idea to paint a series of miniature portraits of well-known people. As I was a little bit famous even then, I was supposed to be one of the sitters.

But soon Gary got disillusioned with the project. And then – and I know this sounds very dramatic – he threw his easels and paintbrushes into the Thames and said goodbye to painting for ever.

Meanwhile he had been researching a definitive history of Anglo–American vulgarity. This was an attack on the pragmatist and soulless way of doing things just for money. Unfortunately, he sent all his material over to Canada and it got lost. So that was that.

But I am convinced that Gary is that rare thing, a genius. Talent is like a rare orchid that you have to nurture carefully. Most talented people go under. I'm one of the exceptions because I have an ability to organize and plan long-term. But people with exceptional talent are often freaks and some are eccentric enough to get picked on by the herd.

When you think about it there are probably only about a hundred people in the history of the world who have done any good. Those are the people who interest me. I don't care about the other ninety-nine per cent of people in the world. They shouldn't be encouraged to believe they are exceptional – they have to know they are the weeds and not the orchids.

Little girls nowadays don't dream of being air hostesses any more – they want to become fashion designers. I despair of all that, this cult of mediocrity we are swamped by.

In Huxley's *Brave New World* the World Controller says that we don't let people do what they like, we make them like what they do. He electrocutes children if they go near a rose or a book. And they are forbidden to learn about beauty. That nightmare future Huxley described is already with us. We don't need an Adolf Hitler to burn our books now – nobody reads them anyway.

The anarchist philosopher Godwin foresaw this in the late eighteenth century. He was against universal education, arguing that, once education was in the hands of the state, people would be manipulated. He didn't realize that the power of the mass media, working with the government, would make his prediction come true with a vengeance. We are living in the age of the Manipulated Mind. All we educate people for is to read the *Sun* or trash like Julie Burchill.

But Gary is old enough to have come from a time before the onslaught of all this commercial mass 'culture'. When there was still a critical spirit around and before intellectuals had given in to Americanization.

I've sometimes wondered about financing a sort of exclusive magazine, a bit like Cyril Connolly's *Horizon*, which Gary could edit. It would bring like-minded people together and provide a focus for bringing back a sense of style and high culture. But Gary is getting on in years now and is sometimes crotchety, so I don't know if that would work.

But if anyone is interested, I also have a project for a modern-day salon, a meeting place, in the same way that aristocratic salons used to bring together wealthy patrons, artists and intellectuals. I think this would cost around £2 million. But then there must be some millionaires out there who want to do something useful with their money! Why not make it available to intelligent people for a change?

Maybe Prince Charles could contribute. He ought to support culture and art, because culture is the badge of civilization.

Nowadays Gary has become my sort of mentor directing my reading and learning. I have regular long meetings with him, about once a week, like tutorials in a college. He tells me which books are essential, the paintings to look for and so on. He saves me so much time because he knows so much and knows short cuts. Don't read this, he says, read that instead. After all, when you're as busy as I am you only want to focus on essentials.

Gary advised me against reading *War and Peace*. It was too long. But he recommended Proust, who is now one of my favourite authors. Through Gary I also started to seriously read Aldous Huxley and Bertrand Russell, and writers like Théophile Gautier. In fact Gautier is the historical figure I possibly most admire. He kept the idea of 'l'Art pour l'Art' alive until finally it was killed by commercialism in the 1950s.

Malcolm saw Gary as a threat from the start. He said Gary was a fraud and a fifties buffoon, and looked like Rasputin. He was especially pissed off when I suggested we put Gary on the payroll. 'What does he do?' he sneered. Well, quite a lot as far as I was concerned.

In 1981 my Savage collection began a cycle of experimentation with ethnic dress. I also started to experiment with the idea of asymmetric layering.

I showed Buffalo at Olympia and in Paris in March 1982.

Malcolm had told me this idea of wild kids who lived north of Hadrian's Wall. These kids would come swarming over the border like old-time Scots attacking the Romans. They would come down from the hills and turn up in a disco south of Hadrian's Wall and everyone would get excited because they looked so fantastic and cool.

Looking at these kids everybody suddenly felt boring and decided to go over the wall to the village of the 'buffalo girls' and find out what was going on. Here they found discos where kids made up their own music like scratch and rap. They also danced together in a new way, sometimes in formal square dances, sometimes in couples, but always with gymnastic dance routines.

To me this was a very strong image which captured the imagination. I think you always do need a story for every collection. Even for every garment. Before models go on in my shows I often tell them the story in my mind, to get them in the right attitude.

Malcolm was also putting together some music for Buffalo. But this time he had decided to front the music himself. No more Johnny Rottens or Annabellas. He showed me a record cover picturing some Bolivian women and from that I developed the ideas mostly on my own.

The themes were muddy colours and things very roughly put together in slouching and eccentric shapes. I liked the idea that these women thought owning a bra was a status symbol and used to wear bras on the outside. My taking on this idea led to Jean-Paul Gaultier and others copying the theme – and then, of course, Madonna.

But the revolutionary thing about this collection was that the line of the clothing came from the body moving underneath. The body was dictating the way the clothing moved. Again this had been a consistent fascination of mine since Pirates – and even before.

Malcolm thought I should show Buffalo in Paris. He said Paris is always the real arbiter of fashion. But we were rejected for the ready-to-wear show in the Tuileries gardens.

A friend of Malcolm's, Pierre Benain, then organized a show in Angelino's tea-room, across the street from the Tuileries. A sort of salon of the rejected like the Impressionists used to display in before they were recognized.

But Buffalo flopped. It was too new and far ahead.

By this time we had another shop in St Christopher's Place, just off Oxford Street. It was called Nostalgia of Mud. That was Malcolm's idea – sometimes he was all dazzle, like a poet. We used this theme of mud harking back to primordial slime. In the middle of the shop was a bubbling fountain of mud and the interior had an encrusted feel. The front was decorated with mud-coloured bunting and wooden maps of Africa.

My next collection was Punkature, in October 1982, a development from Buffalo and Punk. I worked on this completely on my own. I banned Malcolm from even seeing it until the last moment as I thought his input and presence would be distracting.

It was around then that London street fashion really got moving. I was in the forefront of that. Lots of people who couldn't really cut patterns thought, I can just make things from squares. And they all began to do it.

I started working on garments made from rectangles, inserting lots of gussets to give them their shape. But my patterns were the best because I worked them out on my own body. I didn't just make a box you could put on. I got extremely involved in the way things were cut, and I worked on garments for a moving, living body.

I developed a way of working with little dolls or miniature tailor's dummies, just to see how cloth falls into place. I would try things on my own body too, to see how a garment fits and falls and what it feels like. It's very important to me what something feels like on you.

The whole thing about this new collection was the cut. I'd come to see that this was the essential thing about fashion. What couture literally means is 'cutting', or a special way of cutting.

Along with this I was experimenting with the look of 'distressed' clothes and fabrics.

Again we took the show to Paris. And this time it was much more of a success. At the end of the show I didn't really want to go on the catwalk like other designers do – a sort of triumphal appearance. It seemed corny. In any case I really am shy!

But Malcolm laughed and said: 'It's part of your job, girl!' He pushed me out there. It was strange for once to be under the lights with all those people clapping and cheering as if I was the star instead of the fashions. I enjoyed that, because, although I'm shy, my shyness seems to vanish when I get in front of people.

I think the success of this collection was a turning-point. It certainly was a turning-point design wise in my own mind. Now I realized I really was a designer. Before then I'd never thought of myself in that way. I was just an interpreter of Malcolm's ideas. But now I knew that these ideas had originated and grown without any help from Malcolm. I knew I could go on alone if need be. I was creatively independent.

How was I to know this new beginning was also to be the end for Malcolm and me? For by now things were definitely very wrong between us.

It was the Italian connection which finally did it. At a party after the Punkature show in October 1982 I met some Italian fashion publicists who were really enthusiastic. One of them was Carlo D'Amario, who is now my business manager.

Carlo helped me set up a second showing in Milan and through this I began to make connections with the Milanese fashion industry. I saw this as a way out of the limited British scene. To be successful, fashion has to be international and not tied to any particular country.

Also, in the UK I found it practically impossible to get any backing. In Britain they have this laissez-faire attitude towards small businesses – that they will just spring up on their own without government help. If I were French the government there would have subsidised me. But over here all the bank managers wanted to know was whether I had a house I could mortgage. And if I ever asked for an overdraft they would look at me like I was some kind of irresponsible deviant.

So for some time I'd been totally self-financed and therefore unable to meet the kind of orders I was now getting. Whereas in Italy they understand small businesses, and will give you what you need to make a million garments instead of 200.

My next collection was Witches. This was sparked off by images of Haitian voodoo. But although this set me off, I really wanted to develop my new ideas about cutting and tailoring – how the cut and the fabric of clothes could define the body in different ways.

If you change the fundamental design of clothing, the fabric begins to play and touch around the body in different ways. It begins to undulate and move around unexpectedly. This gives the person wearing it a sense of style and a self-awareness about their body in a public space which is very sexy and also quite grand and heroic.

I wasn't just trying to make a kind of shell which stays rigidly in place about half an inch from the body. My clothes were dynamic. They pushed and they pulled, and also slightly fell off. After all, there's more to clothes than comfort!

And I was interested in how they might occasionally slip and need readjusting, because that in itself created a set of gestures and a special sort of display that went with the clothes. I think that sort of feeling as a fashion statement really began with punk and the straps on bondage trousers. Wearing those, walking down the street, you really did feel like a hero.

All of a sudden I was in demand. Fiorucci wanted me to design a collection. Lucia Ralphieli featured my designs in *Vogue*, and I began to be approached by Italians to start mass-producing my designs.

Around that time I also started to go out with Carlo, and that – strangely perhaps – made Malcolm jealous. The trouble really started when Malcolm heard I had signed a deal worth around seventy-five million lire with Fiorucci. Malcolm now showed me his really nasty side.

He claimed we were legally co-owners of Worlds End. I had no right, he said, to engage in contracts on my own and he threw in that he also hated Carlo, whom he called a spaghetti merchant.

Malcolm accused me of being a Judas. He shouted that I had betrayed him. I was astonished, after all the women he had gone out with and all the times he had been unfaithful.

I was also astonished that he thought Worlds End was still his business. I'd stopped thinking that around the time of the Pirates collection.

Anyway, Witches was shown in Paris in March '83. I'd been so hurt by Malcolm that I decided to keep him out of the workroom until a week before the clothes were shipped out to Paris.

Witches was a real hit. There was a huge party after the show in a gymnasium with palm trees. Lots of Italian designers and promoters were there and Madonna gave her first European appearance that night.

And then Malcolm realized, I think, that it was getting out of his control. At that point he tried to tie me up legally. His lawyer sent a telex to the Milan factory producing the Witches collection. It claimed I had stolen the patterns for my new line from the Worlds End workroom – as if those patterns had been his in some way!

This telex was, of course, complete rubbish but it put a panic into the company involved and production was stopped. This was a huge embarrassment to me and cost me a lot of money.

Then Malcolm tried to get everyone in the London workshops to gang up against me. He told these people who had worked for me for so long that now they were working for him. And he is such a good talker and so plausible and persuasive that some of them went for it.

Because of that I nearly lost both my shops.

Then Malcolm changed all the numbers of all the bank accounts, and all the locks on my workroom. Next he switched all the money belonging to me into new accounts. I was devastated. It seemed like the meanest kind of treachery. I just couldn't believe he could do these things. Really, he tried to destroy me.

By this time all these machinations of Malcolm had put the whole company into a complete mess. Nostalgia of Mud owed nearly £10,000. Then Malcolm had the cheek to say: 'I'm pulling out, I am handing it all over to Vivienne. She wants it more than me.'

At this stage I realized I could have nothing more to do with Malcolm, nor with any of those people who had taken his side.

Carlo supported me through all this. Sometimes, when I was ready to give in, he insisted I should refuse to back down on my demands for complete creative control.

But in the end Nostalgia of Mud ran out of stock and had to close. All this meant that my next collection, Hypnosis, focused around sportswear fabrics, could hardly be produced enough to supply Worlds End. And there were also, by that time, many other stores who wanted my designs whom I couldn't supply.

At the end of this it seemed my career was finished. I still had my reputation, but there was no operation behind it. No effective backup. The Italian industry had been frightened off by Malcolm's plots and I could still find no backing in England.

And then, when in 1984 I finally did a licensing deal with Armani's partner Sergi Galeotti, Galeotti suddenly died of Aids and the deal fell through. This was especially annoying because I'd previously also been approached by Zamosport, which went on to back Romano Gigli, but I had chosen Galeotti!

All this was my real and final break with Malcolm after all those years and I couldn't believe how much it hurt. It was like walking through a door into a world of pain. I felt as if I had died and was watching myself in this other place. I hadn't realized before I was capable of such passion. It was almost like a spiritual experience. I think I cared so much because I had put so much into our relationship.

After we separated I was so upset I could hardly put one foot in front of the other. I was crying so much my boys were really worried. I felt I was about to burst into flames – that I would explode. It took me months to get over it.

But I did get over it. And after that I did enjoy seeing Malcolm now and again, just because I knew I was free of him. I looked at him and I had no tremor of emotion – I was indifferent. God, it was so great to feel that!

I will never have that kind of intensity of attachment to anybody ever again. I cried so many tears over Malcolm and once I got over him I decided that was it. Never again would I cry, not for anyone. And I never have. Not even when my father died.

In some ways my relationship with Malcolm was horrible. But then the path to wisdom begins with loving people. You learn from the hard blows. While we were breaking up I couldn't believe how dismissive he was about everything I'd done. He said that without him I would just be a factory worker, a nobody. He gave away all the items from our past collections just to prove how unimportant I was.

I no longer have any of that stuff – which is worth a lot of money now. But in a way, having gone through all that I felt exorcized.

Yet I owe him so much. He would always come in at the last minute and tell me how to exploit my ideas more, how to make things count. He would edit my work, get my ideas down on a board, sort the story out, give it clear lines, show me a clear way of approaching it. He would unscramble my programming.

He also taught me not to be frightened, that creativity was all a question of attention to detail and working through problems one by one. There was no magic to it – just painstaking work.

After all the chaos and heartache of Nostalgia of Mud it took me a long time to climb back personally and professionally.

But in March 1984 I showed my Clint Eastwood collection at the Cour Carrée du Louvre. This was based on a Hollywood Wild West theme, and mixed nineteenth-century city clothes with denim and Red Indian ethnic pieces. And then in October 1994 I showed my Mini Crini collection, also at the Cour Carrée du Louvre, and then at the Limelight in New York.

I had been struck by how sexy crinoline was. I think there was never a fashion more sexy, especially in that big Victorian design. How wonderful to come into a room and occupy six feet of space, to dominate every area you were in and have your own space underneath your legs in that great bell shape.

Crinoline and the corsetry that went along with it are often seen as fashions which hampered and constricted women. But people wore corsets for comfort and pleasure; they enjoyed them. I also imagine that crinoline felt very sexy to wear. It was an archetypal female fertility symbol and that was very appealing to me.

The 'mini crini' I made moved and swayed, constantly revealing different areas of flesh. Sometimes it was quite wiggly and sometimes stiff, depending on the fabric. It was perfect for the summer.

The press seemed to dwell on the fact that I sent models down the catwalk in mini crinis with no underwear! But although this crinoline revival was derided by the media, it was soon taken up by other designers – for example, Lacroix, Valentino and Versace.

By November 1990 I had fought back and finally opened a boutique that was just mine, called 'Vivienne Westwood', right in the heart of Mayfair.

My sons had helped me over this crucial period. Between them they saw to the business and sorted out what had become a mess. Ben concentrated on the production side and Joe saw to the business and finances. They saw I was being ripped off by lots of people – I do have a such trusting side to me – and they took over until the operation got so big we had to bring in professionals.

I also got to know my boys a lot better. For a while we were all living at the Clapham flat and it was a breath of fresh air to have them and their friends constantly around the house.

From here on was my most creative period. In October 1987 my Britain Must Go Pagan collection took the idea of teenagers who slash their jeans and fused it with the last time clothing used to be slashed, which was the late Middle Ages and the Renaissance.

I also put together aspects from the 'Queen's wardrobe' with Sherlock Holmes hats, and combined cut-away mini kilts with eighteenth-century bustiers.

My March 1988 Time Machine collection took a more classically tailored turn, working towards a lean and long outline with longer skirts and higher platform soles.

Then, with Civilizade in autumn '88, I took on a rococo mood which exploited harlequin themes, diaphanous fabrics and half-glimpsed underpinnings. In March 1989, Voyage to Cytherea began a more intensively erotic approach, combining Romantic references with lean silhouettes. I followed these ideas through into Pagan 5 with my body suit, which was decorated only with a gold fig leaf over the crotch, or an erect penis drawn like a stylized graffito.

Now the American fashion guru John Fairchild, the editor of *Womenswear Daily* – probably the most influential fashion publication in the world – suddenly rated me as one of the six most influential designers ever. That took quite a few sceptics' breath away. But as far as I was concerned, it was a statement of fact.

After that I appeared on the Dame Edna Everage television show and the *South Bank Show* devoted a programme to my work. There was also my appearance on *Wogan* when the audience seemed to think my fashions were a cause for laughter. But I didn't mind at all. As I said to Sarah Stockbridge afterwards: 'That went down quite well.' I was mindful of what Malcolm had taught me about publicity.

I had studied Watteau and Fragonard and all those rococo

masterpieces. They seemed to spell out a visual basis for a new age of elegance. It was elegance that I thought was now needed. It was elegance that was potent and even subversive. In a world of vulgarity, it was elegance which stood out against crassness and helped people think for themselves.

We live in an age of such dreadful vulgarity – human beings have never been dressed so badly. It's horrifying. I hate to look at people sometimes; it makes me feel ill the things some people wear. I don't know how they can put such dreadful things on their bodies. So many young people today are mindless. They dress in these awful baggy shapes. They look like hyperactive morons. It's their rock and roll mentality. They have been seduced by American culture.

When I was young I also thought it was enough to look as if you were active. You dressed to look active because that was a way of poking the establishment in the eye. But nowadays I'm appalled by all this brainless activity. The reason why people look so awful now is that every year they get more brain-damaged.

You could say I'm an élitist. But I think it's from the élite that true values begin. But I am not a misanthrope or a recluse. I like to say things and do things which somehow affect the quality of life and make it better. Perhaps that isn't possible, but I have to try.

In 1990 I showed Portrait. Here I played with cross-dressing and gender ideas. The models paraded in chalk-stripe men's-type suits, with shirts and ties and contrasting body suits with frilly satin codpieces and corsets printed with images by Boucher.

Later that year I put on Cut, Slash, and Pull. I was again linking the street fashion for torn and frayed jeans with the Medieval/ Renaissance fashion for slashed clothing. My notes from that collection read: 'There was once a battle from which the men returned with clothes slashed and pricked from the sword; the gallantry suggested by this effect was so pleasing to the eye and the imagination that it produced a fashion craze lasting nearly a hundred years. So I decided to do a bit of cloth slashing.'

In fact, I did quite a lot of slashing. I slashed through jackets again and again to show the shirt underneath which was slashed in its turn. The effect was dramatic and very sexy!

I also became interested in revolutionizing menswear. So I paid attention to the shirt. A man's shirt, after all, is really the sexiest thing. It's worn right next to his body, and he only has to undo a top button or loosen his tie to suggest an element of *déshabille*.

In particular I was thinking of those turn-of-the-century men in elegant loose shirts, with interesting features around the neck. The machine-cut slits in the cotton and satin of my garments enriched their surfaces, and gave them a gallant, swashbuckling look.

At the same time I wanted to alter the basic line of men's tailoring to get away from the broad-shouldered 'macho' image, that nasty boxy look of 'falling off' American-style suits.

It's not possible for a man to be really elegant without having a touch of femininity. For this, as with all clothes, tailoring is all important. You can say everything you want to through tailoring.

What fascinates me is to achieve a kind of tailoring that fits and conforms to the male body. Not in a shapeless way like cardigans, but in a shaped way that makes you more aware of a male body and its masculine features. I love tight shoulders on men's jackets, and sleeves which demonstrate the muscle in the arm. I love it when a man bends down in a jacket and you can see the shape of his back through it. Especially if he's a big man – the kind of man I think most sexy!

With ties I like big knots, especially those double Windsor knots. It's a great pity men don't vary their necklines more with scarves or bow-ties. Bow-ties are really great. The best advice you can give any man is how to knot a bow-tie!

I also like it when there's a sort of hand-made quality to men's tailoring. When things aren't all that structured or so starchy. It's nice when you think someone's wife could have made his suit. That has a human feel to it, rather than a mass-produced, pressed-out look.

The subtle tailoring I use does have problems on the manufacturing side. British manufacturers, especially, aren't used to what I want them to do, and sometimes they do it shoddily. That reflects badly on me. But the problem isn't in the design – it's in the manufacturing process.

In 1990 I got the Designer of the Year award. I think would have had it before but some people couldn't forgive me for surviving. In a way their hand was forced by the acclaim I'd been getting overseas. It was also obvious by now how many people had ripped off my ideas all over the world. People said I wasn't commercial. But a couple of months after each of my shows you saw my ideas in the shops.

Beginning with Dressing Up, in March '91, I began to research into the tradition of great couturiers, especially Christian Dior. It's been forgotten how radical and anarchic Dior was. With the cut and structure of the New Look, for example, he changed the relationship of clothes to the body.

Dior spent a lot of time underneath frocks in museums trying to work out how they were constructed. I do the same. This is very important because it's the lack of historical knowledge which is making couture increasingly crude and predictable. Fashion today is not referential enough.

People are not experimenting with the cut or working on the body, so they just recycle the same old shapes and are content just to fiddle with details. That's why people who copy me often get it wrong. They think it's in the detail, when it's in the cut.

The idea of technique was what I learnt from working with Malcolm. He showed me that creativity isn't a mystical process. You don't really have to have an idea. It's the way you do something that becomes the idea in the end. It's ultimately technique which generates ideas, not ideas which generate technique. The form is the idea. A beautiful form equals a beautiful idea. That's what design is about. With technique you never run out of ideas. As you cut and measure and look at fabrics, ideas come and associations are suggested – ways to progress and push things further.

And technique is not necessarily about free expression. To quote André Gide: 'Art is born from constraint, survives with controversy and dies with liberty.' The terrible mistake of our century is to be obsessed with self-expression, to put 'creativity' first. You hear all these people saying: 'I could write a book' or 'I could compose some music.' But of course they can't. They might have some idea in their head, but working it through, realizing it, is what counts.

In the end, it's how something is expressed that matters. Style is everything.

For the October '92 Grand Hôtel show we took over that prestigious hotel in Paris. Here I appeared for the first time as a model on my own catwalk. We also had Marina Ogilvy-Mowatt, the rebellious daughter of Princess Alexandra, making her modelling début. She was very good but did have some trouble walking on my famous six-inch platform shoes.

The theme of the show was 'amour'. It opened with a traditional nuclear family but was followed by all sorts of odd and perverse couplings. The male models were dressed in skimpy underpants blazoned with images of the penis. They had to undress the female models – who all wore huge wigs – on the catwalk.

By March '93 the heels on my platform shoes had reached nine inches high. This led to poor Naomi Campbell actually falling arse over tit on the shiny lavender catwalk. But though she took quite a tumble and was in some pain, Naomi just giggled and carried on. She'd been wearing a tartan kilt which exemplified the British theme of that season's Anglomania show.

At a time when other designers were trying to revive punk, I went for unadulterated glamour. I had tartans sewn into bustle-backed skirts, nipped-in waist jackets, grey and camel trouser suits, luxurious fake furs and gigantic ball gowns in silver satin and shocking pink, gold lamé lace and tartan taffeta.

By 1994 my business was well established. It was doing £8-10 million a year. I had three shops in London and several abroad, and ongoing deals with a French mail-order company and with Littlewoods in the UK, plus lots of licensing deals.

We had organized the design into two labels, Gold Label and Red Label. The Gold Label group was designed and manufactured in London, and Red Label was manufactured in bigger quantities in Italy with prices quite a bit lower.

*   *   *

I still saw Malcolm now and then. For some reason he always seemed nervous when he saw me. He would sometimes write me congratulatory letters and slip in that he was proud of me. But I didn't need him to be proud of me! He always was a bit egotistical in that sense – he doesn't like anything he thinks belongs to him to slip away.

I was also now in demand as a lecturer and had various professorships. For instance, I would go to Vienna for two days every month to help students work through ideas. One of these students, Andreas Kronthaler, caught my attention. He was working on some stunning medieval-style designs. What also interested me was his turquoise eyes and his strong, sinewy body. The complete antithesis to Malcolm.

It also seemed that Andreas was attracted to me. I invited him back to my Battersea studio to work with me. Andreas was half my age but we soon fell in love. He was such a pleasure to be with and in some ways perhaps even more freakish and eccentric than me!

Eventually we decided to marry. That was really so that he could get a work permit and continue working in England. I didn't even tell my mother about the marriage. We wanted to keep it a secret. He didn't tell his parents either. In fact our parents found out when a few months later the newspapers found out and rang them.

For the wedding I wore a pair of grey trousers, a lemon-yellow twin-set and very high heels. The only people at the ceremony were Joe and Ben, the staff from the register office and some immigration officers from Croydon. These officers were quite suspicious about our marriage. We had to go to a number of interviews. They asked Andreas personal questions like 'What is the colour of her carpets?' and 'How many cats have you got?' They thought maybe it wasn't a genuine marriage.

After the ceremony we just came back to work.

Andreas is very young, but he knows an awful lot. He has a passion for art and for beauty and for reading. He is a bit aesthetic, mind you, with his head sometimes in the clouds. I remember that what really upset him about the French Revolution was all the great works of art which were destroyed by the revolutionaries. He cared more about that than anything else.

100

I am rather different. What struck me was the poor people who died under the guillotine. But that hadn't even occurred to him.

Just before a recent show Andreas told everyone about a dream he'd had. A model appeared headless, with her head under her arm. Andreas took the head and placed it on a table. He stood back and asked: 'Now what shall we do with her hair?'

We go everywhere now. To parties, ceremonies and shows, and even to Royal Ascot.

It's like a second life for me and he's got such flair. The most talented person I've met for twenty years. On top of which he is so patient and good-tempered. We live together in the same Clapham flat I've had for over twenty years and get on very well.

I think if you want to be happy in a relationship you shouldn't expect too much. But you do need to think you can give that other person something special, however small, that they can't get anywhere else. That's your security.

Even so, a close relationship is always a compromise with freedom. If you're not careful you end up spending too much of your time on what you don't want to. And time is so short! Time is the luxury, not money.

Andreas has a tremendous input into my collections nowadays. He wants to make women look beautiful. That is his main aim in life. And he has some really big ideas. My ideas weren't as grand until I worked with him. I wouldn't, for example, have gone in for those great trains. I would have said: 'But what about the dry cleaning bills?' But now I think that's fine and I even like the idea that the train will pick up all sorts of rubbish like cigarette ends from the street. I think it's great to get your clothes dirty.

Men idealize women so they have these big ideas. And while it's difficult to distinguish a man's way of designing from a woman's, I would say that women are more practical and men more idealistic.

In 1985 my father had died of a heart attack. He actually died in my mother's arms on the floor while they were ballroom dancing.

Mum was so upset, completely crushed. She didn't know where she fitted any more. She was unhappy at home in Devon, and then when she came to visit me and Olga and Gordon in London, she was unhappy there. For a time she stayed with me in Clapham and even served in Worlds End. Bit by bit she got her stability back.

She is so proud of me now. She wishes my father could have seen my present success. She goes to all my shows, coming up to London to stay in the Clapham flat and travelling with the whole company. She's not shy of making comments either, sitting in the front row, and sometimes making quite an exhibition of herself.

Nineteen ninety-four was my big year of the behind, when I brought back the bustle and put bare bottoms on the catwalk. Again I was redefining the shape of women and challenging what it was acceptable to say or accentuate. This show was called Erotic Zones and I also exaggerated the bosom. Several of the models appeared topless.

All this outraged the puritans but I couldn't see what they were making a fuss about. What was the problem with seeing these lovely nubile young women in the flesh? How many women do you find who are that perfect? People should enjoy looking at them. I was only sorry I was too fat to model the outfits!

Some people accused me of exploiting women in this show. What rubbish! I actually idealize women, so how could I exploit them? The only people who would say that kind of thing are feminists. Personally, I'm not a feminist as I can't stand puritans.

What could be more natural than putting the world's most beautiful women into clothes which enhance and exhibit their beauty? In any case, the models love doing my shows.

As for complaints that Naomi Campbell appeared with a flashing traffic cone on her head, that Kate Moss wore a tiny corset which exposed her breasts, that Nadja Auermann was walking up and down the catwalk nibbling a carrot, or that one pair of pom-pom slippers was decorated with vibrators . . . The catwalk is theatre. It's about provocation and outrage.

I love to stick my elbow in when I think people are starting to get complacent. I don't set out to shock. But there is this little devil inside me that rings a bell when I'm about to do something with shock value. I like the danger of sticking my neck out, even when I'm not sure what I'm trying to suggest – that just makes it even more exciting.

But there's also a sort of naïveté about me. Like when I wore a see-through dress with nothing on underneath at a reception at Kensington Palace. When I saw the pictures next day I looked almost naked. You could see everything! But that dress is not see-through till you get flashlights on it. I wore it out of a *joie de vivre* really.

All right, so the dress is a tiny bit see-through. But I thought, can they see through it? No, I don't think they can. Well, not very much!

I really am fascinated by beautiful women. Sometimes, when I look at the models I use in my shows, it makes me want to cry. They are so perfect in every way. It seems almost uncanny, almost inhuman. I sometimes wonder whether they are goddesses or monsters. They look very extreme, bizarre. They send a shiver of electricity through me.

I think the human being in general has a most beautiful shape – that upright posture we have. They say that once the human animal stood up on two legs it freed its hands, and the brain developed. That upright posture is so beautiful, and particularly so in a woman. I think it's enhanced by high heels. These change a woman's posture and figure, making her bottom stand out in a sexy way, and giving the possibility of playing around with that vertical dynamic.

And I think it's great to change silhouettes, because the eye gets used to a familiar shape. And that's what fashion is all about. When you change accepted shapes you direct attention to the body itself.

The Japanese have always loved what I do. Sometimes Japanese clients will come up and touch me – just to have touched Vivienne Westwood! I don't mind. I also like it when people come up to me in the street or give me a kiss for no reason.

But fame hasn't stopped me doing things my way. I still go shopping. I ride my bike to work. And I still don't have a TV. I do sometimes buy myself books, and I did once buy a large Victorian brooch of rock crystal with an intaglio bumblebee – which I foolishly lost. I'm the least acquisitive person I know.

I was asked in Japan recently, 'What is fashion?' I think I gave one of my best answers ever. I said fashion is really about being naked. So for a young girl, her rosy, nubile flesh might be the best thing she can wear. But for someone like me, at my age, it's 'Please can I have a pair of high-heeled shoes?'

Fashion is always about sex. But then, what is sex after all? It's self-expression. There's nothing worse than going somewhere and wishing you had put on something more adventurous. Even if you are in the most boring place in the world you can still be dressed wonderfully and then you will be the centre of attention. There is nothing better than that.

Well, maybe seeing someone better dressed than you are can give you even more of a lift.

When in doubt, overdress.

I don't think that fashion is the be all and end all. There is more to life. But I do think it matters what people wear – it can change them inside. There are certain things I just could not wear – for example, anything from Marks & Spencer. And the worst designer in the world is Laura Ashley. She makes women look like children – poor girls in bedsitters are made to look stupid.

Looking as stupid as that must have an effect on your politics. Whenever I've put on a pair of jeans I've had to take them off immediately – they've made me look straight, politically uncaring.

As for the future I should feel that I hadn't fulfilled my potential if all I ever did was fashion. I'm very conscious that there's much more to life. For example, I think of all the books I've never had time to read. Perhaps one day I'll find the time.

I hope my work has done something to better humanity. I've constantly tried to provoke people into thinking afresh and for themselves, to escape their inhibitions and programming. I've tried to put humanity and intelligence back into the design process. And to escape conformity. One of my favourite quotations is from

104

Aldous Huxley: 'Orthodoxy is the grave of intelligence.' The greatest function human beings have is to be as critical as possible.

The ancient Greeks believed in scepticism, and they valued art as the ultimate achievement of civilization. They were enlightened and so, for example, they didn't brand homosexuals as criminals. We should learn from them.

I know my work has some importance. If nothing else, it can stand as a critique of the world we so miserably inhabit.

The only effect one can have on this world is through unpopular ideas. These are our only means of subversion and therefore of hope. I'd like to think I've done something for the sanity of the world, a sanity which nowadays seems in short supply. Particularly in view of the ecological disaster which is occurring because people have not heeded the last paragraph of JS Mill's *On Liberty*.

My greatest fear is that the ignorant and overconfident will get more power than they already have.

As for dying, well actually it's rather a joyful thought. I'll be quite content to rot. When the Emperor Hadrian knew he only had a short time to live because of an illness, knowing how quickly a lifetime is lost and the short time left to him, he wrote a poem to his soul and the last line was: 'Let us go into death with open eyes.'

And now, if you don't mind, I think I'd like to go to the pub.

PART TWO

Growing Up as a Genius in the Sixties

'There is going to be a great disaster in the libraries.'

Charles Fourier

In the mid-1960s Harrow Art School was a white stone Victorian building fronted by wrought-iron railings, with stone steps leading up to the entrance. On these steps lounged art students – pretty girls chattering to boys with insolently long hair, flowery shirts and red trousers. I passed it on the bus every day to and from school. I would lay aside my library book and drag at my cigarette as I stared from the top deck.

Envious desire was born in the schoolboy. I chafed inside my uniform. However customized by an askew tie, a missing cap, a graffitied satchel, my costume still did not fly with my dreams; it signified servitude. I thought what bliss to be down there, with those girls, attracting the wary glances of passers-by, in red trousers of my own.

I knew about this place from the inside. My friend Tony's elder brother was a student there, a 'painter', living what seemed an orgy of 'pissing about', boosted with sex, drugs and folk music. Challenged for being late one morning, Tony's brother had protested that his eggs took 'a long time to boil'. The cool wit of this remark entranced me. This was beyond school. And the reported judgement of a tutor that one student's work was 'so bad it was good' astonished me with its categorical inversion – this was not just cool, this was where I wanted to be, where probity and logic were tipped so neatly upside down.

The interior of the building, which I had furtively scouted out, was multi-layered and *ad hoc*, with all kinds of unexpected passages and stairwells and dead ends, and strangely positioned rooms and studios. Some studios were only accessible from the outside, making the building even more confusing, and were used for drug taking and snogging, or dossing by itinerant beatniks.

For years after I left the college I had dreams about being lost and yet curiously 'found' inside this dreamlike interior – confused yet content, wandering in a labyrinthine adventure, looking for . . . what? For my class, for the plot, for girls, for a store cupboard, for girls, for where I was supposed to go next.

So architecturally as well, the college contrived a kind of deviancy – madness and disorder and complication being as inscribed in its real estate as in the reigning authority.

The college principal – an eccentric then on the verge of retirement – was reputed to play with toy trains in his office. The cries of 'choo! choo!', it was said, could be heard by people passing his door. Nero fiddling while the college ran amuck. For the tutors, it was rumoured, were even more wicked than the students – 'Nobody gives a fuck'. My heart soared at the thought of this regime. Why, everything must be possible there.

In other words this was a place of excess, a liminal setting, a place where I might set into motion and realize my furtive adolescent experiments and gropings towards a transcendental Ego – the wish to shine but to be seen only as pure illumination. Here, maybe, I could begin to achieve a work commensurate with my self-image.

One day I would paint heroic pictures – pictures appropriate to my heroism – and live in an open-plan studio with a woman who would model nude for me. My forehead would sweat with big ideas and her nipples would redden under the caress of my paintbrush. There would be other nudes too – betrayals and reconciliations – how could I help myself in the company of allurement, especially when propositioned? And frequent trips to Paris and New York in the company of my exasperated agent: 'Fred, you must stop yourself destroying these masterpieces!'

To my mother, I stressed my desire for self-improvement. I said to her: 'I want to be an artist' in a calculatedly sober tone, as if I had said: 'Mum, I've decided to become an estate agent.' The announcement was also to myself, for I needed to hear myself say out loud: 'I want to be an artist' to clarify the notion sufficiently to begin a plan of action. How did one become an artist? What were the first steps? Obviously, art school.

I thought about those art college girls. My virgin hands ached for their skin, to soothe my rough edges in their culture, lose my inhibitions somewhere between their mascara-coagulated lashes and the swollen hips I imagined through their long, flimsy skirts, skirts which trembled as they walked, as I did whenever I thought of approaching them.

What was the price of entry? Surely, genius. No woman, I had heard, could refuse a genius. A genius just lay back and considered the offers. Look at Picasso, look at Billy Fury. Geniuses received letters from women in far-away places – photo enclosed. Easier than the wear and tear of the chase. I would let my work be evidence of my worth and women would be pledged in advance.

On learning I intended to leave school at fifteen to go to art college, my mother asked me how I proposed to earn a living. The notion seemed laughable. A living? Dear mother, how could she know my heart? What was 'a living' to a genius? She might as well ask me to invest in a pension. I wanted simply to LIVE. The 'living' would emanate naturally from my works, from my exploits and renown. In any case, all those famous people in the newspapers and *Paris Match* never seemed short of a bob or two. Obviously sustenance appeared like a good fairy in the wake of success. My obstinacy also saw off other objectors. My English teacher, for example, who thought I was blowing university for a fantasy. How true. But so what? More problematical was my complete lack of visual talent. To remedy this I began Saturday-morning drawing classes at the art college.

These classes were attended by pensioners, aspirants like myself, and people who seemed to be there for a desultory socializing. One Ted used to turn up and spend most of three hours taking the piss. I recall him in the studio with pointed shoes and bright-green socks staged defiantly on the table, sneering inanely and burping.

The tutor, a handsome young man with a crumpled beige corduroy jacket, took all this bemusedly, working his way around our easels with a 'how-long-before-I-can-get-out-of-here' look. He told me about cross-hatching, perspective and volume. I chiselled and slashed at sheets of cartridge paper, rubbing in charcoal with my fingers, splashing on white gouache, caricaturing the rotundity of apples and zigzagging around the whitewashed bottles we were meant to represent. My tutor smiled and recommended 'restraint'. I felt that on the contrary I should 'let go', pour out declamations, make angry marks, score piercing insights in the lightning moment.

These classes did little to improve my draughtsmanship. But they did inadvertently launch me on a career of pseudo-perdition. For like all art colleges in the sixties, Harrow was a beacon of modernity, excess and transgression. (All these went together then.) And I soon came to the attention of Richard.

Richard was a homosexual, in his early twenties, loosely attached to the college – I never worked out if he was actually a student or just hung around – and the focus of a homosexual undercurrent in the college; yet another frisson to the place. Richard was determined to corrupt me and claim my soul for his 'queer' underworld. Realizing I was an intense sort, he gave me a racy biography of Arthur Rimbaud. But while Rimbaud's poetry stirred me, his sexuality made no impression. Undeterred, Richard took me to quite a few homosexual parties around Harrow on the Hill, at which there were many servicemen from the nearby USAF base in Ruislip, and to several nightclubs – for example, The Pink Elephant at Piccadilly Circus and, especially, The Huntsman in Berwick Street.

But try as he might, by intellectual conversion or erotic suggestion, Richard couldn't interest me in himself. Several other men at that time also approached me – and in fact Richard was continually and eagerly making introductions. But the notion bored me in advance – another man's body seemed a dull thing; a version of one's own. Where was the interest or mystery? I knew all my own nooks and crannies. I knew a man's heaviness and musty smells from my own, even in the slightness of youth – or extrapolated from the memory of my father, and I could not find a desire to discover such sensations in another. How claustrophobic, I thought, to make love to a version of your own physique, like worshipping a mirror.

I imagined the hardness of men's bodies; their big thighs and hairy arms, their lack of natural grace and lugubriousness of movement, were drab – those masculine effects which the queen tries to dissimulate in a mocking translation of a woman's quickness and physical fluency. I wanted to abandon and lose this sense and sensation of myself as a male and find an opposite; someone 'different' in personality and shape, smell and carriage, tastes and clothes. Only a woman would do.

Even so, as a boy, I enjoyed the company of these articulate and cultivated men. Who else would talk to me so knowingly about Rimbaud and Van Gogh? Or put me on to Norman Mailer and Jack Kerouac? And leave it at that! For in retrospect, I am surprised both at how safe I felt and at how safe I was.

I introduced a school friend, Martin, to this scene. (Also father-less, Martin was equally free to stay out all night.) But I think Martin was shocked and uneasy and he stopped assisting at my weekends. I too was sometimes shocked, but I absorbed the emotion as proof that I was emergent, that my game plan was unfolding.

All these clubs and pubs – like Dan Farson's in the East End – became a touchstone for my new life, and my frequenting them a rite of passage. The mixture of night-life, Soho and the forbidden, was magic. We travelled in cars from venue to venue until the early hours, when I would be dropped within walking distance of my home.

Sometimes I went on my own to The Huntsman, which was always packed and hot and energetic and exciting – drugs in sachets, strange dances, rumours of raids. Preposterously, I would appear in my school uniform – open-necked white shirt, navy-blue blazer, grey trousers. I couldn't afford anything else. I was let in free, probably passing for a rent boy.

Occasionally I tried to approach young lesbians, with a vague notion of propositioning them. Their glacial beauty, cold and remote eyes, their indifference and reputed unavailability thrilled me. I wanted to get close to them, to mix among them as an honoured guest, even as a freak schoolboy. But they looked at me in bemusement and moved away, back into the crowd of queers.

My two best friends then were Gordon Swire and Tony Gibney. Tony was a red-haired working-class boy of Irish extraction, passionately committed to DH Lawrence and only (so he claimed) aroused by black women.

Gordon's family had come down from Tintwistle in Derbyshire in the late fifties. Bullied at school for his Northern origins, Gordon transformed himself into a debonair Southern suburbanite, burying his accent under a West London drawl and affecting an uneasy snigger whenever he reminisced about 'Uh, yeah, Tintwistle'. As if even the fact of recollection was a joke to be savoured. Gordon in fact reacted in this way at every mention of what might be a personal or private topic.

Gordon's parents were a gentle-mannered couple who sold children's clothes in the front of their post office. When she heard my mother was widowed with two small girls Mrs Swire insisted on donating two of the prettiest pink dresses in the shop, with coats to match. But my mother was resistant to this kindness. She'd served in the Free French Resistance (where she met my father) and was prone to assess her generation sternly. Who were these Swires? What, for example, had Mr Swire done in the war? Well, not a lot. He'd been a storeman in an aircraft factory, a civilian job which, according to Gordon, he wangled to avoid conscription. Gordon thought this a hoot. But my mother was unimpressed and the gifts were returned. I recall the puzzled hurt on Mrs Swire's face when I took them back with a mumbled apology.

Gordon had a car, a black banger, and we would all go on expeditions to central Harrow, Heathrow airport or the Hellfire Club caves in High Wycombe. And most weekends we went looking for parties.

Party hunting around the Ruislip-Harrow-Pinner circuit in the sixties began with the reconnoitring of certain pubs with a reputation for party intelligence. You would visit these and have a drink, mill about, eye the girls. Then someone would arrive with an address.

We would travel in Gordon's car, crammed also with freeloaders, and possibly a couple of girls, and arrive at some poor fucker's leafy residence, unannounced and uninvited, and without a bottle to our name.

Getting in was usually easy. If the front door was barred we just went round the back. Or one of us would scale a drainpipe to an upstairs window and open a door for the others. And if we were still unable to get in we would show our disappointment by lobbing a half brick through the front window as we drove off. All this was part of the game of Saturday night. Laughter and tears, drink and stink.

The sex at these parties was often desperate and clawing, a kind of abstracted sex – deep French kisses which went on too long to be credible or purposeful or even enjoyable, sad soggy snogging in piles of coats left on beds or all up the stairs – 'Excuse me mate, where's the bog?' – or the monotonous rocking of cars in the street outside. If you look at popular films of the time you might think that automatism, that vacancy and clockwork inanity in the sex scenes, is just poor acting. But these parties were just like that, just like amateur theatre. In those days we didn't have the references from sex education to *Emanuelle*, to Madonna; we were making it up as we went along.

We didn't realize, for example, that we should gasp and moan orgasmically – we hadn't been shown how. In all the parties and clubs I went to from fourteen years old I saw a lot of sexual contact, but I never heard a classic orgasm until one afternoon in 1967 in Paris in the hotel room next to mine, where I was reading Truman Capote's *In Cold Blood*, and this woman had a beauty that went on for twenty minutes. I was dying to see what she was doing.

Bed was my bohemian province. Here I slept, dreamed, had erections, and read for hour after hour. Here I smoked and drank tea, and nibbled biscuits as I read. Twisting my body in all positions to avoid cramp, turning those countless pages. My bed was my ark of solitude, a nest of solipsism. I learned self-sufficiency in it – how to be alone in the world; to be transcendentally lucid; to be Myself. The world made bed. It became a surrogate for my body, I was so often in it, a suburban Oblomov. I dreamed I was joined to it. I dreamed I was dreaming in it. I dreamed I was trapped in it.

Sometimes I slept all night and then all day. I would rise as it was getting dark, and then go back to bed to read. Day merged with night and my dreams inhabited the day. Falling asleep with the light on I might drop into a hypnoid half sleep. Once in this state I had a waking nightmare. I was on my back, paralysed and transfixed under the light-bulb. A cigarette was burning in my mouth. It burned down and down towards my lips. I was terrified the column of ash would snap and tumble into my eyes. With a supreme effort I twisted and ejected myself into a waking state.

My bed was also a political arena. My mother was appalled at my erratic sleeping hours. Beds, she thought, should be slept in at night, made in the morning and left pristine all day. Not inhabited at all and eccentric hours, and then left unkempt, crumb-infested, as tousled as the hair of a vagrant mistress. This had to be fought through. My bed was my own space. She had to be dissuaded from sweeping into my bedroom when I was away, plumping and airing, and practically disinfecting the place.

My little sisters had a different idea. Quite often in the early mornings one, or sometimes both, would climb in with me. This was an occasion for delicacy, for naturally I had erections while asleep. They would snuggle up and cuddle me. I would return their caresses, seduced by their warmth, and we would exchange confidences. I was never tempted to excite myself or have orgasms with my sisters present – it would have seemed a betrayal of our pleasure. Nor did I desire to experiment with them as sexual partners.

But as an adolescent I was plagued by wet dreams. I would awake to that familiar aniseed odour and stickiness on my pyjama bottoms. I would go into the bathroom to wash myself. Then I would wash my clothes, then dry them with a hairdryer. I felt debilitated, evacuated, remorseful, as if I had lost a vital energy. I would rinse my face in cold water to try and restore my facial muscles to some kind of tension, erasing the soporific relaxation, the post-orgasmic mask. I would go for an energetic walk to restore the normal distribution of tensions in all my muscles. I would eat a hearty breakfast and drag lustily at cigarettes. Gradually my body returned to reality. It assumed weight and presence, I could feel my leg muscles glowing and the tobacco in my mouth and on my fingers where I sucked and licked the sharp yellow nicotine.

I think my wet dreams were so intense because from the age of fourteen I tried to give up masturbation. This was in accord with my project. I needed to conserve my genius, coil myself tightly within myself, not let it out to spill or dissipate my soul. Wanking, therefore, was not desirable. I took Freud on sublimation for a fact. Art stood instead of sex. But sometimes I lapsed. Once, when reading, of all things, Edgar Wallace's *The Tramp*, my erection snaked its warmth into my hand. I recall this because the circumstance seemed so piquant I wondered if the moment – the loss – could be redeemed by transmutation into a poem.

I eventually got into art college with stick men. My Saturday-morning portfolio was unimpressive. But I was interviewed by the incumbent principal, Mr Illingworth, a new man determined to sweep away art college cobwebs.

The new idea then was to briskly instate the notion of a pre-college year with a Bauhaus philosophy of art training. Flicking disdainfully through my portfolio, Illingworth lighted on a sketch-book. In this I had begun a series of cod-Surrealist backgrounds inhabited by stick men, since I couldn't draw people. When he asked what these 'meant' I came alive; he realized I knew my Jung and André Breton and evidently thought the rest might follow. My mother now agreed to buy me a bottle-green corduroy jacket, which I rolled in the dust before wearing as it seemed conspicuously new.

I had prepared myself for the smells of tobacco, turps and alcohol, slashes of charcoal crumbling across cartridge paper, the squeak of Conté crayon. But soon, here I was, at last an insider, and expected merely to sample a bewildering selection of art college 'disciplines'.

We had to go from, say, jewellery to pottery in one day, the idea being that we should try everything before committing ourselves for the next three years. But while I enjoyed the tactile activity of pottery, clay didn't have the transcendental kudos of oil paint. And where did jewellery fit into my prospectus for genius?

My fellow students were a disappointingly respectable bunch and I was socializing more with the old crowd. Soon, however, I noticed around the college an intriguing young man with a shock of auburn hair, who always wore a tartan scarf knotted rakishly around his scrawny neck. He went around with a tall and morose student, darkly handsome and fetchingly sinister. These two always sat together in the canteen, at the table nearest the entrance, and they made a great show of being haughty and secretive – consumed in intimate derisions and chuckling disconcertingly at passers-by, throwing out trails of half-heard insults as people came or went. No one was safe from this pair – not the sternest tutors, the prettiest girls. Everyone ran a muttered gauntlet.

Eventually I dared sit at their table. This was greeted with guffaws and cynical looks, but I introduced myself and gradually insinuated my observations into their caustic commentaries. These two were Malcolm McLaren (then known as Malcolm Edwards) and Patrick Casey.

Pat was an Irishman with *outré* tastes. Precociously, he lived with a woman, who, he claimed, liked to be tied up and whipped with his belt. (This was a new one on me.) He also refused any conventional medium for his work, insisting on drawing everything with coloured ballpoint pens.

Malcolm was much more interesting. His dominating characteristic was his way of laughing, of dissolving and directing, and thereby manipulating, every situation in explosions of contagious laughter.

I recall us passing the window of Heal's in Tottenham Court Road. Malcolm was suddenly doubled up, pointing to a kitsch display of children's cots – pink and flouncy. I wouldn't have given it more than a wry smirk, but his observation was infectious, and I not only joined in, but thereafter was more aware of the risible aspects of such displays. He had enlarged the scope of the ridiculous.

His laughter on this occasion – which stands for many others – had also challenged me. He was 'calling me out', daring me not to consider this display in the uproarious light in which he painted it – in the light he had decided or wished it should be considered. In other words, this was an education in taste.

He wore clothes as a model does – they hung on him transiently, the statement, the cut or cloth, louder than the wearer, cleanly semiological. Thus his tartan scarf, cocking a snook with its ruffian knot and proletarian connotations, at the earnest Carnaby Street fashions sported by other students. But as if to prove the point that clothes were nothing more or less than point proving and point scoring, he might also turn up one day, transformed in a purple tie and pale mauve houndstooth button-down shirt, the acme of tasteful combinations – I can do this as well. He 'wore' behaviour in the same way, sporting attitudes or displaying gestures and opinions as if they too were off-the-peg and replaceable items, shirts to fix cuffs on, or hats to doff, rather than anything intrinsic or integral to a self. He was the complete dandy, inside and out.

He was also the biggest liar I had ever known. He told fibs and his self-fantasizing bordered on delusion. Every event in his life became aggrandized, every step of his life heroic. And very soon we were all implicated. Because, of course, he would tell lies about everyone else, soon nobody knew what was true or false any more; speculations flew and confusion was rife.

I used to wonder if he knew he was lying. I'd watch him spinning a yarn and notice his cheeks and neck flush, his speech become rushed and his eyes turn slightly upwards, like someone in a semi-trance.

And when I sharply challenged him in those early years (before this aspect of his personality had hardened into a matter of psychological survival and commercial strategy) or when we exchanged a certain knowing look of risibility – now come off it! – there would also come a point where he would virtually admit: 'OK, it's a fair cop, Guv', and we both knew that he knew that I knew he was just a lying cunt. I would then grin complicitously and he would chuckle and become unusually affectionate, perhaps even venturing a remark which involved calling me 'Freddie'.

I used to inspect my handwriting for signs of genius. Was it hurried enough? Tortured enough? Did its curlicues and waves exude inspiration? I compared it with the scrawls of accredited geniuses like James Joyce and DH Lawrence, examples of which were helpfully illustrated in biographies. I would rewrite my poems a dozen times and still not get them looking right – still a schoolboy's hand. Maybe if I lost the slant? Or should I be more careless?

I looked for instances of my script unaffected by deliberations, for the real me, for my spontaneity – was that any closer? Unfortunately not. So I tried writing less self-consciously. An impossible trick when you are trying. Twice I incinerated all my manuscripts – burned my poetic bridges. I torched them one by one in the bathroom and dropped their blackening carcasses into the toilet bowl. Then I pulled the chain and opened the window. I wanted to be born again. In another calligraphic style.

I would gaze at portraits of geniuses with the desire that other boys might gaze at pin-ups. Nietzsche, Freud, Bertrand Russell, Edith Sitwell. My look soaked up their faces, memorized their expressions. I was looking for similarities, structural regularities, inventing a private physiognomic register, internalizing it for my own reference at anticipated moments of my future biography. It was always about that look: portraits which combined an intensity, a far-off gaze, a penetration into the soul, the revelation of turmoil within, a photographic trace of renown.

I was duped by this genre of genius portraiture, failing to realize its contrivances. I thought it was all from Nature – inspiration captured on the wing. That look of harsh interiority, furrowed and sombre self-discipline, the ruggedly casual poses, the chiaroscuro lighting, the omnipresent fag. It was what I wanted. Please let me have it! I searched the mirror for resemblances, however incipient. The silken-faced boy who gazed back enraged me.

But I could manifest a genius's stare well enough to alarm people, who sometimes mistook it for hostility, when it was only the heat of

Top left: Vivienne (right) with Gordon and Olga. 'The same pram did for all of us.'

Top right: 'Whenever I [centre] dressed up I just knew I looked better than anyone else.'

Middle: 'I loved these longer walks. The views were spectacular and there was an undercurrent of danger.'

Bottom: 'A teacher would stand at the bottom of the stairs and look up to see if anyone was wearing the wrong knickers.'

'Intellectual things are far more interesting than sex.'

Left: Vivienne and Sarah Stockbridge. 'I sometimes wonder whether models are goddesses or monsters.'

Below: With Naomi Campbell. 'I am fascinated by beautiful women.'

Left: Tizer Bailey. Thinki[ng]
of Jimmy?

Below: Vivienne talking t[o]
Gary Ness. 'He threw his
paintbrushes into the
Thames and said goodbye[to]
painting for ever.'

Left: Vivienne and Joe Corré. 'Even as a young boy Joe always acted like a little husband.'

Below: With Andreas Kronthaler, her second husband. 'He is such a pleasure to be with and even more freakish than me!'

'Personally, I am not a feminist as I can't stand puritans.' . . . 'It is elegance that is pote
and subversive. Elegance in a world of vulgarity.'

my brain emanating as the steadily penetrating glow of my eyes.

Still, something was missing. What, apart from an *oeuvre* – which was in the pipeline – did I lack?

Well, I was particularly concerned about the lack of wrinkles on my forehead and round my eyes. This signified my inexperience, my lack of facility for genuine decadence. So I used to practise frowning in the bathroom, exercising my forehead up and down, vainly hoping to etch a few respectable lines. I would also continually scrunch up my eyes meanly (James Deanly) to install wrinkles round my eyes (a trick I also practised to get into X-rated films). But my skin remained clear and elastic, my face was sweetly oval, my profile was fetching, and, worst of all, my cheeks were soft and sometimes even rosy.

As I engaged in my facial contortions before the mirror I was aware I was 'cheating'. Such lines should be in earnest, not cosmetic. They had to be earned through sleepless nights, participation in great events and the completion of brilliant works.

Meanwhile, excuse me, I was in despair over my boyish looks. I was so fucking pretty! Perhaps if I scowled even harder? I practised all the gradations, flexed every facial muscle. And sometimes I just looked at myself in a sullen trance or in emptiness. Often on Saturday nights, before I went out to meet my friends, when I had buttoned my long, tight waistcoat, knotted a silver tie over a white linen shirt, I gazed, sometimes for an hour or so, combing my hair as an alibi, or smoothing toothpaste over my shaving cuts, but mentally rehearsing all the moves, the things I might become, and looking for facial correspondences to each mood, visible emanations of my identity-to-be.

No wonder my sisters complained about the time I took in the bathroom.

Stories circulated that a gang of our tutors roamed the Ladbroke Grove area, beating up tourists. This sounded too good to be true. They did, however, skulk around the college in Italian jackets.

Ivor Fox, our main tutor, was in his early fifties, with a grey goatee beard, a crumpled and faded corduroy jacket, and a face to match. If you wanted to consult Ivor during opening hours you had to cross the street to the Havelock Arms, where he sat almost all day on a bar stool topping up a whisky glass. Ivor painted still lifes in coagulated greens and browns, one of which hung in the staff room. His colleagues sniggered that he painted it with snot. While I was at Harrow Ivor began an affair with a second-year student. He asked her to model for him at his Chelsea studio. Naturally, this was in the nude. She had hardly taken up her pose when he excused himself. He returned to the studio also naked, and with a paintbrush gripped in his teeth. She fell in love and moved in with him.

Our art history tutor was Theodore Ramos, RA. Theo was knowledgeable and wise, the most sophisticated man I had ever met. He was Spanish-looking, with a dandyish disdain. When his son ran away from boarding school, Theo gave him a present for initiative. That was cool. Theo told us that, according to Freud, people became artists for the love of women. I could see that. He informed us that musicians were not real artists. They lacked the intelligence. Only imbeciles would spend all that time practising. Theo thought that cleaning Old Masters was a scandal. The patina of grime was the seal of antiquity. He also said you could tell how good artists were by how worried they looked. Anxiety betokened intensity. I have since found this a good rule of thumb. In Theo's hallway hung a large Jackson Pollock. But he himself did portraits, mostly of nobs. Theo lived in Chelsea, on the King's Road at World's End (just opposite where, six years later, Malcolm McLaren and Vivienne Westwood would found their boutique).[1]

Theo's seminars were brilliantly witty and provocative. Having delivered one he would suddenly look at his watch and declare: 'I've got to get out of this place!' (meaning Harrow) and then dash from the building. Sometimes Malcolm and I would sprint along beside him up to the Underground station, firing questions and getting breathless gems back.

I introduced Malcolm to Tony and Gordon. We made a gang. We went to parties. We might pretend to dance, caricaturing the moves of those days with absurdist variations. Or we would start arguments about modern art in the kitchen, or hide other people's Pipkins in the garden. Or we might take over the record player – a strategic position from which to alter consciousness. At one party, given by a

Christian poetess in Chiswick, I began playing Edith Piaf instead of the Beatles. Malcolm warded off the protests. Drawing himself up into a Shakespearian posture, he bellowed: 'Edith Piaf . . . and Elvis! . . . ARE LIKE THAT!', entwining his two forefingers and glaring maniacally. The inanity of the remark was compensated by its ferocity. The protesters sloped away.

Some weekends we went to the West End, to clubs and Soho coffee bars, taking in a band – any band, we were hardly fans – watching mods and their girls, and hanging out until the last train had gone. Sometimes Gordon, who was the only one with girl-friends, and hence other duties, was not available with his car and a lift back. And sometimes he had come without his car. No cash for a taxi, no night buses. We would walk the twelve or so miles back, taking around three to four hours, to South Harrow and Ruislip.

We eventually discovered a short cut, which was to walk along the railway track from where the Underground trains emerged from tunnels to run overground. We would crunch the gravel or negotiate the sleepers, or balance along the gleaming rails. But only Tony was rash enough to walk on the 'live' rail (which was, however, disconnected at that time of night). We followed these ghostly parallels, passing deserted and locked-up stations and signal boxes.

Along the way we entertained ourselves with cultural disputations. I might argue that DH Lawrence was just a fucking wanker. Tony would riposte with quotations from *Sons and Lovers*. Or we would quarrel about the merits of the musicians we had heard, or disagree about avant-garde films showing at the handful of art houses then in London, or exchange noisy explanations of novelties like Bertolt Brecht. What did this 'alienation' mean?

These discussions were about the elaboration of extremisms. That was what we enjoyed. Rather than discussing and dialoguing, looking for accommodations, we were exploring antithetical positions, egging ourselves along. How far out could an opinion be? We shouted and railed, and once I nearly came to blows with Tony on the railway line just outside Northwick Park station about the superiority of the Beat poets over Norman Mailer.

Malcolm, not being a literary sort, didn't know all the references.

He would exploit his ignorance, however, to play the jester, interjecting at a sensitive point a completely baffling aspersion, or a madcap comment, which we would relish for its mischievousness, and then move on to the next sensation. Gordon, who was more grown-up and well-balanced than the rest of us (and the only one with a sex life), would snigger in his sardonic way, or try to calm us down, or turn the conversation to bands or girls.

At the mention of girls, Tony would become introspective and brood. He had hopes and desires. He seemed to implode with them. But I had gone off them.

This was after a disastrous flirtation with Diana, a jewellery student from the college. We went to the Marquee together. I paid and she was enthusiastically grateful. She said I would be really handsome when I got older – imagine that! Then she left college. She explained she was pregnant by another student. They were to marry. I thought of suicide. Then I took a toy to her house – a present for baby and the pretext for a last persuasion.

When we were together in her living room I noticed her face was pasty and her skin dry. The details of her house, its homely wallpaper and chintzy softness, suffocated me. I fled – into the arms of art.

For I had taken another cue from Malcolm – women got in the way. Genius was manacled by foolish things. What counted was the creation of an *oeuvre*, a vision, the execution of a purpose. Why had I temporarily forgotten this law? It was treason. To myself. I had been seduced. Still, maybe it was not too late. I was only sixteen.

The path was made easier through Malcolm's own calculated disdain for 'girls'. I was impressed by his bravado. He was, he let it be known, of sterner stuff than hanky-panky. He was in the college library pondering André Masson, he was in the studio drawing fanatical self-portraits, when everyone else had gone to the pub.

What underlay this imposture of Malcolm's I have never decided. It may have been a defence against the fact that this freckled and plain youth, with a shock of hair always standing up and seemingly wagging itself independently at you, was not the centre of female attention. Malcolm attracted the amused passing attention of the more louche and older female students, who sampled a conversation, decided he was nuts, shrugged and moved on.

But only partly. Because I think that in the end, like me at that age – he was one year older – what really absorbed him was this concoction of a genius-as-personality, by any means possible, ruthlessly using all the social cues and cultural titbits available – the creation of this romantic thing: a suburban version of transcendence; the genius at work and at home; the self at a threshold created by relinquishing domestic comfort and abjuring common sense.

I went to Carnaby Street and bought scarlet hipsters from John Stephens. They fitted tightly across my bum, making me feel safely upholstered. I wore collarless shirts, fastened with granny brooches or military medals purchased in junk shops. I got drunk nightly.

But, however drunk, I maintained my solipsistic priorities. Even through the pounding haze of a quart of port I remembered my reputation. Don't get too near that man, he knows such things – a rare and corrosive scholarship; all the deadly influences, from Ginsberg to Walter Pater to Aleister Crowley.

I chain-smoked. Or I distributed my consumption to provide the illusion of a desperado constantly at the end of a trail of cigarettes. (It worked. Someone recently came across a fellow student at Harrow. Asked if he remembered me, he reminisced: 'Ah yes, Fred. He was a chain-smoker.') For preference the strong and esoteric brands – cork-tipped Craven 'A', Three Castles, Passing Cloud, Gitanes, Camel. All a man's taste – pungent.

I practised sticking fags to my lower lip, lifting my head up just enough to breathe while squinting against the smoke. This gave me the appearance of scowling through a fog. I would fill my being with those acrid clouds, as if inhaling a bitter destiny, sucking the fire deep into my lungs and into my heart. I would impatiently snap the tips off proffered cigarettes as a satyr might decline condoms – tips were for wimps. I would slide a packet conspiratorially from my jacket pocket. Flick it deftly open. Offer it round. Extract a white tube. I liked to leave packets face up on tables so I could enjoy the design as an additional aspect of possession.

A boy in a fog. Insatiable dedication to the blue art. First thing in the morning, sitting on my bed. On the top deck of the bus to college, daydreaming through puffs. In the studio, fag dangling from lips, or perched smouldering on an easel. With coffee, clenched in nicotined fingers, camouflaging my mouth at strategic intervals, enhancing a careless gesture. In the pub between sips, inhaling to match the burn of alcohol.

And in bed at night, with a book, mechanically flicking and blowing ash from sheets, pillows, pages . . .

Mentors like Samuel Beckett and Sartre were stern. If you wanted to be of account you had to read 'everything'. But where was this 'everything'? How could I map out this transformative mental domain? I found it by hopping from one reference to another – Beckett backwards to Proust, Simone de Beauvoir across to Camus, returning to Rousseau. And, naturally, the classics. I read these, as autodidacts do, right through, even the title page and the ads on the end papers. *The Decameron* in the Modern Library edition, from Day the First to Day the Tenth, 800 pages, skipping nothing. Flaubert swallowed in Everyman. Livy. Plotinus. Herodotus. I loved this arcane stuff, the archaic creak of those names. Esoteric escapades to bandy about in my head. Tristan and Isolde. More's *Utopia*. One day I would drop these into my prose as whiffs of allusion across the masses to that other fine spirit, my reader. And naturally, Nietzsche. In the Penguin edition. (I was stung by a sneer in the film *The Pumpkin Eater*: – 'Put away your Penguin Freud.' So what was wrong with Penguins? Had I been consorting with inferior editions?)

But I read all this in a vacuum. There was no pattern to it. A random pedagogy. One 'classic' after the other, with no syllabus other than availability, or the accident I'd heard of their 'classic' status. From existentialism to Aquinas, *The Big Sleep* to *The Golden Ass*. The more obscure the book, or the connections between texts, the richer my 'mind' – as that uneasily and uncertainly projected immanence would doubtless become. The drier and denser the text, the more good it was doing me. What joy when I discovered Wittgenstein's *Tractatus Logico-Philosophicus* in Foyle's and carried it home to my bed.

*   *   *

Malcolm was eventually thrown out of his home. His parents objected to him staying out all night.

For a time he dossed in the outside studios at the college. Then, when this became dodgy (suspicious caretaker), he slept in the graveyard at Harrow on the Hill. This lifestyle hardly mattered to his appearance, which was always wild-haired and unshaven, and he continued coming to college. At this time he was penniless and I supported him out of my allowance, giving him money and taking food and cigarettes up to the cemetery. We would smoke and talk there, surveying the views across Middlesex.

However, Malcolm's mother had complained to the college. The principal, Illingworth, and Ivor Fox were alerted to Malcolm's vagabondage, and Malcolm was now obliged to disappear.

The tutors took this very seriously. I was interrogated. Where was Malcolm Edwards? How should I know? Illingworth and Ivor Fox searched the college. Then, ludicrously, they both set off in Illingworth's car, touring the streets of central Harrow, looking for their missing student.

I took Malcolm to my house, hoping he might be able to stay there. My mother, however, took a dislike to his lack of manners. What a rude boy! she said to me when he was out of earshot. In any case, there was no space.

Malcolm sketched me in my bedroom while my sisters looked on and we wondered what to do next. As he drew he commented on my 'worried' expression. This pleased me as measuring up to Theo Ramos's specification of an artist. We then walked the short distance to Gordon's home. Gordon's parents were also disapproving. But Gordon suggested Malcolm could sleep in his car. This was parked in the courtyard behind the flat.

So Malcolm took up residence in the car. He was now able to report to the college that he had a proper residence (i.e. could receive letters posted to Gordon's address) and they decided to leave it at that. So every morning Malcolm would go up to Gordon's for a breakfast of instant coffee and cereal. Gordon was enthusiastic about Shredded Wheat and pressed it on all his guests whatever the time of day. Sometimes I too would arrive for breakfast. Then we would take the bus into Harrow or be driven by Gordon on his way to the Technical College.

Gordon's elder sister was Vivienne Westwood. She was a married school teacher and had a small child, Ben, whom she would bring round when visiting her parents. Being a married mother who earned a living put Vivienne in the category of grown-ups, and she was not then privy to our student goings-on. But she took a sisterly interest in Gordon and seemed proud of his success with girls.

My recollection now is that Vivienne had been intrigued by Gordon's guest, having seen this wild-looking redhead asleep in the car several times. (Malcolm would sleep late quite often, on display to the residents, and an added embarrassment to Gordon's parents.) One morning when I was at the flat, eating Shredded Wheat with Gordon and Malcolm, Vivienne arrived. She tried to make conversation with Malcolm, but Malcolm was particularly anti-social that morning. We all lit up and left for Harrow. But Vivienne, it seems, was in love. Not that we knew anything at the time.

Malcolm soon got into more trouble at college and was obliged to leave. He had alienated most of his tutors and his mother had begun making more mischief. Even the peaceable Swire parents were agitated.

Theo Ramos came to Malcolm's rescue. He introduced him to a set designer and Malcolm became a sort of apprentice, kipping in this man's open-plan studio flat. When I visited I was told that Malcolm's new patron disapproved of the 'mad look' in my eyes. Undeterred, I began assisting Malcolm with his chores, cutting and painting slabs of polystyrene for a set at the New Arts Theatre in Great Newport Street.

We did this in the subversive spirit of 'pissing about'. The result was that some aspects of this set – supposedly a Hindu temple in a jungle clearing – were so incompetently put together they were kicked off the stage by the enraged producer, who began prancing around the stage in a tantrum, demanding to know whether the whole thing was 'a fucking piss-take' or what? This unexpected piece of theatre amused us. But the set designer was mortified and fired Malcolm on the spot.

In the nick of time Malcolm's maternal grandmother, Rose, appeared. She had always been close to her grandson and disapproved of his having been thrown out of his home. She gave him money to begin a journey around various sleazy digs.

Malcolm now lived in a flat with a Greek shoemaker in Berwick Street. At that time he was greatly disturbed, and had regular noisy nightmares which kept waking his landlord. He was evicted. He then moved into a house in Notting Hill used by prostitutes. Malcolm vacated this soon after a conversation I had in the kitchen with one of the girls, who mentioned the cutlery had been used in a recent abortion.

Rose now found Malcolm a room in the house of Mrs Gold, a Jewish friend of hers, assuring her that Malcolm was just a nice Jewish boy, just a bit down on his luck.

In this bedsit Malcolm did some of his best work to date. He remarked that it was more interesting to tackle a small problem intensively than a large one slackly. I was particularly struck by a series of Klee-like experimentations in gouache.

By now I had decided my talent lay in literary areas and was spending my days in reference libraries. In the evenings I would go to Malcolm's bedsit and report on my researches. Then we would review his day's work. Nescafé and cigarettes were consumed. Often then, it was too late for me to travel home. Still talking we would get into Malcolm's bed in our underclothes. We would continue the discussion until one of us dozed off.

Yet there was no sensuality in our relationship. We were both hard young men. We had no love to give, no time to spare for nonsense. Our customary greeting was: 'What you been doing?' Nothing else mattered. I recall the roughness of these associations – the sour tastes of tobacco and coffee, the painterly mess and unkemptness of his room, dirty cups and spilled clothes (we both used to piss in his sink rather than go down the corridor), the astringency of our conversations, and an energy to break the artistic pain barrier.

Mrs Gold had never been keen about her scrawny and avid tenant. She complained to Rose about the mess Malcolm made with his paints. Rose passed it off as a trial endured jointly – two good old Jewish girls humouring a Jewish boy. But Mrs Gold's suspicions were further aroused when Malcolm began refusing her entry to his room. This was because he had begun experimenting with environmental sculpture which turned his room into a rubbish dump of tree stumps, shavings and ironmongery. The sounds of hammering and sawing resounded through the house from late morning to late evening.

Mrs Gold became alarmed. Malcolm now began heaving planks of wood up the stairs. What was the blighter up to? Then one afternoon she managed to slip in while Malcolm was out buying Woodbines. Uproar and recriminations! Rose was summoned. When I arrived that evening Malcolm had fled. Rose and I packed some of his belongings and took them on the bus to where he was holed up in her flat. She cackled with laughter all the way about 'the bloody state' of Mrs Gold, and 'the bloody state' of Malcolm's room.

Rose had by now moved away from the Edwards family home in Edgware. Vitriolic rows with Malcolm's mother and stepfather – quite often about Malcolm – had become embittered, and she and her husband, Mick, retreated to a tiny flat above Clapham South tube station.

Rose was about five foot two and thin as a stick. She had a shrill cockney manner and an unnerving laugh. She doted on Malcolm and relished his scrapes, greeting each revelation with a whinnying rasp of hilarity.

I had never seen a household like theirs. My first thought was that they all hated each other. An explosive malice punctuated every exchange. Everything was shouted at a market trader's pitch and with that rhythmic aggression. Malcolm habitually addressed his grandmother with contempt – rude was hardly the word – 'What's that you're fucking saying? Speak up, girl!' 'God all Christ all fucking mighty! What's she on about now?', waving his hands in mock disbelief.

Rose might suddenly yell at me about my mother: 'How is she?

130

Still in France, is she?' Malcolm would shout: 'For fuck's sake! You asked him that last time!' Ignoring this, Rose would look slyly to see if I was sharing the joke before asking me like a sweet old lady: 'Fancy a spot of toast, dear?' Malcolm: 'He don't want no fucking toast! Can't you see that? Toast? What's he want toast for?' Me (anything for a quite life): 'Yes. Toast.' Rose triumphantly to Malcolm: 'See!' Malcolm, laughing in mock exasperation: 'Oh, all right, Jesus fucking Christ almighty, make some fucking toast then! Jesus!'

Mick, meanwhile, would be sunk in his armchair glowering at everyone, not saying a word. Suddenly and with no warning he would sit up and bellow in an enraged tone: 'WHERE'S ME FUCKING TEA?' Then he would sink back. Rose would laugh like a hyena, then say: 'Oh, he wants his tea, does he? Silly bugger! He'll get his tea all right!', winking at me. Everyone would then forget about Mick and his tea.

After a while I realized this display of hostility was actually their version of intimacy – a way of shouting and cursing your way close to someone. It was also a good emotional training for the hard process of selling, and of selling yourself. (The only other family I've known which worked on this theatrically dysfunctional mode was the family of an Algerian Jewess I courted in Paris. Here too uproar and screamed contempt was the everyday norm and Saturday dinners were blitzkriegs of vituperation and calumny batted this way and that across the couscous.)

Gordon passed his A levels and become a film student at the London College of Film Technique. He rented a large house in Chiswick with a number of other film students. Eventually, Malcolm moved in with Gordon.

It was then that Vivienne made her first move. She left her husband Derek and, with her son Ben, also moved into this house. I thought this was odd – like taking a downward step, a grown-up becoming a student.

Then Malcolm began complaining to me. Vivienne was pestering him. Fucking woman! What should he do? This pestering involved attentions which, according to him, had got to a point of lewd absurdity. Whenever they were alone in the house she would walk around in states of undress. And one night he claimed she had walked into his room naked and climbed into bed with him.

He declared he had felt nothing, and done nothing, not even protested. I believed him. That was his style. But at some point this 'pestering' turned into an arrangement. He began to look shifty. His eyes coloured when I mentioned her. He kept up the same harsh and brittle posture with her as with everybody – don't come near me! And in public they behaved as coy strangers rather than lovers. But I also noticed a softness in her manner to him. She gazed at the poor man with affection. I knew that glutinous tenderness, its coils. I became concerned. Would he succumb?

I didn't believe so at the time. Neither of us thought her a looker. She seemed overly pale, and her skin clammy. Her hair was limp and her look too often beseeching. She also seemed so much older than us, with her past and a child always tugging at her.

And what nowadays famously passes as querulous self-assurance, a witty play on notoriety, seemed merely querulous. Why should we bother with her timidly ventured contributions? Her efforts to match our proud intensity?

However, weeks and months passed and one day Malcolm confessed he was 'sleeping' with her. He said this apologetically. I felt he had betrayed our project. I also thought he would dissipate himself in this relationship. After all, what was she? Just some fucking school teacher.

But Malcolm found a way to redeem himself. He turned Vivienne into his servant. He began appearing in clean shirts – even ironed! She kept house for him. She gave him money. He told me she scared him.

He had enrolled at a college in Chiswick, and this was where he began experimenting with fashion. He devised a set of outlandishly proletarian boiler suits in vivid primary colours for himself, and Vivienne made them.

I noticed that the intensity of her devotion to Malcolm was making Ben jealous. I also noticed that Malcolm was becoming jealous of Ben, curt and exclusive. That seemed curious – a battle between a toddler and a man about a woman the man refused to admit he wanted. Ben would get into bed with his mother and Malcolm would shout and complain. Ben was banned from his mother's bed. In all this Vivienne was compliant. She kept her waspish side back – she really wanted this man. Malcolm was her new life, a chance to begin again.

I surmised that their sexual relationship was intermittent. Malcolm also told me she meant 'nothing' and he planned to leave her as soon as he moved house.

Then Vivienne became pregnant with his child.

At first he blustered and declared it was 'probably not' his. Then that she had 'tricked' him. Indeed she had. (She admitted to Judy Vermorel years later she had been only pretending to take contraceptives.)

Then they moved as a family into a ground-floor flat at Aigburth Mansions near the Oval.

After a while I noticed that Malcolm had become more settled, dangerously – as I advised him – patrician. He even complained that the flat was in a mess, the washing-up was never done! Was being a husband and father good for an artist? I thought perhaps not. The cost of Farley's Rusks, after all, sapped the fund for Rowney Cryla Colours. I had dabbled in sociology and I told him that being a father was just a social definition. Society was a sham, a hoax, a series of floating 'roles' and 'representations'.

Malcolm thought all this over and abandoned his responsibilities. Not that Vivienne minded. Like many women of that time, she was prepared to take it all on. Their poverty, his fecklessness, my outrageous advice. But I think Ben suffered. I found him once as I was walking down from Oval tube station. He was standing in the rain on a traffic island in the middle of Clapham Road, a shrivelled mite. I was shocked by the bewildered unhappiness which seemed to scar his face. I took him home and murmured to Malcolm that he needed proper shoes. His plimsolls were soaked. Malcolm postured. 'Plimsolls are good enough!' Vivienne giggled. Malcolm and I went to the kitchen, where he poured us both a glass of red wine.

*   *   *

133

I soon got to know Vivienne better, as one of our circle rather than as an outsider or the subject of Malcolm's ungenerous reports. She had abandoned her frumpy dresses and now become stylish in slacks. Her hair was spikily cropped and dyed in shades of platinum, sometimes with mischievous pink highlights. I was impressed by her zeal for the revolution, more intense than Malcolm, whom I sometimes had to admonish for his love of bourgeois comforts – at one time he even talked of installing a three-piece suite in the Oval flat. Vivienne also had a determination and pluck (no other word will do), and an oblique sense of humour that I found congenial.

How she grew up wasn't something she often talked about. From the mid-sixties to the mid-eighties, all the years she and Malcolm were together, Vivienne was a bit like a Victorian housewife – ushered in with rustling skirts before her paterfamilias. She suppressed herself in the light of what she saw as Malcolm's brilliance, always ready to take a back seat. It was as if she didn't want to burden his greatness or spoil his stories with her own unseemly and plain beginnings.

She said she came from this place up North, Tintwistle (pronounced 'Twistle') in Derbyshire. Said it with a wryly diffident and apologetic smile. Not a lot to boast of was the picture. Malcolm, after all, boasted – as he boasted of everything – in a big voice with expansive gestures – of descent from Portuguese Jews, the aristocrats of Jewry, so he said, a breed of diamond merchants, failed actors and petty swindlers. He'd laugh coarsely as he recounted all this and you knew he was actually destroying the domestic vision, with its cloying recurrence or hindrance to his master plan. For Malcolm in those days was fanatically contemptuous of any kind of family, or talk of the past.

Everything with him had to be relentless projection. Only the future mattered, where we might all still count and 'do something'. That future which we lacked in a present which might maliciously close in and imprison us in merely fatuous hopes – a million miles from the celebrity he craved, just one of an army of losers.

So any hint of a recollection in a conversation was immediately scorned, venomously and high-handedly dismissed. It was a weakness which might detract from stern tasks. The conversation was switched to such tasks – the next art show to digest, how to wrest from Van Gogh's diaries a recipe for fame?

Malcolm was running madly from his childhood – as I later understood, from a nightmare.

I had left Harrow Art School in a cloud of disgrace shortly before Malcolm. Unlike him I had no taste to continue a student existence. I wanted to study without the burden of a syllabus. But I had to live. So I did stints of work in between my real existence.

Work. I hated work. It sickened me. It signified dead minutes, dead hours, dead days – what the situationists called 'dead time' – a phrase I later seized on from their propaganda. 'Work' was everything I didn't want to do, it defined what I wished desperately to avoid. It was everything that stood between me and my project. It was the contradiction of desire, the inert, desiccated obverse of all I valued and prized. It was death. Summed up in that dull, dread, flat word – w-o-r-k.

I even made a study of the topic, hoping to exorcize it. I collected relevant books and read up on the history of work and the work ethic – Samuel Smiles, the Protestant ethic, time and motion studies, Henry Ford. I discovered the Nazis had decorated the gates of Auschwitz with the motto: 'Arbeit macht frei.' 'Work is liberty.' That filled me with bitter satisfaction. Was work really necessary? Was it not yet another gigantic irrationality of the social apparatus?

Whenever I awoke and remembered I had to go to work I was seized with depression. I felt nauseated. Darkness filled me. I experienced myself as that vast aching, numbed desert which stretched in front of me. That vile place to go to, that time to eke out, those stupid cunts to talk to about nothing.

Once I had a job as a park keeper. I turned up to the park keepers' compound. I thought of the day ahead. I paused at the gate. It was now or never. Commit myself to a dead day – or bolt. I went to a park bench and lit a fag. Eight-thirty turned into 8.45. Now I couldn't go anyway. I would be late. I felt relieved. I went home.

It wasn't the physical activity or the actual work which appalled me. It was the boredom, the stultifying waste of myself. And the indenture of my subjectivity. Every second spent in a place of work at someone's behest was a second torn from my project; an irretrievable moment of my soul had vanished, a moment when I could have been properly absorbed in myself.

In those days, to claim unemployment benefit you had to work continuously for about four weeks. Then you arranged to lose the job – apparently through no fault of you own (no one ever checked) – and could get back on the system for a spell of creativity. So I had many menial and temporary jobs – as did all my friends.

To get these jobs you had to make out you wanted a permanent position. For interviews I perfected a downcast look with a cockney mumble. It was because I let out I had some O levels that I was refused a job as a bus conductor. The interviewer's eyes narrowed as if I'd admitted a criminal conviction.

Opportunities for such work were plentiful. And in that time of affluence and full employment many of these jobs were superfluous. Many work practices were simply about 'hanging it out'.

But this only increased the agony and injustice. You were wasting precious time doing absurd and pointless tasks at a maddeningly slow pace. For if as a temporary worker, new to a job, you performed it at an average or – God forbid! – impatient rate, you disrupted an equilibrium built over years by the permanent workers. Why, the employer might realize that he could get by with one worker instead of three. Or that a task could be polished off in three hours instead of three days. So you had to learn the rhythm. Not to go 'fast', not be a 'flash cunt'.[2]

One psychological means of surviving the regime of work was to 'fuck about', or, still better, to exercise the right of 'industrial sabotage'. This afforded respite from boredom, and opportunities to test ingenuity and daring. It was undertaken with zeal and conviction and garnished with surreal touches. These incidents were related to friends at weekends in pubs to guffaws of appreciation and incredulity. (The girls often didn't think these stories very funny, but we put this down to female realism and sobriety getting in the way of poetry and splendour in the warehouse.)

I once had a job as a storeman. With Bert, the permanent storeman, I had to patrol sacks of chemicals used in the preparation of a well-known foodstuff. This was presumably in case they grew legs and ran off.

We spent all day in our gloomy basement domain. Sometimes we would entertain. A worker from the factory upstairs would arrive to collect a sack. He would fill out a docket and Bert would self-importantly check it out and then slip it in a wooden box. Such encounters entailed passing the time of day, discussing last night's telly, or the football. The visitor might also stay for tea and biscuits.

Every day Bert would read the *Daily Mirror* for several hours, make tea, potter about, make tea, play cards with me, make tea, go out to place a bet in the betting shop in the afternoon, make tea, go out to see if his horse had come in, and then begin preparations to go home which lasted about half an hour. Bert had this job so well cased he even had an assistant – me.

I brought transcendence into our workplace and into Bert's life. I discovered that if any sack of chemicals was found to be damaged it had to be binned. My idea was to see how many sacks we could have binned and get away with it. What would be the management's breaking point?

Armed with a Stanley knife, I began mutilating sacks. When I had got up to thirty a day Bert became nervous. He had quite enjoyed this glimpse of sublimity in our work – I think he even felt oddly proud of me, as if I had initiated events he had always dreamed of. But he didn't know how to caution or slow me down. To snitch would have been a breach of honour. But the mad ferocity of my onslaught – its irrationality – baffled him. I think he was relieved when my four weeks passed and I left.

I also worked on building sites. The trick here was to find a site where the work was almost done, the holes dug, the bricks laid.

Otherwise it was too much of a fag. Trundling barrows of cement or carrying hods of bricks was for students or Irishmen.

At one such site, a new block of flats in Ruislip Manor, there was a particularly festive atmosphere. The chief painter would turn up on his motorbike at about 10 a.m. and join us for tea. He would do a spot of painting. Then, at about 3 p.m., he would load his pillion with several jumbo cans of paint and roar away.

The plasterers here had invented 'plaster fights'. These sometimes spread over the whole site, engulfing the other workers in hilarity, with lumps of wet plaster whizzing all over the place, smashing on walls and cascading over unwary passers-by. These plasterers also took pride in their ability to 'fuck up' their plastering jobs. They would deliberately use the wrong mixes, or introduce foreign substances – such as urine – into the plaster. They would then point out the resulting unevennesses and lumps to visitors, doubled with laughter, and anticipating the woes of future residents.

More genteel was my spell as a telephone clerk at a carpet warehouse. We clerks would concoct outlandish 'orders'. These were elaborate nonsenses designed to destroy the maximum amount of the most expensive weaves. They were ordered by strange-sounding individuals with unlikely addresses. Thus: quality Axminster cut into a star with three triangular holes. Of course, the warehouse lads knew it was cobblers – the order was another fiction, a gift to hilarity from those young mods on the switchboard. But they diligently cut these patterns out, and packed and dispatched them into the void.

I got my job at the Tavistock Centre in Hampstead through a temp agency in Bond Street. Here I was told to move a number of patients' files, dating from the 1930s, out of the records store into the basement. This should have taken me about two days. But I began reading the files.

I worked out a system of appearing at regular intervals in sight of my supervisor, carrying a bundle of files. This was to allay suspicions about why I was spending so much time in the records store. I also arranged a stepladder by the door to forestall surprise entries. Settled in a chair, I then read through scores of case histories.

I was taken aback by the detail in them – the meticulous records of such intimate aspects of people's lives. I was also surprised by the tone of many of the commentators and psychologists involved – it was careful and protective, almost loving. I had previously been fascinated by the fragments of such records in published case histories. But here were the real things – entire, uncut, imperfect, still smouldering. Not a clinical and retrospective knowingness, but the ambivalences, uncertainties and insincerities of conversations, evasions, silences. A child's guardedness, an adolescent's angry confession, a psychologist's remorse and self doubt.

I became so absorbed, reading in that store, I could imagine the shifts of menace or affection in certain exchanges. I was scandalized by the hurt coiled inside the drawings of a disturbed child. I was haunted by the reported shy wave of an unmarried mother with her two partners, all three leaning on a fence as the social worker drove away . . .

I wanted to read all these files. But I dared only hang the job out for four weeks. Anything longer and I was sure I would be discovered. When I finally told the supervisor I was finished she complimented me on my efficiency!

Essential features of our working world were the 'caffs'. These 'greasy spoon' cafés were dotted around high streets and provided breakfast, lunch, impromptu office space, and recreational facilities. Caffs were prized for their gruff conviviality. The only women seen here were the counter assistants, who were often the proprietors' wives and daughters. A family atmosphere prevailed. Men could burp and swear, turn up unshaven and puffy-eyed in vests, exchange filthy jokes, refine dodgy deals, pour as much tomato sauce as they desired over their chips, and talk freely about women's arses or 'melons'.

The food was always variations of two egg, bacon, chips, spaghetti, two slices. 'Slices' were slices of white bread thinly smeared with margarine. One café proprietor, when asked for an extra 'slice', would hurl an entire Wonderloaf across the café to the customer. This ensured the fame of his establishment. I used these caffs as refuges from the weather or respites from the library, scrawling notes for poems and descriptions of the weather beside large cups of stewed tea.

My peculiar work for Hermann Baur at Serena Ltd enabled me to explore and compare such caffs all over London. Indeed, I thought at the time of compiling a guide to them, a homage to catering insalubrity – the rudest proprietor, the worst cup of tea.

Hermann was a German friend of my mother who had fled the Nazis in the thirties and brought his wholesale business in women's underwear to London. His premises were just off Oxford Circus. He supplied the UK with Serena bras and girdles and other items of lingerie. Hermann was a cultivated and thoughtful man. Each morning he played a revered piece of classical music, such as a Brandenburg Concerto, before setting off to work. At the office he was punctilious and kindly, a feverish worker with a permanent expression of concern.

Hermann took pity on me. I think he knew what I was up to – romantic genius had also been a prevalent adolescent quest in Weimar Germany. He eventually offered me a 'job', which I could take up more or less whenever I was stuck for cash.

Every so often a Serena order would be sent out minus a bra or a couple of girdles, or with a wrong size. I would then collect the missing or corrected items and set off by bus or tube to a lingerie shop in a distant high street.

I was a courier in ladies' underwear. It was entirely unsupervised. No one could check how long any journey should take, so I could spend an afternoon in travelling to, say, Finchley and back. Naturally I stole as many hours as possible for my own pleasures and explorations. I mapped out local caffs and investigated local libraries, gaining an encyclopedic knowledge of both. I loved to travel across London, daydreaming or reading on the top decks of buses, a packet of D cups on my lap, meandering out to Lewisham, Silvertown, Rickmansworth . . .

My book collection had by now become a strategy and conspectus for my project. It was a growing map of my mind, showing me places I had been and where to venture next. I added to it conscientiously, building it as a parallel and materialized domain of all the books I had read so far. As such, it expressed my interiority – I beheld myself in it. It was a version of me in arraignable form, my consciousness commodified.

At home I would sometimes spread my collection of books all over the floor and, when I ran out of space, also over my bed. Then I would sit on the edge of my bed to inhale this display of covers, relishing my possessions as identity and habitus. In this way I was inside my books as much as they were inside me. I would, however, have been ashamed to be seen doing this. I made sure no one was in the house, or I locked my door. It was a private pleasure, a solitary moment, alone with all my knowledge spread all around me – my trophies, my erudition. My business alone. Someone prying at this moment – an Other – would have opened me to a social rather than a private definition of what I was about. I would have been revealed as a consumer practising consumption.

I also began stealing library books. Such books, however, sat uncomfortably in my collection, neither satisfyingly inside or properly outside it. Their municipal covers and library stamps made them unsettling intruders on my shelves, reminders of cupidity and weakness rather than stores of knowledge and trials of strength. They were also mundane – not the results of a market transaction, a glamorous unfolding into possession through purchase, but tainted with a humdrum municipal stolidity.

I tried erasing the library stamps with an ink rubber, but this left unsightly blemishes. I tore out the tell-tale front pages, but the books seemed sadly amputated – you got into them too abruptly, without the ceremony of the 'prelims'. Besides, their spines were branded, and so shelved among other books they fairly cried out: 'Stop thief!' I therefore stole only the most essential and otherwise unobtainable items, such as the phrenologist Lombroso's *The Man of Genius* (Swiss Cottage Library) and Gombrowicz's *Ferdydurke* (Theobald's Road). The essentialism of such texts – their centrality to my project – superseded their origins.[3]

Other suspect and unwelcome books came as gifts from relatives or well-wishers. These joined with the kind of books you got as school prizes, tiresome and impermeable lumps with sweaty covers, books I could hardly bear to open and was glad to give away.

141

Likewise, any digest or abridgement was anathema. It had to be the whole book, as nature and the author intended. Moreover, it had to be the real thing in every sense, a pure encounter with the text. I impatiently tore out the scholarly introduction to Goethe's *The Sorrows of the Young Werther*. What was this fool of an academic trying to pull? Who was he to come between me and JWG? I would only bask in the direct voice, the very words, the exact tone, of the great man himself. I wanted no commentaries to intervene or dilute my proximities to genius.

Especially dubious were those books occasionally bought me by my mother. She, in her candid generosity, had no inkling of the dark and subtle connoisseurship I was building. Her gifts were as embarrassing to me as a child spotlighted by the coo of: 'Look how he's grown!' She gave me an illustrated French edition of Saint-Exupéry's *Le Petit Prince* for my sixteenth birthday. It was inscribed 'A mon petit Prince'. Dear God!

For I had long superseded Saint-Exupéry and relished the Surrealists' jibe about him being 'a fool in an aeroplane'. But how could I intimate that to her? She would have been hurt. Not even indignant, but uncomprehending. She also gave me Khalil Gibran's *The Prophet*, a mystic windbag whom I accepted without a word and I have never had the heart to discard. However vulgar and absurd, it carried the scent of her goodwill.

But therein lay the problem. My library was not about goodwill. It was fraught and mean, possibly even dangerous. Who knew what frictions might arise with de Sade nestling against Virginia Woolf? It was as potentially explosive as the contents of my head or my underpants. Not a collection of paperweights or knick-knacks. Not furniture. Not reassuringly perfumed like my mother. It should reek of that sour and musty bouquet of old books and fresh discoveries. It should smell of abstraction: resistant, difficult, hard. It was a dedicated and necessary collection, not an arbitrary and contingent gathering. It was the deeply serious evidence of my serious depths.

Most prized were my paperbacks. Freshly bought and newly opened, they wafted a perfume as clean and promising as new toys. They lacked the patina and hazardous speculation of old books, but they had the cachet of novelty, and the crackle of modern design. They could be neatly slipped in and out of pockets, their reassuring bulk set on the hip. They were portable, like dress accessories. And if you had the right depth of jacket pocket they could be transported with the author or title cunningly displayed – a movable sign of erudition and taste.

My first volume of Husserl was a pleasingly ascetic shiny white paperback, with a formidably terse text which seemed to deflect understanding as stylishly as the cover reflected the light. Whereas Berger and Luckman's *The Social Construction of Reality* was matt black with stark white lettering in Courier typeface – well suited to its bustling and definitive summations. Did I really think that?

Paperbacks could also be flexed and dimpled under the light, and their lustre covertly fingered as they were read. As literary objects, as objects of literature, they also had a unique and paradoxical totality – they were all one, blurb and text and design bonded together in hermetic perfectibility. The way paperbacks were tightly glued, rather than sewn, at the spine, also made them tight wads, satisfying impactions of culture. Paperbacks eschewed the decorum of 'jackets'. There were no dust covers to stray or be crumpled, no way to undress them of the publisher's promotion or author's portrait, revealing waxy and ungarnished 'real books' inside. A paperback was a paperback. It came clean and entire, like a modern girl slickly wrapped in tights, not fussy with petticoats.

The paperback revolution of the sixties subverted and undermined cultural values as it disseminated them. Like the effect of paper money in a traditional society, paperbacks cheapened and trans-valuated *oeuvres* and reputations by rendering them accessible, common, comparable, and in some senses, commutable.

Paperbacks liquefied the preciosity or aura of 'the book', enabling the dissemination of some of academia's rarest discourses through wider and wider currents of mass media, and releasing high culture from its holding and sanctioning institutions, to drift and fend abstractly in the wider operations and dimensions of the market. In that way, paperbacks foregrounded and mediated the dispersion of university and fine art disciplines into mainstream and eventually into popular culture, a popularization which has had profound effects on those disciplines themselves.

In the sixties there were plenty of alarms about this 'commercialization' of academic knowledge, a sense from established academics that their stock was being daringly shoplifted beneath their eyes and dignities, lightly dissipated and combined in errant and drunken formations, bandied and misused and traduced by slack-jawed youths and smart alecks.

All that was true. The knowledge at last was out there for the taking. The complete works of Balzac, Kant's *Critique of Judgement*, Gérard de Nerval. Glistening to be picked like ripe apples in a supermarket. No longer secured in specialist libraries or guarded by 'disciplines'.

You could, moreover, take them in any way or in any progression, and for any use or misuse, as your consumer's inclination fluttered. No need to start at the beginning or go through the arguments and debates in the proper way in the proper order. Why not begin with Wittgenstein and then graduate to George Steiner – and then how about Gertrude Stein? All those 'steins' ought to be good for something.

The paperback industry was also, in this most expansive and imperialistic phase, hungry for rarities, probing and convening taste, looking for ways in, how to resuscitate and rehabilitate even the most marginal poet, the greatest prat of a visionary, creating myths to mine exoticisms and pathologies with commercial zeal and po-faced scholarly 'introductions'.

As they ran out of the Greats, paperback publishers began to ransack all the most covert and marginal interstices of high culture, rediscovering and resuscitating lost or neglected or unlikely 'masterpieces', bearing rare gems before the public – lunatics, delinquents, pornographers. They thus began to reorientate the sense of high culture around its margins, and this was a very appealing fact for my own and my friends' marginality.

*   *   *

Gradually, the interstitial hesitations and cultural stuttering of my group, our alienated perceptions, our forlornness, became a confident assumption of eccentricity – the future belonged to people like us as first 'culture', and then society itself, was reorientated around its margins.

First I was amazed and delighted to find Stendhal's reflections on love in translation – what luck! what wisdom! Then Kierkegaard on seduction – what craft! Soon even Breton's *Nadja* appeared. What next? Lautréamont? Sure enough, Maldoror crept out of the closet into the window of Better Books. Justine? Surely not! Then it was Charles Fourier. What a man, what a genius . . . what a sublime wanker!

This was the beginning of that consumerization of academic and other high-cultural discourse whereby the phenomenology of consumption became identical with the acts of citation, argumentation, debate, etc. – all the processes and etiquette of this discourse.

Nowadays, all such discourse is framed as consumption and feeds from consumerist energies and priorities. Are you for or against Lacan? Do you rate Foucault? Such questions now have the same inflection as your taste in coffee or your advertised sexual proclivities. They fit with your 'lifestyle' and define your particular self. They address your 'identity' before they begin to address any problem.

Paperbacks were therefore one material basis and precondition for 'post-modernism', a dummy movement created by my generation as an alibi for its reading habits, our taste for marginalia and oddities.

The natural guides to this pot-pourri of deviant culturalism were aesthetes, connoisseurs and bibliomanes – such as Walter Benjamin, Bataille or Borges, who were duly ensconced as the founding fathers – or retrospective 'classic' texts of a mastery of knowledge in the mode of consumption – masters of guise and guile and bookish inflection, succeeded by their acolytes, philosophical stylists like Barthes, Foucault, Derrida, Deleuze, Kristeva . . .

Hence too the apposite ubiquity of that notion of the 'text', floating with self-signifying nods through a sociological vacuum – an apt metaphor for the material culture of paperback publication free-floating in the market which it transforms – texts free of academic moorings, texts wrested from syllabi, schedules and tenures, and assigned to the solipsistic gaze of the consumer; that rare self – Me alone.

As my collection began to multiply and diversify within itself, I began a sub-collection of books by mad people. This was before the notion became fashionable, and I had a request to appeal for such material in the *Times Literary Supplement* tartly declined by postcard. I prowled the Charing Cross Road and sought out secondhand and dissident bookshops. There was an anarchist bookshop called the Wooden Shoe in St Giles High Street, by Centre Point. This was run by a shaven-headed Scandinavian with a reputed prison record. Just the man to recommend a rare edition of Alexander Trocchi. Better Books in the Charing Cross Road was different too, but it had too many gassy Americans and poetry readings about it for my taste.

But it was in Better Books that I found the first translated selection of articles from *Cahiers du Cinéma*. An article on revolutionary cinema entranced me. From the first staccato sentence to the last resonating claim, I knew this was a style I admired. This was an early example of that guttural cultural studies commentary, now *de rigueur*, a writer who leads you to understand he knows the references so securely that he has become blasé, cunningly letting the learning show like expensive cuff-links under a carelessly frayed sleeve, inviting you into his special gang of jesting and scoffing scholars. I wanted to be in such a gang, and it was then I began thinking about Paris. Everything seemed to be happening over there.

A favourite haunt of our group was the Tolmers Cinema, in Tolmers Square. This showed the kinds of 'deleted' popular movies available nowhere else at the time – movies nowadays screened on late-night TV or in retrospectives – Norman Wisdom comedies, *Hercules Against the Moonmen*, fifties sci-fi, *The Charge of the Light Brigade*. This disrespectful jumbling of genres was appealing.

The place smelt like a doss-house with a tang of disinfectant. The floor was littered with empty bottles, chip wrappings, and the debris of packed lunches. The clientele was students, bohemians, and pensioners who would doze in their seats all day or chatter in a desultory way throughout performances. The atmosphere could be raucous, the pensioners joining in with us bohemians as we cheered Norman Wisdom on to greater feats of destruction, or jeered the colonel of the Light Brigade.

On either side of the screen were two emergency exits. These would frequently clank open to admit someone who would creep in to take an unpaid seat. On one occasion one of these doors burst open and a window cleaner with a bucket and a long ladder over his shoulder marched across the screen casting an interesting shadow and then disappeared through the opposite exit door. He was taking a short cut across Tolmers Square.

We especially enjoyed trailers. These compacted the kitsch appeal of the films – a banality so condensed it became surreal. Malcolm and I were also intrigued by what appeared to be the excitingly avant-garde, even rash, editing techniques which appeared in the most unlikely movies. We eventually discovered that the projectionist had got into the habit of randomly chopping bits out of film reels. This was to make the movies shorter so he could go home early.

This misdemeanour was used as the basis of Malcolm's first public showing as an artist. He had met an artistic entrepreneur who ran the Kingly Street Art Gallery. This was a sort of artists' collective which aimed to show a wider selection of work than was available in Bond Street. It had a wishing pool inside into which visitors threw copper pennies. I waded in one afternoon and retrieved enough coppers to buy admittance for both of us to the Academy cinema, paying the cashier with piles of oxidized and slimy green coins.

Malcolm had now decided he was an 'environmental artist', and persuaded this gallery owner to turn his premises over for transformation into an 'environment'. This environment was actually a kind of obstacle course made from rolls of corrugated cardboard, empty shoe boxes and other debris. You had to crawl through tunnels and negotiate false floors.

Retrieving edited-out sequences of an Audie Murphy war movie from the projectionist's special bin at the Tolmers, Malcolm re-edited these out-takes together and arranged for a projector to beam the result into Kingly Street. He sent invitations on duplicated maps of the London Underground.

Everything went well at first. Audie Murphy crackled and flickered, people came and went, wine was quaffed. Then two coppers turned up. They wanted to know who was in charge. They explained this was an illegal display. What about health and safety? Just then a drunken soldier, one of a group of squaddies, crashed through a false floor on to some people below. There was cursing and pandemonium. The show was closed and everyone went home.

Malcolm met Henry Adler at a Vietnam rally, when they were arrested together for trying to burn an American flag. Henry was a South African Jew. His wealthy father paid him an allowance which kept Henry in books and cinema tickets, and paid for weekly sessions with the trendy existential psychoanalyst David Cooper. Henry had a nice sense of the ridiculous, his as well as ours. He looked like Groucho Marx without a moustache and his ungainly body moved with furtive zeal.

Henry was a modern London *flâneur*, an assiduous and subtle cultural consumer at a point when the consumption of culture was becoming a kind of work in itself, a specialized knowledge and activity which could generate more and more culture and was opening new markets for the dissemination and exploitation of culture.

Henry's own consumption of culture was a serious and dedicated frivolity. Henry knew exactly what was current and what was coming up – the best bookshops to browse in, the latest Godard movies (he even went over to Paris to check them out before they got to London). He recommended theories hot from the Left Bank and esoteric Beat titles from America. He strongly recommended that the best time and place to hear Bach's *St Matthew Passion* was on Good Friday in St Paul's Cathedral. He got us free tickets for the Dialectics of Liberation conference at the Roundhouse. Henry took

Malcolm and me along to the first Arts Lab in Hanway Street, where films were projected in a room with a foam floor and no seats. Here we squatted for Kenneth Anger's *Scorpio Rising* – a thrilling shock in those censored days.

Henry was encyclopedic on movies. Seeing a film only once was a lamentable cop-out and lack of seriousness. He would go to an early showing of say, *Duck Soup*, then sit through the next three showings. Film spectatorship was a kind of hermeneutic meditation for him – meanings would unpeel themselves from successive showings and be recounted to us in what was a prescient anticipation of what later became film or cultural studies. (He showed us, for example, how to read the Marx Brothers as an expression of the defiance of Jewish immigrants against Wasp orthodoxy.)

In the sixties, London was rich with educational resources. There was a profusion of extramural and evening classes which were heavily subsidized. We all made the most of such opportunities. I attended courses in sociology, film criticism, French literature, and statistics, and Malcolm took extra drawing classes at the Sir John Cass College in Whitechapel, and an acting course at the City Lit. Vivienne, of course, was often stuck at home with the children, or working to earn her and Malcolm's keep, but she would hungrily quiz us about our cultural explorations and ask us what to read and see.

I would also attend lectures and seminars at the colleges of friends. No one ever challenged my presence. I went to many screenings and seminars at the London School of Film Technique in Covent Garden, where Gordon was studying. And I taught myself photographic printing at Goldsmiths College by simply walking into darkrooms, asking questions and using the facilities.

Libraries were also plentiful and well endowed and I belonged to as many as I could fake references for.

This educational network (of which the art school scene was also a vital part) was the basis of London's growing 'underground' scene. The liberal access to books and ideas created appetites and clients for the theatre groups, clubs, bookshops and cinemas which began to cater to an audience receptive to experimental and 'radical' ideas.

There were many people, resident Londoners and visitors (Henry being a good example), using this network to define themselves through these new tastes, which then became enough of a consensus to sustain an international market which eventually identified itself as a collective sensibility – the 'underground' or counter-culture.

But for a long time this network of courses, events, venues and retail outlets was frustratingly disparate and uncoordinated. You heard on the grapevine or stumbled on things. This was where people like Henry were invaluable as conduits or heralds of novelties. Such connoisseurs made it their work to plot and master this expanding cultural terrain.

Few of the 'straight' publications reported these things or publicized them in advance – which was when you needed to know. The impact of the London listings magazine *Time Out* was therefore considerable. *Time Out* mapped out and presented within its covers an accessible image of what could then emerge as the London 'scene'. And it defined the scene of the punters rather than the stars – advertising where people like me and my circle could be found, as opposed to Mick Jagger or Twiggy. *Time Out* in this way was much more significant than such often-cited sixties magazines as *IT* or *OZ*. Simply by drawing together an eclectic brew of demos to go to, bands to check out, secondhand markets, poetry readings and bookshops, it consolidated a taste and defined an 'alternative' lifestyle through available options of 'alternative' consumption.

By simply detailing what was going on *Time Out* also gave the scene a pattern and a tone which you absorbed through browsing and musing and comparing its sections. This resulted in the illusion that all the events and commodities it reported had a common source or identity, or that they all shared an interwoven destiny in a collective project of avant-gardist 'lifestyle' – the counter-culture. Thus Collet's bookshop became mysteriously connected to Habitat, which was somehow something to do with the forthcoming anarchist meeting next Saturday upstairs at the Lamb and Flag, an event which nestled auspiciously close to a review of the new Kinks album. In this way a notion might form that the Kinks owed anarchists a living, or that Habitat was ethically obliged not to 'sell out' in accordance with the imperatives of radical magazines sold in the back room of Collet's. (This was the rationale, after all, of the Angry Brigade's bombing of Biba.)

The open-air rock concerts of the late sixties, which were the first signs of this fantasy of a collectivity, are nowadays taken as evidence for the mood of that collectivity. But they only achieved the sense they have now through retrospective media spectacles of these events. As photogenic fillers they survive and transform our memories. But no one I knew then would go anywhere near such events, and we were irritated when the Rolling Stones ruined our Saturday afternoon stroll across Hyde Park by summoning a few thousand imbeciles to a 'free concert'.

Only the situationists had the temerity at the time to point out that the counter-culture was just another phase of consumer culture – which was one reason why until the late seventies they were an utterly despised and embarrassing voice, censored by the New Left orthodoxy.

I had sometimes toyed with the idea of university. This might, after all, buy me time for reading. Malcolm and Vivienne approved. But I had only one A level, and you needed three. Then I spotted an ad placed in *New Society* by the University of Sussex about a scheme of entry for the under-qualified. I made enquiries about a course combining history and philosophy, posted an essay on empiricism, and was asked for interview.

There I met a group of fellow applicants. Among them was Olivia. She was small and elfin, dark-haired and dark-eyed, with a sharp look which contrasted with her rather docile expression. She looked like the girl in a photo I had surreptitiously torn out of a *Photography Annual* in Whitechapel Public Library. I had kept this picture as I might a literary reference – a reference to my desire which I consulted from time to time. And now here she was in front of me.

Her name also struck me: Olivia. What a poetic, flowing sound – all those vowels, and the sensuality of the 'O', and also an Italianate flavour. Not to mention the pseudonymous novel *Olivia*, by 'Olivia', which I had bought in a Kensington bookshop in the hardback 1950 Readers' Union edition, a slim volume whose black cover was tastefully embossed with a pink (ageing to mauve) ribbon, dashingly knotted in an art deco flow. Olivia and I exchanged words, but she was suspicious of my penetrating gaze, and preferred the conversation of other applicants.

It turned out we had to take an 'intelligence test'. I had read about these and formulated a prejudice that they were hopelessly mired in American behaviourism, and thus philosophically flawed and a waste of time. I ventured this to the psychologist conducting the test. He looked piqued. Then I noticed some of the questions required 'yes' or 'no' answers. I leapt on this and declared the test simplistic. Some of these questions cried out for more qualified responses. He was now well pissed off and snapped at me to just get on with it or leave. So I spent the allotted time devising banal and unlikely answers, undermining what I calculated to be the intellectual and emotional parameters of the test, and adding surreal marginalia.

After that it was interview time.

I took the view that people should recognize me by what I was in my work – these people had my essay. They might also note the determination coiled in my look and exuded by my forehead. Not to mention the nifty lapels on my Italian sports jacket. I expected these two university boffins to have the same stylistic acumen as my old art college tutors.

I was quizzed by two men, one of whom I took an aversion to. He was a fool with a pipe. He kept on about the philosophical niceties of *Alice in Wonderland*. Now this was one of my favourite books, so I agreed with him. But the bastard wanted to know why I agreed. Obviously testing me out. Why should I tell him my ideas? I looked at his dowdy tweed jacket and his shoes, which looked like brown paper bags. Then I went into dissimulation mode, evaporating every question offered and dissolving my presence in a fog of deliberately confusing and contradictory cues. The interview fizzled out with them looking perturbed.

On the way out I went looking for Olivia, but she had gone.

Of course I didn't get in. But I had met Olivia. What next?

I asked a girlfriend to ring the university a week later. This girlfriend claimed that Olivia had lent her some money. Unfortunately Olivia's address was now lost. Could the university please supply this?

It transpired that Olivia lived just outside a small town in Essex. I pored over Ordnance Survey maps in my local library to get a fix on the place and its surroundings. I sent her a letter. I reminded her who I was. I said something like she would no doubt be surprised to get this letter 'out of the blue', but that the best things sometimes came 'out of the blue'. (I pinched this sentiment from Samuel Beckett.) I got no answer.

About a fortnight later I packed an overnight bag while playing an Archie Shepp record. This contorted and dissonant jazz set an appropriate mood for my adventure. I caught the train and arrived in her town and booked into a hotel.

Next morning I set off with a map and a notepad – as always, to record my impressions. She lived about two miles out of town. As I left houses for fields I began to enjoy the sunshine and the walk. The road towards her house was long and straight, with a track for pedestrians on the left. I saw two figures coming towards me about a half a mile away. An older woman and a younger one. As they approached I was gripped with panic. Was the younger one Olivia? I wanted to turn round, to escape over a nearby hedge. But I walked on. It was indeed Olivia. Presumably with her mother. I approached them in the dense and nonsensical clarity of a dream, scribbling my impressions as I walked. Olivia looked astonished. She said something to her mother, who considered me sharply. We passed without a word. I didn't look back for at least five minutes. By then they had disappeared.

I walked on to her house. It had the kind of middle-class privacy which invites curiosity. A thick hedge, carelessly lush undergrowth, a newly mown lawn with garden furniture scattered over it. The details of her life, waiting for my intervention. Which would never come. My interest was academic, theoretical. It was precisely to establish and explore my absence from her life; her absence from mine. Her absence made me real; the idea of her helped me exist. I think that even had we stopped to talk on that road, even if we had begun to court one another, I would, in one way or another, have continued that game of dissimulation and referral, evasion and

153

fantasy. Getting to know her merely in order to keep her apart from me, and her away from me – maintaining her strangeness.

I went into a nearby pub for a pint. It was full of British nonsense – brass horseshoes, wooden beams, a florid landlord booming with good humour, and a couple of local lads – the kind she might date, red-faced and beefily opulent, sure of themselves and secure in their Englishness. For an aspect of Olivia's fascination had been this notion of an Englishness which she represented. She was an Englishness which I missed in myself. Not that I aspired to it. But I would have liked to have had it as a casual option, a leaf in my book, a quality to renounce.

Was there hatred nesting at the core of my desires? Edging up to and confusing all my identities – French, Ruislip, suburban, Catholic, savant, bohemian. And lyrical, ironic, despotic . . . I was a Romantic, at home only in my heart. An internationalist like Leon Trotsky, on the run, hounded, exiled. Once, strolling along Bond Street in the footsteps of Mrs Dalloway, I saw the TV chatterbox Dr Jonathan Miller. Nod in recognition? Complain about his latest production? Kick his arse after the hilarious fashion of surrealism? But I ignored Miller. He pretended not to notice. Fucking bastard. Like all those other bastards in the backs of Rolls-Royces and Daimlers. I sometimes spat at them from the pavement. I watched their astonished, horsey, English faces disappear in the traffic. I would also pause by twee window displays and Bond Street art galleries, pretending to gaze in, sucking juices from all corners of my mouth, and then gob until the window ran, bubbling with spittle. Sometimes I would then loiter and study affronted passers-by.

When I walked in a venerated English place, among privileged English people, next to Peter Pan's statue in Hyde Park, among the catalogues of the British Museum Library, in the menswear department of Harrods, I felt out of place, under surveillance, angry, out of breath. I especially despised the uniformed lackeys in such places. They exuded a supercilious knowledge that I was a suspicious character, not quite right – too Latin-looking, too concerned. Obviously a secondary modern product.

The back of my neck felt under scrutiny. My spine went stiff, and I stumbled. Which foot to put first? I froze. Olivia. Remember her? What was she to me? Should I steal their coats? Or fuck their daughters? Or steal their language? Or fuck their words? Olivia was a signal at the core of my vacuity. She seemed to fit. As effortlessly as I was disproportionate. As cool as I was passionate. As right as I was wrong. I was the problem, and she was the solution. Lucky Olivia. Filled and fulfilled, as English as her assured tread and spryly erect spine. Poor, unsettled me, ungainly, intrusive, stooped, foreign, extraneous, expectorant . . . All the wrong things. But all the same proudly enquiring. I had the light of investigation, the clarity of research about me. I caught the train back to Ruislip. The Olivia enigma was noted, if not sorted, the episode closed. Desire had looped another loop.

At Aigburth Mansions Malcolm and Vivienne began hosting the odd soirée. They hoped to bring people together, to start something.

At one of these dinners I met Robin Scott and Jamie Reid, both then students at Croydon Art College. Malcolm was most genial. We all drank Spanish wine and feasted on Vivienne's stew. There was a selection of cheeses with a bowl of fruit. We talked politics and art. Robin was handsome and sensible. He had brought his guitar and strummed along after dinner, singing in a deep, rich voice. His girlfriend was also there, a mousy girl we thought would not last; the rumour was she was about to be jilted. In the kitchen Vivienne was complicitous – how could we help this girl keep her hooks in Robin?

I was unsure about Jamie. He was alternately benign and cutting. Mostly he growled just below the threshold of audibility. Every so often you half caught a pithy dismissal. But was he just a duffer or simmering with the revolution?

All of us would do something in music eventually. Robin, as 'M', was a one-hit wonder with Pop Music ('Everybody's doin' it . . . Pop pop, pop music!'). Jamie became the Sex Pistols' art director and then worked with many other bands. I co-wrote the Sex Pistols' biography as my first publication and then pioneered the study of music fans. Malcolm and Vivienne, of course, masterminded and clothed the Sex Pistols and influenced countless acts thereafter. And finally

Malcolm became a performer in his own right with several top twenty hits. (This was the more remarkable since Malcolm had an inability to keep time and could not sing a note. At Chiswick he had threatened to 'combine' music and the visual arts. A sort of Wagnerian notion of total art. Absurdly, he had even 'taken up' the piano, thumping the keys in exasperation when they failed to flow spontaneously with melody.)

But only Robin talked much about music in those days. Pop or rock music was peripheral to most of my friends' lives.

In 1967 I was working for Express Dairies in South Ruislip. My job was to unload milk floats of empties and restock according to each milkman's specification – x pints of white top, y cartons of yoghurt. I worked from late evening to about three in the morning. These hours suited me as they left my days for reading and writing.

I soon realized that much of what I discarded as past its sell-by date was edible. I therefore began selecting deleted delicacies and taking them home. Early one morning I was walking home when a police car pulled up beside me. Two coppers got out and asked about the carton of yogurts under my arm. I was driven to a police station and charged with the theft of six yogurts of assorted flavours, the property of Express Dairies Ltd.

In those days the police were routinely corrupt. I had already been framed as a schoolboy for 'stealing' a defunct electric razor I'd retrieved from underneath a bus seat. So it was no good protesting these yogurts were binnable – the police would have lied or fixed the evidence, and I might have risked imprisonment. So I pleaded guilty. I did, however, protest in court that I'd been 'framed', and to my satisfaction this was reported in the local paper, albeit sceptically. My first appearance in print.

But my troubles had only just begun. For now I was allocated a probation officer who decided to take an interest in me. This well-meaning man evidently thought my lifestyle and values bizarre if not perverse. Why was I writing a novel when I should be earning a living? Why was I studying books outside of a recognized educational establishment?

He was baffled when I challenged his right to advise me, and then, citing RD Laing and other psychiatric references, questioned his career choice and emotional stability. He also failed to appreciate that my appointments with him were merely an absurd formality, and began turning up at my house to complain – somewhat bitterly I thought – whenever I stood him up. He was behaving like a jilted lover.

By this time I had already decided that swinging London was a bore, and I should move on.

The day before I left for Paris, in September 1967, I paid a final visit to the Tate Gallery. I lingered by the Pre-Raphaelites. When would I see them again? Then I went into a nearby café and sent Malcolm and Vivienne a farewell letter. I inserted a recent cutting from the *Guardian*. It concerned a murder case in which the only clue was 'three long blond hairs'.

On the night ferry over I tried to rehearse a spirit of exile by staying on the windswept deck. This fantasy was nearly spoiled by the remarkable coincidence that travelling on the same ferry was a woman who had worked at Hermann Baur's lingerie firm. She kept winking at me. But I turned my back and maintained my reverie until the Gare du Nord.

In Paris I booked into a Left Bank hotel, and set about registering at the Sorbonne. In order to do this I had to fulfil a number of bureaucratic obligations – standing in line and so on. I was also confronted with a number of problems to do with my eligibility for grant aid, and my dual (French–British) nationality.

I began terrorizing the French in a way I found very effective. I discovered that a show of Anglo-Saxon hooliganism so completely threw them that they would accede to almost anything. Thus I began storming in front of queues, bursting into offices, refusing to leave until my case had been heard – immediately! – pestered officials, reducing some to fury and others to tears, and generally carried on in the vein of Arthur Rimbaud.

Looking back, I suppose the apparition of this rather pretty young man, with an English accent, and a set of uncompromising demands, must have seemed quite sexy, and rather amusing – more of a frisson than your average day at the office.

I also think that at that point in '67 the French had not caught on to the anarcho principles circulating in my milieu in London, and had no defence against a solitary youth who knew his Bakunin and James Dean and wasn't taking any fucking shit from any fucking bastards.

I enrolled on my course, which was called French Civilization (a university entrance course for foreigners). I listened to the debates on Radio Sorbonne and attended lectures. I explored the book-shops, and frequented the Cinémathèque.

But the French students seemed dull, and so very nice. I wrote glumly in this vein to Malcolm.

Then I went to my first Parisian demo. This was a routine anti-American Vietnam march. London demos like this had always annoyed me – the cunning way the police marched alongside you, anaesthetizing fervour and absorbing the chants of 'Ho! Ho! Ho! Chi Min!' in comforting lines of bobbing black helmets. British protesters also seemed to 'march' with a finger up their arses. Was that any way to topple capitalism?

My group had often tried to inject malice and vandalism. The only time we really succeeded was at a march to Rhodesia House, when the police miscalculated and the way was suddenly open down the Strand to South Africa House. In the scrimmage which followed only missiles were wanting. I saw one person hurl a dustbin into a plate-glass window, while a fusty old gent excitedly used his rolled-up umbrella to poke in side windows. I was reduced to smashing similar windows with my elbow. I think I managed three before I had to scarper. That was an occasion we celebrated later in Lyons Corner House.

But this French demo was something else. As it began there were no police in sight, only several hundred demonstrators and a lowering atmosphere. Suddenly a row of CRS riot police, hel-meted, goggled and carrying riot shields, and looking like sinister shiny black insects, came into view stretched across the Boulevard St-Germain. Then they opened fire.

In those days, as all through the '68 events, the CRS used a variety of weapons. Blast bombs were so shockingly loud that you could see everyone in the vicinity of an explosion jump at least a foot into the air with shock. Then there were missiles which sprayed on impact a yellow powder which filled your throat and lungs with a burning so painful you could hardly breathe to run away. (Veterans could sometimes neutralize these powder bombs because in the second or so between one landing and exploding it was possible to run up and cover it with a dustbin lid.) Then there were tear-gas bombs, thrown or fired with abandon. Helmeted demonstrators responded to this barrage with a hail of stones and bricks, attacking the police lines with staves.

All this was new to me. It seemed to portend the revolution. These Frogs knew how to pick a fight with the cops. Perhaps I should stay after all.

But trouble was brewing for me at the Sorbonne. For I had unwittingly besotted two members of staff. The first was my lecturer in French grammar, a spindly and agile homosexual of about fifty. He would dart about the streets in the rain, impatiently brushing away people's umbrellas. I took up the invitation of extra lessons at his flat. However, when these lessons got to the stage of a hand clasped to my knee, I lost the map of what to do next. I carried on going to his lectures while avoiding his recriminating eye, but felt increasingly uncomfortable. I just didn't want to go to bed with him.

Nor did I wish to sleep with a woman in her late twenties who worked in the student accommodation bureau. She had also become infatuated with me. We went out to cafés together, and she was earnest and wonderfully chic, and more attractive than a brat like me deserved. But I chafed at the time I was 'wasting' which could have been spent finishing *Oblomov*, or catching a rare Prévert brothers movie at the Cinémathèque. It didn't fit my plans at that time to be in love. I had come to Paris to fill my head, not my bed.

In retrospect, I think my very intransigence may have attracted these two. Perhaps it was a challenge to get through to me, or perhaps they enjoyed trying. They failed. Partly because I was sublimely and obdurately unaware that there was any problem. Get through to what? What for? But they had their revenge.

This woman had found me a comfortable attic flat near the Etoile, attached to the apartment of a wealthy old biddy who delighted in making friends of foreign students. The flat was rent-free, but the price was company. This was the kind of small talk a genius abhorred. I recall increasingly uneasy conversations and long silences. Soon she began avoiding me. This suited me fine. (I recall closing the final page of Breton's *Nadja* in this garret with the full moon piercing through my window. I knew then that I was in Bohemia.)

At the time I was penniless and used to forage in neighbours' dustbins for scraps of food. Perhaps this got back to my landlady. Nor did it help when I put up a homeless Italian painter for a few weeks. Giorgio was every bit as glowering as myself. But she couldn't evict me; it was winter and I was protected under French law.

The next bit happened like a dream. One Saturday morning three important-looking men turned up at the flat. One of them introduced himself as the 'director' of the Sorbonne. He announced that I was 'a problem'. Two members of his staff had complained about my inconsiderate selfishness. One was now taking professional counselling. My landlady had asserted that I was 'terrorizing' her and that my presence was preventing her from 'enjoying' her property. I had, moreover, flouted Sorbonne regulations and circumvented procedures.

In fact, he said, there were only two other students at the Sorbonne who had caused him as much trouble. I asked for their addresses.

But he was not there to be amused. He had come to eject me from the flat and from the Sorbonne. He offered me my fees back immediately in cash, waving a wad of notes in front of me, a handsome sum for a starving boy, but only if I would promise to leave the flat immediately and never enter the Sorbonne again.

Of course I took the money. And my revenge a month later, when I entered the Sorbonne as one of its occupiers, part of an entire generation which had suddenly become 'a problem'.

Paris was a private city of circles of people which hardly touched or mixed. Mostly you met the interesting people by chance in hotels as you criss-crossed the Left Bank looking for better or cheaper accommodation, or you struck up conversations in cafés. In this way I met an American writer, an assiduous drug-taker, who showed me the novel he was working on. It was sub-Burroughs tosh. But he introduced me to a network of Americans in Paris who supported themselves by dubbing foreign movies – mostly Italian 'spaghetti westerns' or propaganda films from the Eastern bloc. We would drive out to a suburban studio to make crowd noises, scream with terror or perform bits of dialogue. I played the part of Lenin's elder brother on his deathbed in a Soviet biopic of Lenin, passing on the revolutionary message in gasps and wheezes – a communist death-rattle.

I also associated with a network of Italians and South Americans. I met Ana, an Argentinian, petite and fiery, who was, she proudly claimed, the daughter of a doctor who had once 'known' Fidel Castro (or was it Che Guevara?) in Buenos Aires. I flirted with Ana and we travelled with a group of Spanish anarchists to Madrid at Easter '68 in a car garishly decorated with anti-police slogans. Surprisingly we were let through the Spanish border (Franco was then still in power) with only a flicker of a Guardia Civil's eyebrow. They must have thought it was a student prank.

Loosely connected to such émigré circles were gangs of French working-class drop-outs. These I first encountered through the doss-houses I sometimes resorted to. In those days there was no social security for young French males. If you were destitute the government gave you fifty francs (£5), and told you to fuck off and earn a living. Not surprisingly, many young men turned to petty crime, forming gangs, which often inhabited a particular hotel, each room being illicitly occupied in shifts.

One such group was headed by Jacques, a self-proclaimed anarchist. Jacques was a choleric and burly teenager who led his gang on daring shoplifting forays in high-class supermarkets. I joined in several of these and learned about shopping bags with false compartments and the art of creating a diversion. The contrast between the poverty of Jacques' gang and the feasts they nightly gorged on was comical. Jacques was a gourmet, and insisted on stealing only the finest foie gras, the plumpest steaks, the choicest wines. All this was fried up and decanted back at the hotel, where Jacques would pass round fags and joints and poetize about the collapse of capitalism, which he predicted would be sudden and bloody.

The existence of such groups and their inclination to anarchistic ideology helped to precipitate the unexpected ferocity of the May events in Paris. It was when such young people – who had nothing to lose – collided on the streets with members and affiliates of the Situationist Internationale and their various offshoots – people who were out to lose everything – that events spiralled out of the control of institutions and pseudo-institutions, from the students' union to the various 'revolutionary' groups like the Trots or the Maoists, all of whom tried in vain to wrest madness back into a semblance of political discourse.

Paris in May '68 was an ideological 'slippage', a vertigo of discourses which projected political non-sense centre stage.

I began working as a porter in the Paris fruit and vegetable market, which in those days was still in the inner-city district of Les Halles. Lorries arrived in the narrow streets every night from all over Europe. The area was also thronged with prostitutes touting lorry drivers for a quick shag in nearby hotels, and gaggles of gourmets in search of the select restaurants the area was renowned for.

While I did this work I stayed in a hotel which was also a brothel. I aimed to get home when business was dying down and the creaking of stairs, door banging, and occasional arguments had abated. Before retiring I would select a café for a *vin rouge* and a smoke, often to a background of 'A Whiter Shade of Pale', the lugubrious jukebox hit of that spring.

One early morning I walked into a café. I ordered my *rouge* and lit a Gitane at the counter. Then I realized the place was full of French prostitutes and Algerian pimps. They were all dressed up in a nightmarish version of Sunday best. The pimps were in creamy suits and white or fawn shoes with exotic ties over button-down shirts. The girls, halfway between tarty provocation and the sort of finery I've only otherwise seen on Jewish women coming out of synagogues on Saturday, or on West Indian women at church or for weddings: costumes of an incandescent pastel.

162

The tables had been pushed back, clearing the floor. A pimp sauntered over to the jukebox, and a tango came on. A number of pimps and girls got up and began to tango with the mean dexterity appropriate to this dance. Their moves mimicked the slavish defiance of the whore and the disdainful dandyism of the pimp. (Later I learned that the tango had originated in Argentinian brothels precisely as a dance between prostitutes and pimps.) I asked the barman what was going on. It was the wedding of a pimp and one of his girls. By now I was getting the odd glare and left as inconspicuously as I could.

I became aware of the crisis in French education through reports in the newspapers about events at Nanterre and elsewhere. Soon demonstrations started in Paris itself. I was quickly bored with the liberationist rhetoric of these initial student protests, which in themselves were destined to go no further than the Grosvenor Square 'riot' of '67 – less a revolution than a rugby scrimmage.

What initially made the difference in Paris was the misjudgement of the French authorities, who alternately panicked and prevaricated. And then, with lightning ruthlessness, the situationist-influenced groups and their hooligan allies catalysed this misjudgement and precipitated the 'events'.

When, after the first round of student protests, the Sorbonne was closed down it became a geographical focus for protest. Because of its position, sprawling behind boulevards and winding approach roads, and because the CRS continually broke these demonstrations into smaller groups, the whole of the Left Bank around the Sorbonne over a period of weeks became a battleground, with paving stones and tear-gas canisters flying, and scuffles and running battles which affected everyone, including café customers and shoppers. Gradually this radicalized the area against the police presence.

More and more working-class youths began to turn up from their suburbs, out of curiosity and in the hope of giving the police a good bashing. Knocking over café tables and chasing the CRS down cobbled streets was more fun than hanging out in St Denis. So these youths, to whom the Latin Quarter had hitherto been exotic territory, began to map out and claim the area.

This was not at all to the students' liking. They were often openly dismayed and resentful at this sudden incursion of louts oblivious to liberal idealism and polysyllabic rhetoric. These were not the mythical 'workers' which marching students invoked in their chants. The students were also perturbed at the ease and panache of the street fighting of these newcomers, and their lack of proportion and propriety.

While students might hurl missiles at the CRS, they knew the boundaries. Theirs was a legitimate protest. Their violence was retroactive and protesting, rather than aggressive. They declared they would not be provoked by the authorities into 'going too far'. They felt themselves to be victims of a terrible misunderstanding which would eventually be cleared up in the light of rational debate.

But these freeloaders, the hooligans, were not playing this essentially middle-class game. They were not calling Papa's bluff in the knowledge of an eventual share in the patrimony. In fact they didn't give a toss for Papa or his sons or daughters and, moreover, they were just beginning to have a really smashing time.

This clash culminated on the night of the barricades, Friday 10 May. All that day protesters had been marching round the Sorbonne, chanting and skirmishing with the CRS. However, Papa was beginning to lose his nerve, and plans were afoot to dissolve the crisis and effect a tearful reconciliation. The CRS that day were relatively restrained, and rumours were rife about secret talks at the Ministry of Education. After which, vindication and the reopening of the Sorbonne. And then everyone could knuckle down to exams and get ready for the summer break. Reality would resume its normal service.

But in the event these talks, which were being reported live on transistor radios carried by students, took so long that a delicate and fateful 'situation' arose. For the CRS had cordoned off a section of the Latin Quarter adjacent to the Sorbonne. Into this free zone, over a period of several hours, filtered several thousand protesters, sightseers and miscreants.

Everyone was anticipating a student victory that evening. So at first there was a relaxed and comradely atmosphere. After a while, however, we all became apprehensive. Would it not be wise to make some kind of protection, in case of a sudden CRS attack? Cars were shunted into the middle of some streets. Was this enough protection? Café tables and chairs and debris from building sites were added to what then suddenly became perceived as versions of the famous revolutionary barricades – echoing the French Revolution itself, not to mention the Paris Commune of 1871. As the evening wore on, these barricades began to be fortified in some streets with makeshift piles of *pavés* – cobblestones. By now many of the students had begun to be openly concerned that things were indeed 'going too far'.

Because the hooligans, sons of the street and veterans of building sites, seeing these isolated and rather amateurish barricades, now understood this interesting game, but knew they could do it better – properly. Quite suddenly, all over this area of the Latin Quarter, barricades began to go up in earnest – real barricades – five, then six, then seven or more feet high.

As this was happening I saw several confrontations between students and barricade builders. One student, for example, remonstrated with a group of louts who were digging up *pavés*. The bespectacled idealist admonished the gang for 'adventurism'. He then picked up the loose stones one by one and 'hid' them in a wastebin.

At one point a column of Maoists turned up, marching in 'military' formation down the Boulevard St-Michel. They took one look at these barricades, denounced them as 'counter-revolutionary' and marched off – to hoots and whistles of derision.

By now it was too late to stop – the night was out of control. And after a while it became such fun that everyone forgot why they were supposed to be there and joined in anyway. Fuck the Students' Union – let's live a little!

A building site was gleefully looted for weapons and barricade material. Someone started up a cement-mixer. Someone else was using a pneumatic drill to excavate *pavés*. People formed chains stretching down streets, passing debris and *pavés* to the barricade builders. Side-streets became denuded, resembling soft, sandy passages. ('Under the paving stones is the beach.')

Some people had broken into an office and were showering passers-by with documents and letters while sitting on a window ledge drinking wine. Residents began coming out in their dressing-gowns to offer refreshments and advice, or to shake hands with the revolutionaries. One elderly lady set out a flask of hot coffee with mugs on a car bonnet. A man in a first-floor flat threw open his windows and played a record of the 'Internationale'. In a courtyard people were transforming milk bottles into petrol bombs, as dextrously as if on a production line, then stacking them in crates.

By about midnight we knew we had reached the famous situationist 'point of no return'. We were boxed into the Latin Quarter, physically and mentally, the prisoners of a cultural logic – the unfolding of a historical 'moment', a text which had to be recited and enacted to whatever bitter end awaited us. For we were trapped by the enormity of what we had done – the barricades themselves looked awesome. Was this a monster we had conjured from history? Would this be a fight to the death? Was this IT – the revolution?

The neighbourhood had been transformed into surreality, and we began looking at one another oddly. We talked as if what we were saying meant something else – something we couldn't quite grasp or formulate. It was as if we were collectively rubbing our eyes. Was this Paris? What year was this? Surely not the 1960s. This was nothing like modern life. An urban area had become suffused with a fantasmic atmosphere, resembling the makeshift and fragile décor of a Jean Cocteau film.

But better than a film – we were in it. The imaginary had burst its banks.

I remember my vivid conclusion: Paris belongs to me. For the first time during my stay I felt organically linked, and profoundly at home, in these streets. This was my place and all around were my people. Surely now, from this delirious moment, in this strangely recreated and labile space, anything was possible.

But we were also apprehensive. We started looking around for staves and other weapons. I found an iron bar and tucked it in my waistband. It seemed that negotiations had, in any case, stalled. No way out. We were now awaiting the police onslaught.

It began just after 2 a.m.

The street fighting that night has always suggested to me a metaphorical link between a riot and a collective orgasm. It is not often admitted, but rioting is serious fun, like making love to a city – an exhilaration only matched in my experience by the first time I heard the finale to Bach's *St Matthew Passion*.

As the CRS approached they were met with showers of *pavés* and petrol bombs. They advanced along many streets simultaneously, taking barricade after barricade, the barricade defenders only abandoning their vantage-points at the last moment, to retreat to the next barricade, which they began defending all over again.

Many cars were set on fire – a beautiful sight.

For part of that night I was in the Rue Gay Lussac, which, unknown to me, was also the street defended by members of the Situationist Internationale. They put up a cruel and exact defence, firing ball-bearings from catapults, ambushing CRS in courtyards, exploding cars just as the CRS reached them, hurling petrol bombs so accurately and so far that they ignited several police vehicles.

That night was all explosions – the sharp ones of tear-gas guns and canisters, the dull thuds of petrol tanks exploding, the jolting of blast bombs. There were fires everywhere, running figures and shouting, metallic clatterings, and in the distance the ever-advancing CRS: hard and shiny little objects. We longed for just one rifle to pick them off – perhaps next time . . .

But inexorably they pushed us back, squeezing us tighter and tighter, until we realized it was all up. Where to go now? Suddenly it was said that the student hostel of the Ecole Normale was a sanctuary. We fled inside. I ended in a student bedroom with about a dozen others – all strangers. Someone wisecracked about my iron bar: 'If only your mother could see you now!' We waited until the commotion and the explosions outside subsided. As dawn broke we cautiously left, one by one, aghast at the destruction all around, smouldering, ugly and black, and uncanny in the light of day.

I later learned that several hundred of us had taken refuge in the Ecole Normale. The police had realized this and tried to enter and arrest us. They had been prevented by the director of the Normale –

an extremely important personage in France, who had rung the Minister of the Interior to ensure our safety.

After that night the 'events' of May and June began in earnest. As is well known, a wave of occupations and strikes began, and gradually turned into a national strike which effectively closed France down. Universities, schools, shops, theatres, factories all went on strike, and people occupied their places of work.

Student union officials and trade union organizers as well as various leftist ideologists worked frantically to transform this escalating holiday into a series of understandable grievances and coherent demands – to absorb it into current and comprehensible politics. But this was not easy.

For what, after all, did people want? They weren't sure, and began asking questions and framing problems which had never previously found a popular or radical articulation. Were we not all profoundly bored? Was modernization really such a good idea? Did we actually desire consumer goods? Paris became a talking shop, a massive, unrestrained, continuous and chaotic version of Speakers' Corner in Hyde Park. People would begin arguing in the street for no apparent reason. Soon a crowd would form around the disputants. Then members of the crowd would begin separate arguments, and themselves become the focus of yet more spectators, who in turn became participants.

Rioting became a nightly occurrence on the Left Bank and spread to all parts of the city. And when one night I heard that rioting had started in, of all places, Montmartre, and that prostitutes and pimps had been seen shoulder to shoulder, building barricades and taking on the CRS, I knew the entire city had gone nuts. I also sensed that soon the government would have to act decisively, or else concede defeat. And it was in fact shortly after the Montmartre riots that de Gaulle had Paris ringed with tanks, preparatory to a possible military intervention.

It never came to that. Because the French went on holiday. As July approached, and it was announced that all students that year would pass all their exams – no need to sit them – and as all workers were awarded blanket and generous pay rises, people began talking about continuing the revolution, well, maybe next term, and certainly after the holidays – but in any case the struggle would continue even on the beaches of Biarritz or Cannes!

And the whole thing ended not with a whimper, but an ice-cream cone.

But the repercussions were considerable.[4] Particularly in spreading a situationist mood into culture at large, a mood which later emerged as a commodified situationist chic, through the Sex Pistols and Punk, and which then transmogrified into an ideology of mischief and carnivalesque misbehaviour through all that other 'angry' music.

As soon as he realized the dimensions of what was happening in France, Malcolm tried to join me. I made several excited calls from phone booths in the Latin Quarter, one of them in the Boulevard St-Michel with a riot as background, with suggestions about travel and accommodation. But Malcolm was frustrated by the rail and air strikes which had isolated and paralysed France. In early May I had received a letter from Malcolm addressed to my poste restante in the Boulevard St-Germain: 'Fred, coming over Saturday or Friday, that is 17th or 16th May [he never made it] . . . have been in contact with Henry a lot. Want very much to see the Louvre exhibition of GOTHIC ART! Have begun to paint but must be careful of my own . . . [the sentence peters out] been taking photos, mucking about with film, drawing every day. Beginning to feel for the greats: MASACCIO! Must see his frescos (tribute money!) in Florence this Summer. I have begun to see and BEGIN to understand Cezanne! (Bernini is marvellous). The Rennaisance was fantastic. Joe [his and Vivienne's son] is so sensitive his movements are something that reveal his specialness. Want to see you.'

Malcolm eventually arrived in Paris after the 'events', *en route* to a holiday in the South of France, where he was joined later by Vivienne. I took him on a car tour of the Left Bank battlefields. People were still jumpy and there were CRS loitering menacingly. I insulted a group of them: 'Wankers!', and so on. They suddenly rushed the car with batons flailing. The driver swerved in the middle of the boulevard, did an abrupt U-turn, and shot off with Malcolm screaming: 'Get the fuck out of here!'

Afterwards Malcolm assisted me in attempting to recover a 1940s tweed waisted overcoat I'd bought in the flea market, and a precious cache of posters, leaflets and pamphlets I'd collected throughout the revolution. When the Swedish painter I'd stored all this with told me she'd chucked it out that very morning, Malcolm helped me to smash her windows. We could hear her screaming inside.

When I returned to London in July I was a convert to the power of the mass media. I thought the media would be the arena for radical politics post '68. I therefore enrolled at the Polytechnic of Central London (after hastily taking some A levels) which in those days ran the only course in the country dealing with mass media.

Meanwhile Henry Adler had put me on to some British situationists. This was King Mob.

King Mob was formed as a result of the British situationist Chris Grey being expelled from the SI. Grey was a gentlemanly sort who lived in Ladbroke Grove with his hippie girlfriend. Always a dreamer, Chris boasted to the French situationists that he could call on a hardened guerrilla combat unit of at least thirty. This sounded good to Guy Debord, who rushed across the Channel to inspect the revolutionaries under Grey's command. It was all cobblers, and an embarrassed Grey diverted Debord to the home of Dave Wise, an art college lecturer. Debord found Dave lying on a sofa watching *Match of the Day* on his six-inch telly, swigging a can of McEwans. This collaboration with the 'Spectacle' enraged Debord, who was beginning to smell perfidious Albion. Had he been hoaxed about the British guerrillas?

Learning that Dave's girlfriend was an infant school teacher, Debord demanded to know whether she was teaching them to 'desire incestuous relationships'. She was not. This was the final straw. Debord began to pick books off the shelves, shouting: 'Why are you reading this!' and throwing the suspect volumes all over the flat. Then he stormed back to Paris. Chris Grey was duly expelled from the SI for telling lies. The movement demanded revolutionary 'transparency' in all matters from its members.

So then Chris and Dave and his brother Stuart, together with about twenty others, founded King Mob, a sort of Bash Street Kids version of this continental radicalism. They staged theatrical protests against banality and art, smashing up the Wimpy Bar in Ladbroke Grove because of its décor, and holding a street festival to celebrate the shooting of Andy Warhol by Valerie Solanas. They also debated how to detonate the critique of art implicit in the work of William Blake, and proposed that the only working-class radicals were football hooligans.

Associated with this group was a former criminology student from Cambridge who made his living stealing typewriters from solicitors' offices in Holborn. This person was the brains behind the idea of infiltrating what later became known as teenage 'subcultures', the idea being to channel their frustrations to revolutionary ends.

For example, he stirred up the beatniks then hanging around Piccadilly Circus into occupying a café from which they'd been banned. Then he helped organize a hippie squat in Piccadilly. While this was going on he duped the media, saying he'd arranged a 'truce' between hippies and their natural enemies, the skinheads. These rebels would all now join in a crusade 'against society'. The result of this nonsense was that several thousand skinheads invaded the West End looking for a riot. The police spent the evening chasing booted and braced ten to fifteen-year-olds around Shaftesbury Avenue, eventually herding them back East.

Here was an excellent blueprint for starting trouble, and the moral of the story was not lost on Malcolm and Vivienne.

In late '68 I wrote to the Situationist Internationale at their box number in Paris. I gave them the address I was then living at with Gordon, in a condemned house we had on a short lease in Anerley, South London.

Here I action-painted the walls of my room green, grey and red, and continued my education by reading Hegel's *Philosophy of Art*. Then I read the rest of Virginia and all of Leonard Woolf. I learned with awe – in a book from Lewisham Library – about a Russian writer so intense he sprained both wrists writing and rewriting his masterpiece. I listened to all nine of Beethoven's symphonies in the order he wrote them.

I received another letter from Malcolm, from the South of France: '. . . Vivien's [sic] coming over this weekend, Henry's here, understanding him a little more . . . sleeping around a house in Théoule old man was a Gaullist, thought I wanted to murder him . . . now at Le Trayas sleeping on beach. The sun was constant today. The sea is like Nolde BLACK NOT BLUE. At Avignon a good festival is happening, Living Theatre doing Brecht, and Maurice Bejart ballet. Young film makers from all over plus new Truffaut and a film called Jagnat [?] which Henry reckons on. Saw Le Mepris at Nice, Godard's film of BARDOT, JACK PALANCE AND FRITZ LANG about a film being made. Been to Arles, Aix and the Camargue. George forced me to climb Mte Ste Victoire around Aix, great country, CEZANNE . . . Henry bought a primus and cooks good [crossed out] reasonable . . . WILL WRITE AGAIN. MALCOLM.'

One day a Frenchman turned up at the flat. He was in his early twenties, handsome and dashingly dressed with a Gallic spruceness – coloured silk kerchief tucked under his shirt collar, immaculate cream trousers, shiny Burgundy-coloured shoes. He said his name was Pierre, and that he had come from Paris to visit me on behalf of the Situationist Internationale.

We spent several days talking – or was I being interviewed? He seemed as interested in my lifestyle and sources of income as my politics. He explained that the SI had been struck by my letter on two counts. First, I had concluded with the phrase: 'Towards a Situationist Internationale!' Now what exactly did I mean by 'Towards'? Did I know something they didn't? Was there an argument behind my phrase? I explained I was suggesting the ideas might need more working out, especially through popular culture.

The second reason I had made an impression was somewhat farcical – it was my surname. Auguste Vermorel had been a member

172

of the Paris Commune of 1871, a radical journalist who died defending the barricades outside the Hôtel de Ville. My father had indeed boasted that we were related to the great man, but I never thought revolution might run in the blood. But the SI, it seemed, had been tickled, possibly seeing a name to summon up a past demon of the bourgeoisie.

Pierre disappeared for a while. When he next appeared, I was in the process of decamping from the flat. I had moved most of my possessions to my new address, but I wished, not unnaturally, to break open and empty the electricity meter. This meter was in Gordon's room, which was locked, and Gordon was out. Pierre had the answer. Taking two wine corks from the kitchen he inserted them at the top and bottom of the door. He then rolled and squeezed these towards the lock, first one and then the other, alternately, inch by inch. Finally, there was a loud crack, and the door flew open. He did this with such ease I suspected he might earn his living from such tricks. When I asked he smiled in a bashful sort of way. We went drinking in the West End that night and I left him at Charing Cross Station. I never saw him again.

I introduced Malcolm to situationism at the 36 bus stop, just outside Goldsmiths College in Lewisham Way. Goldsmiths was where he had enrolled in October '68 in his continuing quest for a grant. I produced two issues of the SI magazine (the silver and mauve ones) and showed him some of the illustrations, translating captions and some other passages. Malcolm reacted in the way many others did. He was nonplussed and irritated, yet anxiously excited.

I had felt the same when I discovered these publications in a Paris bookshop some months before the May events. This literature irritated because it was vaguely familiar; as one of the SI slogans went: 'Our ideas are already in everyone's heads.' Yet the familiar was here given a cogent and perverse twist. What had been mere residue in the mind, a kind of dirt or dreamlike aura around familiar stances and habits, was sharply and shockingly defined, crystalline and uncompromising, stated as a position and a thesis.

The careful design of these magazines was also shocking. Unlike all the other roneotyped, smudgy, and hastily produced radical leaflets, magazines and booklets of that period, the SI's publications were sternly professional and insolently expensive, flaunting their boast that, unlike their rivals, they would still be read in a hundred years' time.

They made every other leftism – Maoism, Trotkyism, anarchism – seem half-hearted and insincere, the debris of past misfortunes and miscalculations.

Particularly impressive was the situationists' head-on concern with the realities of mass media in the mid-century. The Spectacle of one-way communication, as they put it.

Why they were so appealing to people like me was that their fervid and brittle critiques encapsulated the revolt of a Romantic soul against this media, the Romantic genius seething with injured pride and baffled angst at the assault of banality – its eating away at the edges of my integral self, the media's interruption of a solipsistic reverie, alone with my project against the world, fortified by those few, my chosen friends, Malcolm and Vivienne and others of a happy band, as barmy as me, as pledged to the cause of endless self-education.

I had often raged against the media, shouting at TV screens, cursing news readers and DJs not for what they said but for their unassailability. I imagined devices to beam hatred into their studios, explosives to cripple transmitters, slogans to devastate common sense. What were the media's banal exclamations, the humdrum duties it invoked. Those fucking cunts! I had, in Zola's phrase, 'all the fury of a timid soul let loose on pure theory'.

This theory was pure because in it I recognized my limpid consciousness – that is, my consciousness of myself as a limpidity, a transparent but corrosive spirit floating through a half-world in which I lived resentfully immersed in the Spectacle, seething at its stupidity. But where else was there for an unknown and unemployable boy to go? I turned in my twilight anxiety and scorn, imprisoned and chafing at this culture of smug surveillance – all those responsible people I hated, going about their poisonous jobs in their poisonous cars, living their poisonous lives with their poisonous families.

Even before I encountered the situationist style my solitary campaigns of graffiti anticipated its rasping tone. My pre-'68 graffiti was a wink and a leer across the separation of my ego from the unknown and innocent eye of a future reader, a nudging and uncalled-for intimacy.

In library books I inked in obscene details to romantic novels, leering and idiotic asides to good sorts like Bertrand Russell, meticulous death threats in political biographies. My comments were mines left on enemy territory.

Such insertions were cunningly designed and placed like the 'happy surprise' of the Romantic landscape gardener. I wanted the reader to stumble upon the chilling traces of this previous inhabitant of the text, to experience the vertiginous thrill of crumbling foundations.

The style of orthography should therefore be bold enough to be instantly readable and therefore instantly alarming, yet with a hint of suppressed mania in the way the letters were of subtly uneven size. The handwriting was spidery and scholarly, but the letters childishly disproportionate enough to prise apart common sense and insert a radical doubt. Buffoonish misspellings alternated with archaisms. For while the misspellt breathed the threat of the cretin, crazed philology added the hint of a scholar gone off the rails – possibly at that moment stalking your children through suburban streets, or peering through your very letter-box AS YOU READ MY WORDS!

In this I was guided by Samuel Beckett, especially the trilogy of early novels – razor-sharp inanity crawling along in archaic or long-winded locutions, as if some maniac had just crawled out of the eighteenth century through a crevice in between the pages of this innocent library book.

On suburban trains my messages aimed to undermine the routines and certitudes of commuter existence. Thus I might cackle gleefully at the impending waste of a day. Or one of the pinstriped bastards would be sure to sport a moustache. I would compare his moustache to the scum around an ebbing bath. The idea was to couch a phrase between the general and specific so that 'dear reader' never quite knew whether he or she was being personally or anonymously targeted. Who, for example, was the 'fat wanker with a blue tie' reading the *Financial Times*? Was this the very 'BASTARD' indicated by an arrow pointing down to his seat?

So I donated mystery to the tedium of their day. Who had done this? Who would dare? What kind of mentality would even dream that up? And was he still here, on this very train?

After I had successfully 'bombed' a train I felt pleased with myself. A job well done. I might celebrate by unscrewing light-bulbs and hurling them on to platforms as the train sped through stations. Or else I would peer and gesticulate maniacally out of the window, bug-eyed and imprinting a momentary image of insanity in the minds of commuters. Sometimes I added to this display with a two-finger sign. My best platform audiences were schoolchildren, who gave as good as they got, jeering and pulling faces back.

Once I was so absorbed in my work, standing on a seat and decorating the roof and spaces over the luggage rack with imprecations against everyday life that I failed to notice another train had pulled up and was travelling alongside mine. I suddenly noticed a carriage full of gaping commuters. I was unsettled by this and wondered what to do next, frozen on the seat with my felt-tip in hand. Oddly, they came to my rescue, by pretending in the best British tradition that they hadn't noticed. They all returned to their papers or uncomfortably averted their eyes. I carried on scribbling until their train pulled away.

Hence my recognition and delight at the situationist slogans spray-painted over Paris during the May events: 'Never work!', 'Culture is the inversion of life', 'Live without dead time', 'Orgasm without restraint', 'Scream, steal, ejaculate your desires', 'The more you consume the less you live', 'Down with the Nazarene toad', 'Knowledge is inseparable from the use to which it is put', 'I take my desires for reality because I believe in the reality of my desires'. All done in the curly orthography required by a *baccalauréat* exam paper. These were a systematized and classy version of my lonely campaigns. Suddenly I was in company – there were other idiots like me in the world.

Situationism was partly this heightened revelation of the latent self-consciousness of every spectator and consumer – the boredom and itch at the heart of mass consumption. What I routinely experienced as an invasion of myself was what everyone else experienced as a discontented normality. But it took only the words, a slogan, a shifted perception, to turn this discontent into rebellion. It was the situationists' ingenuity to say those words.

It was a near thing, an almost miss, which inflected an insider's scorn – not like those old boys from the Austro-Hungarian empire, Adorno or Marcuse, insulated from the mass culture of the late twentieth century by a modernist disdain. Ours was an insider's pique – all the more venomous and urgent.

One of the most suggestive remarks made about situationism was in a 1964 *TLS* article. Michelle Bernstein asked: 'Are the situationists serious, or are they utterly mistaken and destined for unparalleled depths of stupidity?'

Stupidity? This captures the situationist gamble and autodidactic fervour; the fierce antagonism of the autodidact who secretly always wonders if he or she is actually really rather stupid, who cannot quite 'master', or possess those knowledges which reveal 'intelligence',[5] and thus will make everyone suffer – by imposing a droning jargon or a caterwauling effortfulness. (How many conference papers have I sat through like that!)

The situationists solemnly proposed 'Theses on Banality'. Theses on what!? How absurd! 'Art is dead,' they warned. 'Do not consume its corpse.' What a deliciously scandalous and dotty formulation. And then they politicized boredom – and what could be more stupid than that? But also, what more clever?

Through such situationist devices and bluffs, a Romantic (avant-gardist) ideology of genius was given a final, wickedly risible twist as exposé and end-game.

And that is the secret which McLaren and Westwood learned by heart – how to paint your subjectivity in the codes of culture and foment an insurrection of like-minded solitudes.

In some ways the situationist style was that of a collectivity of Max Stirner. Stirner is the long-forgotten author of a masterpiece of solipsistic sophistry, a heroically fatuous attempt to write the 'last chapter' of Hegel's *Phenomenology*. Just as Jean Hippolyte summarized the intention of the *Phenomenology* as: 'The history of the world is finished; all that is needed is for the specific individual to rediscover it in himself', so Stirner set out to do just that. Published in 1844, his book, *The Ego and His Own* was a hysterical outburst of the individual against everything and everyone.

For Stirner, only the 'I' exists – its dictates and requirements are paramount. The self stands in opposition to the state, to law, to morality, to humanity – all condemned as 'spooks'. 'The idols exist through me; I need only refrain from creating them anew, then they exist no longer . . . my intercourse with the world consists in my consuming it for my self enjoyment.'

The book was originally banned, but the order was lifted as the German Minister of the Interior thought it 'too absurd' to be dangerous. Interestingly, however, it enraged Marx and Engels, who devoted three-quarters of their first joint book, *The German Ideology*, to a vituperative and slanderous attack on 'St Max'. Stirner was thereafter influential on a number of notable Egoists, including the anarchist Bakunin and the Satanist Aleister Crowley.

The situationists' stance and voice had echoes of Stirner in their self-conscious absurdism, their defiantly 'up yours' viciousness, and their being completely out of step and off-beam in relation to everything else being said in the 1950s and 60s. Not to mention their neo-Hegelian flourishes and cant, a stylish – or 'styled' – nihilism and their derisively tendentious and piratical use of a 'stolen' academic jargon.

But the situationists had the strength of a group mania – a self-conscious 'movement' constructed on avant-gardist principles, and a tested strategy which saw their 'non-sense' through to a cultural conclusion: they were a collectivity of Egos (with Guy Debord perhaps as Master-Ego). 'Only geniuses need apply,' read their recruitment ad. How could they fail?

Moreover, a hundred years after Stirner, this celebration of solipsism had found its social context and an experiential reality in a Romantic consumerist sensibility and a Romanticized consumer culture.[6]

The 1960s were profoundly marked by consumerism. It was a thoroughly consumerist decade and the 'counter-culture', notwithstanding its anti-consumerist rhetoric, was simply a new spin on consumerism with brand-new goods – from the Beatles to Buddha, a spin which resulted in a decisive acceleration of consumerism's idealistic, fantasy-based momentum.

I've suggested as much above, in relation to features of the sixties as shared by myself, Vivienne Westwood and Malcolm McLaren. So it was no contradiction at all that our Romantic search for genius and revolution, and our fetish of Culture, should end up most famously and succinctly expressed as a boutique in the King's Road, or that Westwood and McLaren's particular revolution should be associated with that motor of consumerism, the fashion industry.

Nor is it odd that we were all drawn to situationism – which at the time was still seen by practically all Left commentators as a marginal and esoteric, if not downright barmy, cult.

For situationism was so prescient about consumerist modes of existence and fantasies of being because it was itself an anguished revelation of Romantic consumerism. And while its ostensible take on consumerism as a subject for critique was the same mechanical hate mail of the Frankfurt School, the situationists' essentially Romantic expressivity, their attention to stylishness, their waspish propositions, a taste for the ferocious apophthegm (as jagged and curious as that word) – all knowledge whittled into a withering rebuke – which is also the delight of autodidacts – amounted to an insistent tone of high subjectivity, a Romanticism which was expressed as the breaking point of consumerist subjectivity, experiencing and countering the monolithic tedium and poisonous ennui, the hyperboredom encoded in mass entertainment and mass consumption.

Like all artists, like all bohemians, the situationists were 'specialists in the self', virtuosos and dandies of 'theory': theorists of a modernized sublime, of a consciousness pitted against the Spectacle, 'so that the immanence in the self reaches out and touches the value immanent in the world'.

So that the situationist voice corrodes the Spectacular appearance of the world through the media and breaks through to an authentic experience, a cry which is couched as a bohemian festival, an overturning and carnival transgression – the Revolution.

The fashionable expression of that revolution, fashion as that revolution, was punk.

There are intriguing similarities between the relationship of the élite Situationist Internationale with their student and working-class 'cannon fodder', and the Sex Pistols' management team's (Glitterbest) relationship with the youthful punks of 1976.

The situationists were full-time revolutionaries, self-consciously intransigent and uncompromising, belonging mostly to an age group half a generation away from the students of '68 – as were Glitterbest from the punks. Both groups therefore had a maturity and experience which fired up and also reassured youthful hesitations and misgivings. The situationists' fluency of rhetoric, and their contempt for all other leftist groups was equally inspiring. They let it be known they were engaged in a 'journey to the end of the night', intent on creating a monster 'situation' from which there could be no turning back.

Like Glitterbest, they scorned underground tactics and secretive cabals, plotting loudly and preposterously in public places and in print so that it seemed like a grotesque come-on for the secret police one imagined were never far away. But, in fact, so fantastical were their claims, so off the wall their ideology, that the Paris police mistook them for nutters and concentrated their attentions on the harmless Leninist or Maoist groups. Similarly it was always simple to find out what Glitterbest was plotting. You only had to sit within earshot of Malcolm McLaren in a pub (up to about fifty yards away!). Only you would not believe your ears.

Like the situationists, Glitterbest had access to an avant-gardist repertoire of examples which suggested that you can never 'go too far'. To go 'too far' was merely to enter history, timidity being the only barrier to success.

Both the situationists and Glitterbest were 'sexy' (in advertising jargon); they had their finger on the consumerist pulse of the times, and a garrotte around the neck of modern art/rock music. They knew that to aestheticize everyday life, crossing the boundaries between art and life, was a hot topic in a culture which celebrated the power of fantasy to transform reality, and that to infuse the mundane routines of reality with dotty speculations and wild fancies could make it all come true. Rhetoric really could work, talking could make things happen – nobody believed that more provocatively or assertively in the sixties than the situationists, and it was from their 'situation' of '68 that the 'situation' of '76 (or thereabouts) took its cue.

And finally, the situationists expressed all this in startling and pithy slogans, a poetry of subterranean intelligence mysteriously appearing all over the walls of Paris, a sardonic come-on and 'answering back' to official and sanctioned messages. Just as, nine years later, the media would be forced to swallow its own vomit and regurgitate its headlines helplessly – headlines which were twisted and subverted through another sloganeering genius, as the careering fame of punk rock took it for a spectacular ride and its 'writing on the wall' seeped as a nihilistic poison into the hit parade.

Nowadays when we recall the sixties it's often through music – the Beatles, *Blowin' in the Wind*, Rolling Stones, walls of sound, Beach Boys, *Stairway to Heaven*, Joplin, Hendrix, Bolan, Woodstock, *Performance* . . . Everything is deemed to flow from and to return to such cultural references. Biographies are plotted against the release of albums and top twenty hits illustrate documentaries on the Cuban missile crisis, the rise of the miniskirt or the crash of Biba, the Prague Spring or Paris 1968. In such accounts, pop and rock seem omnipresent.

But we lived our lives the other way round. Music was a backdrop to our noisy and fragile aspirations. We hardly noticed – and who

181

cared? – which Beatles single was in the charts, or what band Eric Clapton had just joined, whether Bob Dylan was in Europe or New York, or dead or alive. Pop and rock only happened on certain occasions in our lives, and then not a lot of it; it was limited in time, space and technology, and by our taking it for granted.

To start with, opportunities to hear the stuff were rare. No Sony Walkmans or hi-fi sets in the modern sense. And there was practically no pop or rock played on the radio until the pirate radio stations began broadcasting.

No one I knew bought records in the sixties in any serious way, like some people do nowadays – as if their lifestyle depends on it. Records were just sort of around. There were piles of the things at parties and in bedrooms and you might pinch one or two in a vague sort of way. Or you lent or borrowed them and played and forgot about them. Sometimes at parties we spun them across the lawn at one another. Or we stubbed out fags on them or wiped them free of grime with a cuff. I don't remember that they were seen as valuable or particularly collectable except by people with some kind of professional interest, like disc jockeys or nerds. Nor did we often go to performances – too much trouble. And when we did go it was for lots of reasons, but I can't recall when one of them was to see a particular act. Most of those acts seemed interchangeable and ephemeral. Rock was just scenery – something we wanted to move beyond to get to the real action.

Moreover, all these stars were as remote, as bizarre, and irrelevant as . . . well, Australia. I know far more about these people now than I did then, and that's because a pop tune is so mnemonically apt, and because these sixties artists are more present now in the nineties – more featured and played and reported and analysed than they were in their 'heyday'. This is partly because popular culture now has an intensity far greater than in the sixties. And, a corollary factor, because the media itself has a potency, penetration and manipulative skill it was then only improvising towards.

Who in the sixties really gave two fucks for John Lennon? Rich cunt. Nasal whine. The only connection we had with him was when I organized a protest outside the Robert Fraser Gallery, where

Lennon was showing some erotic etchings. We forged several dozen 'original' Lennons in the Goldsmiths print room and gave them away outside the gallery to mark our contempt for the silly wanker's artistic pretensions.

Otherwise we never thought about him. Indeed we peevishly refused to subordinate our lives to speculations about such people. We spent our time trying to invent ourselves, rather than following celebrities.

I think that sometimes my generation succumbs to a pietistic history of itself, reinventing a conveniently commodified sixties through the glow of Sergeant Pepper and other cosy icons. But we were casual and tactical consumers, rather than fans. Being a 'fan' of the Beatles (standing for any other act of the time) was mostly for the little girls who clustered around the Apple door in Savile Row. I only went to Savile Row hoping to bag a mohair jacket from the Gieves and Hawkes sale.

Malcolm himself has reinterpreted his sixties decade as a love affair with Elvis and rock music. But I know this to be another one of those lies whereby he periodically reinvents himself through useful memories. Before he resigned himself to the fact that the music industry represented a fertile playground for subsidizing his mischief, Malcolm was not the slightest bit interested in rock or any sort of popular music. Indeed we all had a disdain for such music and particularly for the culture surrounding it, which seemed obese and abject.

Burning in our ears was the wisdom of Theodore Ramos, counselling that musicianship was for the more stupid kinds of artist. (Malcolm periodically even agonized over whether he was 'too intelligent' even to be a successful painter!) We might go to the Wealdstone Railway Tavern, where Long John Baldry was playing, but we were only there for the beer and the girls. And as fleet-minded and subtle cultural connoisseurs we were also then discovering the wilder shores of jazz, Bartók or the atonal crowd.

Vivienne is much more straightforward about this. She prefers Chopin now as she did then and has never concealed her contempt for 'popular culture' in general, which for her remains always second best.

If all this is a surprise to you, then you have failed to understand the central thrust of punk and of McLaren and Westwood's (and indeed all our group's) involvement in popular music.

For punk was rooted in a contempt for the values of 'the popular'. It was an exercise predicated on a distrust and despair of what electrified the hit parade or excited the tabloids. Far from being, as it is so often represented, an attack from below, punk was a snob's revenge from on high. Far from being a dadaist assault on high culture, punk was a dadaist assault on popular culture.

Thus the notion that 'anyone can do it' was also the idea that it's all crap anyway; the spectre of the Swindle was there from the start. Thus too the mocking of the star system by promoting musical retards and quasi-psychotics like Sid Vicious as 'stars' with 'star quality'. Thus too, the rubbishing of the idea that any special talent was needed to succeed in this area – a lack of talent being touted as a distinct advantage. Far from being a democratizing call, this was a sardonic indictment of popular taste – of what could pass for talent, and therefore a covert vindication of élitism. At the core of punk was the aesthete's hollow laugh

So punk – in the crucial sense defined through Westwood and McLaren (though of course many other people made many other meanings from it) – was an attack on 'mass' values and perceptions as represented by the media. And this attack was mounted from the perspective of an autodidactic reverence for a certain late-nine-teenth and early-twentieth-century (essentially modernist) version of high culture – the culture our group was immersed in and aspired to, the culture we were painstakingly inculcating in ourselves throughout the sixties, throughout Malcolm's eight years as an art student and Vivienne's proxy studentship.

This reverence for high culture is clearly visible in the bravura aestheticism which dressed up punk as punk fashion.

In retrospect, the vivacity and cultural 'overloading' of this fashion, its now classic status as an anti-fashion fashionability, as the source of the articulation of 'street style', probably owed more to Vivienne than to Malcolm. Punk fashion's charm and edgy flamboyance – precisely what made it fashion rather than fancy dress or mere sartorial confrontation – its locking on to fashion values – came from Vivienne's diligent and meticulous, indeed querulous (might I add punctilious?) attention to the detail of Culture.

Whereas her brother Gordon had buried his Northern accent, Vivienne kept hers (today her accent is more pronounced than her mother's). Indeed keeping it was a strategy. She played on retaining it, rolled it around her mouth like a defiant and protective reserve, spat it politely out as an injunction. As she insinuates it still, syllable by syllable into interviews to foil awkward customers with mock naïveté – how would a country girl know that?

Being a Southerner, I failed at first to distinguish that hers is also essentially a working-class accent. I was fooled by her genteel parents with their suburban flat above a post office, Gordon's plentiful pocket money and Vivienne's sister Olga, a university student. The Swires seemed more Pooterish than Tintwistle or Coronation Street.

I realized only gradually how Vivienne's sense of a working-class (even though she is, more precisely, lower-middle-class) identity is burned into her. And it's this which accounts for her elaborate and circumspect reverence for the cultural capital which was absent from her family home and which she has since assiduously stored and now lavishes on her creations.

Interviewers have often fulminated about the interviews she gives, which they say are long-winded and pretentious accounts of her current reading. Maddeningly, they say, she disserts about Aldous Huxley and Bertrand Russell, or about Proust or Flaubert. They see this as baffling and irrelevant. 'Yes, but what about the frocks, Vivienne?'

But this is precisely where the frocks come from. Not from Proust or Huxley, but from that same anxious and solecistic reverence for such figures – for the idea of Culture which their reputation embodies.

These particular tastes may happen to currently come from the cultural formation of her mentor Gary Ness – a standard fifties reading list. But what counts is her assumption of the artist as hero.

She believes profoundly in the Romantic concept of 'genius' as an attribute or subjective quality, a effect which emanates sometimes in lieu or in excess of any works of genius. Not for her Sartre's observation that 'there are no geniuses, only works of genius'.

Vivienne's autodidactic identification with Culture also underlies the sedulous exactitude of her tailoring – tailoring being associated with the landed wisdom and gentility of Savile Row, another version of Culture. It is equally the source of her nervous irritability about getting everything just 'right'.

Hence too her overload of Cultural references – such quotation is an autodidactic fetish.

Pierre Bourdieu, the French sociologist who has done most to link creativity, style and flair with the possession or the lack, or the aspiration to, cultural capital, has written of 'the fireman's gala'. This is the occasion for speeches creaky with awkward allusions and half-understood references, a panic about not getting it exactly right. In some ways Vivienne is a textbook case of the person who has appropriated culture from 'outside' and can't quite work out where it all goes (or where it came from) so she sticks it anywhere she pleases.

If this is 'post-modern', it is so only in the sense I've already indicated, that her marginality was vindicated as the world caught up with (or fell into) the practices of commodified culture. This meshed with the proliferation of a self-educated view of Culture as the prerequisite of a Romantic soul, a subjectivity experienced through consumerist options – options structured as acts of consumption. In that sense, Bouvard and Pécuchet were the first post-moderns.[7]

As an autodidact myself – you will have gathered – it was only when I read for an MA in History that I suddenly realized my distinctive mentality and became self-conscious, losing some of my autodidactic bottle.

In 1974 I found fellow students who had read far less than me but who had read in a systematic and cumulative way, in a way that counted. They simply knew a lot more history than me. I also encountered a tutor, the historian John Harrison, who was making a study of autodidacticism in the nineteenth century. I began to realize that certain habits of my mind, characteristics of thinking and judgement were historically and culturally specific to the sociology I shared with my companions.

We autodidacts care deeply about our knowledge – it is our most precious possession. Attack our notions at your peril – we get irascible and hot, even murderous.

We laboriously do all the wrong things for all the right reasons, immerse ourselves profoundly in rubbish, insist that the 'contents' of our mind must configure – every scrap of information must bear some relation to every other scrap simply because it exists in the same place – our head. We build fabulous systems, splice and mutate disciplines, and plead heterodoxies. We are also prone to paranoia, defensively scorning the academies which are, after all, trying to conceal certain things from the public.

Again, read 'post-modern'.

But then again, Vivienne's work transcends its autodidactic origins through the self-mockery of her own fashionable solecisms. She can't help laughing at herself. And hers is the last laugh. She is the autodidact I knew back then doing a sort of evening course in Genius – but now she is a Professor of Fashion (Royal College of Art, Berlin, Vienna, Milan), the legitimate owner of Fashion trophies, signing cheques in the name of a multimillion-pound Fashion enterprise, a bohemian who made it to the Academy, an accredited 'genius', much to the annoyance of the upper-class 'flair' industry which is Fashion proper – or 'proper' fashion.

You may recall what an unusual character Malcolm McLaren was in his youth. However, you don't know the half of it.

Even in the sixties, a decade which celebrated eccentricity, and in that hothouse of exotic behaviours which was the British art college scene, Malcolm was a one-off. People backed away, or they enthused about his strangeness, or dismissed him as a crazy loser.

He kept going. He was going for broke, playing loser wins. He confided he really expected to end up in the gutter, a broken man, a spent delirium.

For Malcolm knew he had no special talent to claim the acclaim he craved. He couldn't paint well enough to get into the Royal

College of Art (he was encouraged to apply but feared the inevitable rejection), he couldn't act to the specifications of the Royal College of Drama, which he briefly attended after leaving school.

At Harrow Art School he was trying to study for his A level in English. His orthography, like his sentence construction, was a wild pastiche – it floundered and swirled. After hearing me expound the notion of a guttural and improvised style of writing, he rushed this into an essay which temporarily electrified his tutor with its 'creativity'. But after that, and after all, he couldn't write, and failed the exam. So here was a creative writer who couldn't write.

Later he turned into a manager who couldn't manage, a film producer with no productions, a singer who can't sing, and recently, a raconteur who can't remember his lines.

But he knew intensity could masquerade as talent. And that even more miraculously it might produce the very talent that was so desired – up to a point – and up to which point depended on the gamble you were willing to take, and for Malcolm there was no limit – the odds, after all, were stacked so high against this flame-haired, freckle-faced loony from the suburb of Edgware.

Even as a seventeen-year-old Malcolm measured himself immediately and uncompromisingly against the reputed 'masters'. Every watercolour was in anguished competition with Turner, each sketch had to be matched implacably to Rembrandt or Klimt. And the inevitable despair (after all he was no fool and had an eye), spurred him to further feats of contorted bravado – smudging, fudging and bludgeoning his way towards ever more confusing intimations of a uniqueness which failed to materialize on paper as it surfaced so effortlessly in his behaviour.

Everything about him spoke of self-preservation. His trick of laughter, for example, was directed at transforming the material circumstances around him to his own advantage, of redefining it according to his own fashion or stylistic requirements. These requirements were often deliberately in opposition to common sense – they opposed it in order to position his ego as a dynamic of opposition. The laughter was a lubrication for this dynamic and a demolition of whatever stood in its way, toppling fancy things and dainty ways.

He was acutely sensitive to the boundaries and influence of his self, and insisted on his maverick position within a constellation of existing taste. His exploding out of this taste, or existing within it in vertiginous opposition, was his freedom, his creativity, his sense of personal integrity; which was, in reality a devouring of the space of other people by occupying all possible spaces around them. All other positions and tastes dissolved in his acid of derision.

His making of any statement was equally in defiance of any statement that 'you' (that is, the set of all other possible contenders at any moment of his biography) might venture; his hunger was for nihilation[8]; his charm and his laughter, and his summoning others to laughter (part of his 'hystereogenic' character) were aspects of a persuasiveness which sought to hack through the threatening jungle of others, engulf them in his plots.

Malcolm was astute at working out what people most thought they were like – intelligent, shy, ugly . . .

As any psychologist will tell you, people's strongest characteristics contain the seeds of their opposites. Dispositions and self-images, like emotions, are frequently ambivalent. Moreover, people are vulnerable on this score, secretly fearing that this opposite characteristic may be contained within them, hopefully confident no one else is aware of it.

Malcolm would then, with a show of great assurance, roundly accuse a person of being the opposite of what they thought they were. So a dainty Royal Academician became 'an oaf', a clever person became 'a cretin', someone who was pretty became 'horrific'. This tactic never failed.

He also needed to push himself centre stage, in front of everyone else, and he needed to push other people aside. This was manifested in certain compulsive physical acts and gestures.

Most distinctively, he had a curious habit when walking with anyone of gradually edging up closer and closer and then forcing them by degrees either into the gutter or the adjacent wall or hedge. If you looked at him when he was doing this he seemed oblivious to the effect. If you mentioned it he looked blank or laughed nervously – as if this behaviour was on the periphery of his attention and not properly available to inspection.

In the end I developed a technique of either slipping to the other side of him – when the whole process would begin again and then I would skip back to his other side. Or sometimes I nudged him off at the last moment, which was a bit like nudging a dinghy and he would for a while bob and float away in the direction he'd been pushed before inevitably approaching you again, when you had to nudge him away again, and so on. (Vivienne adds that when Malcolm once went for a driving lesson, the instructor stopped the session abruptly, and, clearly shaken, warned that Malcolm should never! be allowed to drive a car.)

This was part of a constellation of apparently inexplicable behaviours and tics which everyone put down to Malcolm's unique personality.[9]

For example, he was remarkably imitative – a talent he would use for one-upmanship or as a derisive show. Once we found ourselves among a group of yobbish mods outside Harrow Art School. Malcolm suddenly began running around in tight little circles, jumping up and down and scratching his underarms like a baboon, grunting like a pig and squealing: 'Oi, fuck that! Oi, fuck this!' This display completely deflated and flummoxed these mods. It was a manic and perceptive approximation of their own behaviour.

He was also very prone to swearing – and swearing in an ejaculatory and innovative manner: 'Shitting cunters! You arsey wanker!' This prolix obscenity would erupt unexpectedly, startling passers-by in the street or unnerving people in a coffee bar. He would also snarl and spit these imprecations, opening his mouth as if symbolically devouring his opponent and displaying his gums and the inside of his mouth in a monstrous pink display.

Then there was his hyperenergy. Walking, for example, he could outpace anyone (except me – as a point of pride) and the faster you walked so he would speed up until both of you were practically running down the street, with him gesticulating madly and loudly all the time and seemingly oblivious to this careering progress.[10]

In the early seventies Malcolm went to Paris accompanied by my younger brother, who was acting as a translator. Phil returned exhausted, complaining that Malcolm had insisted on criss-crossing Paris on foot at a fantastic speed, never pausing in pace or volubility. Moreover, confided Phil, Malcolm was 'fucking mad'. For instance, when signing a hotel register, his jerky and expansive signature had shot off the page and scrawled itself all over the counter.

Such incoordination and 'ticciness' was also a feature of his way of working as an art student. His earliest notable drawings were a series of self-portraits. These were manically overdrawn, slashed and criss-crossed with thick and furious pencil lines, until they looked like black holes of graphite, shiny and dense, layer upon layer of what looked like despair – in some cases the paper was worn through.

Malcolm's eating habits were equally bizarre. He would gobble and chomp loudly with no care for anyone adjacent, splattering people with bits of food as he jabbed and sawed and mangled and stuffed food into his mouth with his fingers, shouting a continual conversation with crumbs and spittle spraying out of his mouth. He was both invasive and strangely uncoordinated. If you went into a lavatory after him you would sometimes find pools of piss all around the pan and on the seat, and evidence he had wildly directed his flow at nearby walls and even into sinks.

At the time I put all this down to genius. Malcolm's uniqueness – his taint and curse of inspiration. So did others.

I was satisfied with the bohemian notion that genius is often mad, that madness and genius are allied. Malcolm obviously fitted that pattern. And, as a teenager, I also aspired to this Dionysian condition.

We equally subscribed to tosh about the unconscious mind and its unpredictable depths which erupted through genius to spray itself into instant masterpieces. If only we could find the courage and stamina to live the life – then spontaneity would do its work.

Malcolm and I pondered the alcoholic crags and fissures on Jackson Pollock's face in the college library. So far to go!

Many years later, in the mid-eighties, after punk, I was scanning the *New York Review of Books* in WH Smith at Charing Cross Station, when my eyes lit on a passage which uncannily echoed all these traits of Malcolm's. This was a description of someone with Tourette's syndrome.

At the time I was thinking through some observations of punk and the Sex Pistols. I'd noticed that a set of gestures and mannerisms peculiar (as I then thought) to Malcolm had been taken up and adapted as a rock and roll rhetoric – a way of being a punk rocker. As I then put it: 'a way of flaunting and carping, a fierce flash and studied resentment'.

I had mapped Malcolm's personality against aspects of punk performance – what I had called his 'harsh orality' against its audience gobbing, its hectic speed (it was often as if the Sex Pistols took the amphetamine called 'speed' to keep up with Malcolm's natural – or unnatural – speed), punk's 'ticcy' and spasmic performance gestures, and the confrontational obscenities coded into its performance, deportment and fashion – likened by Dick Hebdige to a form of sartorial swearing.

I thought it remarkable that the mannerisms of one individual seemed to have proved 'contagious' to the extent that they spread so precisely from Malcolm to the circle around the Sex Pistols, and eventually became a worldwide behavioural rhetoric for rebellion, anger and protest.

It was also apparent that John Lydon, in his brief incarnation as Johnny Rotten, extensively acted out a version of Malcolm McLaren in his untamed student days. When I first saw Rotten perform I was astonished by how Lydon had apparently fathomed and adapted Malcolm's early appearance, his gait and playful spite (though he lacked the ironic overlay and generosity of my old friend), and how he was seemingly pantomiming Malcolm's ambulatory and gestural style. (Jon Savage has also reported Lydon's own astonishment at seeing photographs of the younger McLaren: 'Why, that's me!')

Blakiston's New Gould Medical Dictionary defines Tourette's syndrome as 'a severe form of habitual spasm, beginning in late childhood or adolescence and characterised by multiple tics associated with echolalia, obscene utterances and other compulsive acts'.

The condition was first described in 1885 by the French neurologist Gilles de la Tourette, and named after him by Charcot. Aspects of the disorder had been previously described in medical literature but never so accurately and lucidly as by Tourette, who saw that there was an interconnected pattern, and who also surmised a biological basis, to this constellation of behavioural oddities.

The first phase of research and description into Tourette's was dominated by neurologists who attempted to link it to other movement disorders such as Huntington's Chorea. Psychoanalysts became interested in the syndrome from the 1920s and their work led to a concentration on Tourette's as a psychological entity – an eruption of unconscious or 'primal' urges. However, the failure of this psychotherapy to make any impact on the disorder was followed by the discovery of the dramatic effect on sufferers of the drug haloperidol (which controls but does not cure Tourette's). This led, from the 1960s, to an abandonment of psychological approaches for a biological model. This model predominates today, the consensus being that Tourette's is not a psychological disorder, but has, according to Oliver Sacks, 'an organic neurological basis'.[11]

Sacks has specialized in conditions like Tourette's. It is, he writes: 'characterised by an excess of nervous energy, and a great production and extravagance of strange motions and notions: tics, jerks, mannerisms, grimaces, noises, curses, involuntary imitations and compulsions of all sorts, with an odd elfin humour and a tendency to antic and outlandish types of play.' Describing a 'Touretter' he chances on in a New York street and who is compulsively mimicking passers-by, Sacks notes: 'it was not just an imitation . . . The woman not only took on, and took in, the features of countless people, she took them off. Every mirroring was also a parody, a mocking, an exaggeration of salient gestures and expressions . . .'

Tourette's is notable for its mischievous and subversive manifestations, which can make it disturbing or distressing to onlookers. It is also sometimes characterized by hyperenergy or hyperactivity, by aggressivity and antisocial behaviour, and by sleep disturbances. The majority of patients report obsessive-compulsive behaviours, such as the compulsion to touch or physically approach other people or objects. This is combined with a variety of tics and motor gesticulations.

A distinctive symptom of Tourette's is 'coprolalia', the involuntary exclamation of obscenities. Such obscenities appear suddenly and explosively, seemingly untriggered by any cause. This swearing can be unusually florid and innovative, meshing curses in unusual or absurd combinations.

Now this syndrome is extremely complex and not all of these symptoms are present in all sufferers, or present to the same degree or in the same combination.

But I think I have indicated a variety of behaviours, and reported many anecdotes throughout this book (and elsewhere) which suggest that Malcolm's distinctive personality approximates to the symptomology of Tourettism very closely indeed.

You may recall his remarkable imitative facility. This was called into play on many occasions, and made famous by his mimicking the people and gestures around him, especially in the music industry, from stars to A&R men. In his protracted love affair with the idea of America Malcolm would constantly and annoyingly talk in a ridiculous imitation of an American accent. Strangers took this as a comic talent, but people close to him realized there was an underlying compulsiveness. Touretters are also reputed to excel at improvisation – and may make excellent jazz musicians. Malcolm certainly has an extraordinary talent for improvisation. Recall too, his mercurial and 'hyper' personality, his lack of motor coordination and 'wild' gestures, his compulsion to approach companions or the nearest visible object when walking, his distinctive and inventive manner of swearing – seamlessly weaving the oddest obscenities into his vocal presentation – and then his noisy nightmares, which I also experienced when staying over with him. Oliver Sacks cites a patient: 'Having Tourette's is wild, like being drunk all the while.' As a teenager Malcolm in fact had an aversion to drink. He would refuse offers with the assertion: 'I don't need it. I'm drunk all the time.' As indeed, it seemed. (When he did drink he would get grotesquely uncoordinated.)

It also seems that Tourette's is hereditary and that certain population groups are more prone to it, particularly Eastern European or Ashkenazi Jews.[12] Malcolm is descended on his mother's side from Ashkenazi Jews.

And finally, Tourette's is age-related. The usual onset is at around seven years of age and its effects may become less marked with time or the condition may disappear completely. As the years have passed, this distinctive behaviour in Malcolm has become steadily less pronounced, though I would say residues of it remain.

Now I am not in a position to medically or psychiatrically diagnose Malcolm McLaren, past or present. I cannot therefore state with authority that Malcolm McLaren suffers or has suffered from Tourette's syndrome. I am also loath to appear to pathologize traits which I otherwise have enjoyed and approved of, particularly in relation to their anarchic and disturbing effects on people and institutions which, like him, I have little respect for.

But whether Malcolm suffered from Tourette's or not, there is no doubt that he displayed all the symptomology of this syndrome. I would further suggest that both he and Vivienne Westwood have ingeniously developed and extemporized on this symptomology through their punk and other fashions, as well as through the behaviour they encouraged in the very many young people associated with them.

If we assume Tourette's, many otherwise puzzling features of Malcolm's personality and upbringing seem to make sense. For example, he must have realized from an early age that he was inhabited, as it were, by a behaviour he couldn't control. His body must therefore have been a most distressing and disorientating medium for a boy to be trapped in. Malcolm always gave me the impression of someone thus trapped – anguished and alienated from his own body and self-image, angrily detached from his gestures and emotions.

The condition must also have tried and bewildered his mother, who would have thought she had given birth to a monster, and made his relationship with her impossible. Which it duly became. She angrily refuses to this day to discuss any aspect of the disgraced and disgraceful son she last saw in 1963. (The only conversation I had with her was when in 1963 I went to pick up some of Malcolm's belongings. This plain, dumpy and rather bland woman didn't then strike me as the vindictive, sex-mad and sadistic beast he has since so often claimed, but rather the confused and outraged Jewish mother of a Godless boy unfit to be seen at *shul*.)

Tourette's has only recently become a topic for general and media discussion. Previously there was no ready diagnosis, it was hardly known by GPs and there was little research on it. In fact the idea of such a condition might have seemed a suspicious absurdity to many lay people in the fifties and sixties, especially in relation to the compulsive swearing, or 'coprolalia' – who are you trying to kid? There was no way a sufferer could account for such compulsions, or articulate them within a medical or otherwise reassuring framework.

Now consider this uneasy consciousness of being in some respects beyond volition or out of control of how you appear to others, with your body ticcing and rushing into absurd gesticulations, and your mouth uttering obscenities, and a compulsion to take on and gobble up and regurgitate the gestures and faces around you.

And yet you know you are not mad, you know you are lucid and intelligent. So you need to buttress your fragmenting and elusive self, reclaim it as your own, and assert your subjectivity. So you cast this very out-of-control quality, your abeyance of control, as an excess of control, your own special talent or quality – an aspect of yourself, and of you alone, your uniqueness.

And since everyone around you decries and defines this behaviour as wicked, even extremely wicked, possibly possessed and Satanic, who then are you, a mere child, to disagree? (The first description we have of a probable Tourette's sufferer is in the *Malleus Maleficorum* (Witch's Hammer), the classic text of the Inquisition, in a passage about a priest suspected of being possessed by the Devil. The book and film *The Exorcist* are also based on an exaggerated description of a Touretter.)

So you are labelled as wicked. And you accept the diagnosis. Yes, I am a wicked, wicked boy. But to reclaim your self-esteem you also claim this involuntary wickedness as an innate capacity fomented by you, a special brand of badness, a talent for badness which you will spread all about, seeing it returned as the reassuring sign of your power and integrity.

Badness, malice, wickedness, were preferable alibis to behavioural incontinence. A wicked person was in control. Indeed, exceptionally in control. In control of oneself and, potentially, of others.

All of which seems to fit with Malcolm's fanatically willed and manipulative personality.

Malcolm, moreover, cultivated a bravado around his peculiar mannerisms. He used them. He was unapologetic, even bold about them. He made them seem like a deliberate defiance, a willed and systematic transgression of sociability and institutional polities. That wicked, wicked boy turned into an entrepreneur who commodified wickedness – malevolence off the peg in SEX and by courtesy of the Sex Pistols.

Recall too, punk's recherché taste for extreme wickedness – *the* punk movie, the one that was *de rigueur* for young punks, was The *Texas Chainsaw Massacre*. Malcolm and Vivienne took all the Sex Pistols to see this – like a family outing to see *Bambi*. Also recall Malcolm's recurring fascination with the Fagin legend, a fantasy he has continually enacted in his dealings with young and vulnerable people.

This theme of calculated wickedness reverberates through Malcolm's career. Indeed Craig Bromberg calls his 1989 biography of Malcolm McLaren, *The Wicked Ways of Malcolm McLaren*. This book is certainly required reading for anyone contemplating doing business with its subject. Reading it cold you might recoil from an unpleasant tale of duplicity, corruptness and betrayal. Bromberg is not using the term 'wicked' as a glamorizing gloss – he really means it; he thinks Malcolm is a very bad person who has done lots of people lots of harm.

Now Bromberg's is an extensively researched and in some ways perceptive biography. It is, however, marred by the author's at times hysterical dislike for his subject. Malcolm's undeniable wickedness is therefore only catalogued in a way that eventually extends the myth, rather than explaining its sources or the dynamics involved in the, after all, not inconsiderable cultural resonance of this wickedness.

It might seem tempting at this point to reduce punk (and the work of McLaren and Westwood) to the expression of behavioural aberration. That would be an old and disreputable trick. It was done with panache by Max Nordau in his turn-of-the-century polemic *Degeneracy*, which thundered against the Symbolist and other avant-gardist poets and artists and the associated bohemian circles of the time – his equivalent to rock and roll and punk. This 'decadence' was decried by Nordau as a false artistry, a pseudo-intelligence and a perversion of genuine culture.

Nordau's book contained many gems – for example: 'Wagner is the last mushroom on the dung hill of romanticism.' But it was an embattled defence of bourgeois propriety and order. The examples and artists lauded by Nordau in contrast to the avant-garde are long-forgotten, whereas his hate figures continue to inspire a century later. Moreover, Nordau's text has connections with racist and supremacist ideology. The supposed moral degeneracy he outlined was rhetorically linked to ideas about a biological deterioration of the human species caused by the 'neurasthenia', etc. of modern city life and unhealthy appetites – especially in the sexual realm. Watch out for the master race.

Nowadays any such commentator would be more circumlocutory (Christopher Booker's *The Neophiliacs* being an example). But however tentative or subtle, such an analysis would still fail to account for the talent and pleasure which is in excess of such reductions and squeezes beyond a plodder's discourse – just one of Vivienne Westwood's collections will laugh off the sarcasms of a Nordau or his modern imitators. And only a fool would deny ever having been tempted or tickled by the adventure of the Sex Pistols.

Most of all, such reductionism would fail to account for the enormous and continuous resonance of McLaren and Westwood's joint and separated work.

Note the imitators and groupies who cluster around their enterprise, the transmission and prolongation of their work, the expanding bibliographies, proliferating controversies, attempted canonizations and retrospective shows and documentaries, the endurance of their influence in fashion, design and fine art, the impact of punk (particularly their inflection of punk) on the design of clothes, furniture and interior decoration, and their influence on films and on novelists from Kathy Acker to Brett Easton. And finally, there is the punk succession of Boy George, post-punk, neo-punk, Madonna, cyber-punk, rap, gangsta . . .

Such resonance demands a context, something to resonate against.

It has been amply documented that British art schools in the fifties and sixties especially, served as foci for bohemia, and that this was related to their central role in creating and disseminating popular culture.[13] I have already mapped out Malcolm McLaren's route through the 'art college dance' and some of its implications. It should also be apparent that Vivienne Westwood, through her equally assiduous cultivation of this arty bohemian milieu and the versions of creativity it proposed, was as much a creature of its opportunities and fantasies as her partner.

This art college education was focused through a repertoire of exemplary avant-garde figures and their acts and activities. Such figures were overtly taught and/or suggested as role models. These were often Romantically transgressive in their absorption in extremist politics, their deviant sexuality and other 'disreputable' interests, and their fraternizations with criminality and the exotic, and the cultivation of excess and revolt. They formed, in effect, a canon of deviancy.

But this essentially Romantic ideology, once absorbed, could, it turned out, be improvised for success in some of the most volatile and lucrative areas of consumerist expansion, rock music being a notable example.

Robert Pattison's book *The Triumph of Vulgarity* (1987) has extensively documented the Romantic sources of rock music. 'Rock,' he asserts, 'is not a clone, but a mutant variety of Romanticism.' Pattison points out that rock music is effectively a transliteration into vulgar idiom of Romantic themes such as the fetish of youth, hero cults, sexual outrageousness and a fascination with transgression. He also cites rock's Romantic emphasis on drugs – 'the embrace of totality', its aesthetic of the sublime shock – the shiver of dread – and its pantheistic fantasies (from Mother Africa to Live Aid). Then there is the brooding solipsism of rock figures – 'the Romantic self bound on an expedition to infinity', and their anti-intellectualism – 'we don't need no education' – resulting in that characteristic appeal to mysticism, liminal states and madness. Even the reputed roots of rock in black music is, Pattison suggests, a Romantic appeal to primitivism.

Such Romanticism is strikingly illustrated by Greil Marcus's magisterial account of situationism and the Sex Pistols, *Lipstick Traces: a secret history of the twentieth century*, an attempt to reveal visions of an alternative and subterranean – or 'secret', scheme of history.

As a connoisseur and interpreter of popular music and punk – and there are few more persuasive and occasionally moving – Marcus is fundamentally a professionalized consumer. His book is an attempted grand narrative which also propagandizes his consumerist tastes in music and anti-heroes. What Marcus celebrates in punk is its technique of the transcendental sublime – the opening of the 'horizon' through an aspect of shock, the shiver of illuminating terror, projection towards a 'limit' beyond the edge of the frame of the work itself, a technique which punk qua rock music appropriated from the Romantic aesthetic. But *Lipstick Traces* simultaneously reveals the romantic sublime coded into Marcus's acts of consumption – the Romantic roots of modern consumption, which he continuously rediscovers and reaffirms through his enthusiasm for punk and situationism.

Marcus's method of discovery and expression – a method which is built into his writing as a stylistic appeal as much as a descriptive texture, is that same Romantic technique of the sublime which he finds at the 'core' or the 'beginning' of this or that punk or situationist artefact, an artefact which is then supposed to emerge from its disclosure in the text as that very fact of transcendence, rapture and dissonance, through the dizzying phrase anticipating the vertiginous 'moment'.

Hence the pantheistic romance of situationist (or Hegelian) 'totalization', in which anything can be read as everything, and everything in anything – a whole world, an entire future in the black hole of the opening bars – the sublime vertigo, of a Sex Pistols hit – read as the masquerade of Marcus's outed pleasures – his intellectual and political itinerary – all of Greil Marcus present within – but at the same time exploding out! of his gratitude at consuming these commodities. This is Marcus-as-commodity-Being, unfolding and simultaneously contained by a miraculous expressivity; the moment of genius, witnessed and metonymically enacted – or consumed: 'God Save the Queen!'

In these pleasures Marcus is hardly tapping into a millenarian undercurrent in Western culture – any more than did situationism itself. For both *Lipstick Traces* and the situationist project – not to mention punk – were essentially anguished redeployments of the romantic ethos at the heart of consumer culture.

Also underlying Marcus's argument is a transposition of the Romantic notion of the unconscious to history – its dark depths and dangerous desires, the Id of millenarian revolt or punk rock, threatening to well up into consciousness or reality.

As in the unconscious itself, the desires supposedly encoded in punk haunt normality – they are 'underneath' or 'inside' its official or Spectacular version. It is only through the cultural dreams and the visions of seers and the temporarily (historically) 'mad' in contact with these depths – 'moments' which fracture official discourses – that we catch glimpses of this unknown selfhood of history – antisocial cravings and insatiable potentiality.

Jon Savage's equally monumental account of the Sex Pistols in *England's Dreaming* escapes these consumerist excesses, but it is also the work of a Romantic fan/consumer. In a gleefully complicitous compilation for the instruction of forthcoming generations, Savage affects a benign back seat, overseeing the mayhem he is advertising with an innocent twinkle of expertise. His book is concise and exact; description is Savage's strength. But there is little analysis, only analytic asides which suggest there is a war afoot – squares against spiky heads, us against them, punks against the fuzz, queers against straights – and Jon Savage against anything to do with Margaret Thatcher. This war has little sociological grounding and really seems like a naturalistic projection of Savage's consumerist choices into politics and culture at large. In any case, we never learn what the mechanisms and structures involved in this conflict might be: how it works.

Both Marcus and Savage seem to offer massive wish-fulfilment exercises, to transport themselves into surrogate participants of the history they relate. Both *Lipstick Traces* and *England's Dreaming* read like incantatory, magical substitutes for not having been there at the time, events so longingly drawn out in the description that writer and reader might vicariously step into the shoes of a ghostly witness. This has its advantages, since nothing is taken for granted, and they both have acute eyes and a talent for salient detail. As records, their accounts are invaluable.

But the breadth and scope of their work fails to penetrate through their own motives and modus operandi, or to recognize the common provenance which fuses their Romantic fascination as consumerist commentators to the consumerist logic, and the play of psychosocial trajectories animating these events.[14]

Historically, Romanticism was crucially predicated on its seeking out, and public predilection for, monstrosity, insanity, and the perverse.

The historian Tobin Siebers has put this very well: 'The equation between madness and genius encouraged many [Romantic] writers to study psychopathology, and the result was a profound change in literary form, style, content, and especially in the artist's conduct. The Romantic artist portrayed himself as the carrier of madness and uncanny inspiration, deliberately placing himself in the margins of society and moving frenetically between the crowd and solitude . . . [his] unique talent was in transforming idiosyncrasy into poetry and the reproofs of others into the proofs of genius . . . As the behaviour of aspiring geniuses grew increasingly eccentric, the myth of the mad artist evolved and thrived . . . and by the early twentieth century the belief in the creativity of madness reached new heights of delirium, when Freud's concept of the unconscious made legitimate the Surrealists' desire to immerse themselves in folly.'[15]

In the context of this tradition, McLaren's Tourettism was able to survive and flourish, and eventually be accorded, a shamanic status as the manifestation of dark genius. He was then able to make his considerable mark on fashion and rock – precisely those creative areas within consumerism most susceptible to such Romantic exploitation.

At the same time he revelled in expressing a Romantic demonology, as the deviant explorer and revolutionary, a living proof of the frisson of the obscene and dangerous, the freak and the Other, the taboo and the primitive – the wild child and untrammelled 'mad genius' . . . the reckless Romantic daring to submerge himself through heroic descents into nothing less than the polymorphic slime of the unconscious . . .

The elaboration of this unconscious as a site for perverse expressivity was explored by Romantic writers and artists as well as by psychoanalysts. The definition of certain behaviours as pathological in the first place – the narration, hence the creation, of a taxonomy of available perversions – was bound up with the process of rediscovering, redefining and liberating these perversions through Romantic self-expressivity.

The reigning imagination of our time, that conflation of psychoanalysis, consumerism and Romanticism, typically represents itself as a process of exploring limits, breaking down barriers, laying bare concealed desires and stripping away 'repression' or inhibition. This rhetoric enables such desires to function as a schedule for the emergence of Romantic subjectivity coded through the unconscious as an expanding portfolio of perversity. In this sense the unconscious operates as a conspectus of possible experiences and putative pleasures, as a menu of aberrations.

This popular Romantic unconscious has always represented dark powers and dangers. Horrors lurk within – watch out!. Even the initiated are not safe. Freud referred to the unconscious as a 'seething cauldron' which 'proliferates in the dark [like rats?] . . . and takes on extreme forms'. He warned that 'any amateur attempt' to penetrate it 'may have the most evil consequence'. We read that the early psychoanalyst Otto Weininger did a fragmentary self-analysis and 'the glimpse into his unconscious drove him to suicide'. The psychoanalyst Abraham Maslow described the unconscious as 'bad, evil, crazy, dirty or dangerous'. In a popular 1950 textbook, *Doctors of the Mind*, the unconscious is 'an arch criminal guilty of most of the worst sins of humanity, which Freud spent a lifetime tracking down'.

More alarming still, the 'Id' – popularly represented as the core or centre of a concentrically structured unconscious – is an amplification of all that is most alterior, driven, feckless, sinister, transgressive and deviant about the unconscious. A sort of punk rock of the psyche.

Hence too the notion of the 'psychopath' (a dubious psychiatric classification) in the Freudian sense of someone lacking a superego, an out-of-control enacter of 'sick' dreams and fantasies, a person who is 'all id' – a 'monster of desire'. Such malevolent creatures are the carriers of homicidal or parricidal or incestuous or other unspeakable desires, beyond recall and beyond reason, outside of humanity – and yet curiously human, by implication, all too human.

These ideas have been visualized in a variety of ways. Principally through a Romantic iconography of interior demons as serpents with slime-coated tendrils (from Turner to the Id rampaging across *Forbidden Planet* and the mutating Id-like creature which erupts from the belly of one of the spacemen in *Alien*), monsters which feed inside us and then burst from within to create spectacular wickedness and havoc.

There is also a specifically Romantic 'design' of the unconscious as the décor of aberration, a tradition which culminates in the late-twentieth-century 'design' for sexual deviancy – the look of suburban 'torture chambers', sexual fetish interiors and décor, the objects and appliances of commodified sexuality. Not to mention, of course, the look of SEX and Seditionaries (the interiors as much as the garments and accessories), punks in general, and all the subsequent punk mutations, equally tendril-dripping with chains and bonds and mysteriously sagging or clotted or deviant fabrics, arbitrary complications and dream-like overlays, from bands like Motley Cru to Pinhead in the Hellraiser movies.

It is noticeable today how consumer capitalism is constantly pushing the boundaries of acceptable desire, commodifying former 'perversions' and traumas and exotic behaviours, colonizing and redefining in a positive light the outlands and margins of 'pathological' expressivity and identity.

Increasingly, marginal or deviant attitudes and activities are harnessed to expand a potential consumerist selfhood by extending permissible ranges of passions and obsessions. This process underlies many contemporary moral and ethical debates about control and censorship and the influence of the media.

A striking case of this phenomenon is seen in the popular music industry. Here a variety of sexual and behavioural 'pathologies' have been progressively and systematically translated into ciphers for mass expressivity and mass consumption.

The point here is not the status of these behaviours by any supposedly objective, psychiatric, medical or legal criteria, but their popular representation as deviant and pathological, and their subsequent definition as subjects for Romantic exploitation.

During the 1970s and 80s the process seemed to work as follows. Fine art, avant-garde and art college circles researched particular behaviours through, say, performance art. Such explorations aestheticized a behaviour previously defined as 'pathological'. The artistic exploration of this behaviour gave it a new emphasis as a courageous exposure of self-expressive potentialities and artistic meanings. Hence, 'homosexuality', 'exhibitionism', 'fetishism', 'narcissism', 'nymphomania' – all previously and Romantically isolated as 'pathological' expressivities.

The selected 'pathology' was then translated and developed in a variety of popular expressions by magazines like *The Face* or *i-D*. These

205

behaviours were subsequently styled and commodified by managers, A&R people, rock journalists, designers, photographers and so on – and by the stars themselves, who were sometimes wont to take their performances 'seriously', without irony, in an display of self-righteous self-expression – 'this is the real me coming out' (Sid Vicious, Tom Robinson, Madonna). Hence the commodification of transvestism by Boy George et al, or of sadomasochism – from punk to Madonna, to name but two of these paraphilias and their star turns.

In the same way non-sexual pathologies were translated into culture and effectively marketed as legitimate areas of self-expression, expanding the permissible margins of consumerist subjectivity. Hence 'schizophrenia' (David Bowie) or 'the psychotic' (punk and skinhead bands, etc.).

The music industry in this sense resembled a laboratory for commodifying perversities – a continuous recycling and packaging of behavioural aberrations and quirks – out of the pages of psychiatric monographs and journals into fine art, then music, then mainstream TV, and then the high street.[16]

A key player in all this was the series of boutiques at 430 King's Road, and the associated activities of Malcolm McLaren and Vivienne Westwood.

What gave this enterprise its centrality and edge was its ability to express and commercialize a 'brand-new' aberration, Tourettism, the symptomology of which gave especial zest and mystique to its productions. The creation and dissemination of punk in particular, was, in part, a function of the symptomology of McLaren's suggested Tourette's syndrome being translated into culture. This was not a simple transcription of Tourette's, but a Tourettish emphasis inflected through the personality of McLaren and the cultural uses he and Vivienne Westwood chose to make of this symptomology.

This process is still central to the dynamic of Vivienne Westwood's imagination. It has always underlain her particular type of design intelligence, be it the invention of sleeveless T-shirts, the application of 'deconstruction' to design, or the deviant tailoring and impishly erotic couture she has made her trademark. Her long association with McLaren enabled her to internalize the principle underlying the Romantic dissemination of pathology through a Tourettish expressivity and emphasis, and to develop it for her own work.

Vivienne was always more intellectually curious and adventurous than Malcolm. While he grasps at ideas for what they can give him, she is interested in them for their own sake and will take his wildly improvised insights much further than he can himself. It is notable that Malcolm's post-Westwood work has been shallow, mired in a reputation which coasts on the music industry's celebration of a by now rather clichéd eccentricity.

Vivienne Westwood's work is still electric with the Romantic genius of Tourettism – its diabolical transvaluations, its manic attention to detail which it then subverts, its imitative cacophony, its compulsive disrespect, its perverse mutations and improvisations, its mischievous humour, its ticcy details and its sartorial coprolalia (as an erotic effrontery).

She has also exploited and rationalized her ex-partner's fanaticism to be centre stage and to foist his presence on his surroundings, the relentless requirement to 'make a mark'. Thus she stamps her style and her name and even her face (on labels, for instance), imprinting 'her' style through every detail of every garment, every aspect of production and promotion.

While the input of other designers working for Vivienne Westwood Ltd (for example, her current husband Andreas Kronthaler) is crucial to the technical and expressive facility of her ideas – to how they unfold on the catwalk and get made in factories – the ideas are 'hers' – implacably! – but only in the sense that she still follows this Romantic dynamic of an ever-unfolding and manifold perversity.

Vivienne Westwood has popularized through fashion a version of imagination as perversity – perversity as the sign and the site of imagination.

'The dress was not at all bashful. Like so many of her sort she had allowed herself to be followed by the man, even dawdling provocatively as she passed by shop windows.

Then she suddenly turned into a deserted street and disappeared through a door.

Inside, he found an ordinary room, rather heavily scented, with a large, vulgarly inviting divan.

But he saw that the dress was here! at last in his gaze and within his grasp.

As he contemplated her, desire impelled him to kiss and then inhale her . . . and then he became drunk.

On his knees before his darling dress, which stood up stiffly and disquietingly, he uttered crazed yet gentle words, all manner of absurdities, as if incanting a prayer.

"As soon as I saw you, I adored you . . . Oh, this mad desire! . . . I would give I know not what . . . You are so beautiful!"

After a while she became a little impatient, finding such preliminaries somewhat protracted and ridiculous. Usually, she was direct with her clients, and once she had worked out their predilections satisfied them with precision and skill. But this one was strange.

She demanded with a smile whether he would at least allow her to take off her mantle.

"No, no! The dress in its entirety, that's what I want, the dress!"

And he dragged her towards the divan, embracing her furiously. Then she understood. She cried: "With my dress? Never!"

She tried to stand up, to unhook her collar, but then she felt his hands squeeze it tight. With her head bent backwards she fell inert upon the divan. But he, perfectly unconscious of his crime, ignoring the death of her flesh inside his desire, this lover of dresses consummated his lust."

(Adapted from 'The Dress', in Rémy de Gourmont, *Angels of Perversity*, c. 1890)

NOTES

1. Theo also advised us to see bad films regularly. According to him, you could get a surfeit of good art and thus lose your perspective. He lamented that the National Gallery had too many masterpieces cluttering its walls, suggesting that a few very bad pictures should be displayed to keep a sense of proportion.

2. If you worked indoors, especially in an office, you therefore had to cultivate 'the corridor shuffle'. This enabled you to move at a rate nicely adjusted to an impression of reasonable motility while actually traversing from points A to B at the slowest permissible pace. People doing this would trot with their feet splayed outwards, making little 'kicking' motions towards either side of the wall, as if metaphorically kicking the walls which imprisoned them. Each step they took began with an explosive spurt immediately succeeded by a sharp brake as their foot hit an invisible barrier. In this way their gait gave the contradictory impression of being simultaneously energetic and impotent. They were in fact locomotively killing time. (I have since noticed this peculiar duck-like mincing gait in academics who have been in one institution for too long.) Such workers also seemed to continually and restlessly expand within their places of work as if their bodies were langorously and compulsively yawning. All such gestures were tools of the trade of 'work'.

3. I did have my limits, however. When Helen Mininberg stole a copy of Robert Motherwell's book on Dada from Westminster Reference Library to prove her love for me, and presented it wrapped up for my twenty-second birthday, I took it back and slipped it on to the librarian's desk.

4. In London at the end of the sixties, I had participated in a 'march against work'. We began in the City and ended in an East End park with an audience of several hundred yobs and skinheads who turned up anticipating the promised 'rock show'. When I suggested from the stage that we might now march on the local town hall and burn it to the ground, I was met with derisive incomprehension. They had never heard anything like it. Five years after punk, cities were aflame from London to Liverpool in the worst British riots of the twentieth century.

5. An interesting example of the culture clash inherent in this is Jeremy Paxman's separate TV encounters with Vivienne and Malcolm. Paxman is quintessentially public school, a drawling know-all with an impatient and disdainful approach to interviewing. When asked a perfectly simple question by Paxman on the late night news, Vivienne froze, clutched her temples and was agonizingly struck dumb. Many people have commented to me how embarrassed they felt on her behalf. When Malcolm and Paxman met on a arts review show Paxman was hosting, the mutual dislike was evident. Paxman obviously thought Malcolm a pretentious prat, while Malcolm was almost choking with hatred over Paxman's superior attitude and made a snide comment about Oxbridge people. Neither Vivienne or Malcolm can fend for themselves in the cultural terrain of educated debate and tend to take defiant refuge in their eccentricity.

6. This take on the Romantic roots of consumption is particularly from Colin Campbell's remarkable book *The Romantic Ethic and the Spirit of Modern Consumerism* (1987). This is one of the most important of the recent upsurge

of works which have densened and complicated our idea of what 'consumption' is and what it entails, and where historically it has come from. Jean Christophe Agnew has made a neat summary of this work: 'First, historians have shifted the birth of western consumer culture to the early modern period and deferred the arrival of mass consumer culture to the mid-twentieth century. Second, they have rejected the Weberian dichotomies between Puritanism and romanticism and, correspondingly, between saving and spending and in some instances, they have also abandoned the classic Marxist distinction between use-value and symbolic value. Finally, they have revalued the political and moral dimensions of fantasy, fetishism, dream and wish – the keywords of consumer mystification as it has heretofore been understood. As a result, the productionist, supply-side and hegemonic interpretation of consumer culture has been shaken, if not overthrown, leaving one-dimensional man marooned on a small and ever shrinking island of history.' (JC Agnew, in John Brewer & Roy Porter, *Consumption and the World of Goods*, 1992)

7. Malcolm's seven-year studentship failed to save him from an equally autodidactic take on things. Autodidactic habits are central to the vague and free-floating pedagogy of British art colleges.

8. Once, at Harrow, a tutor snapped at Malcolm: 'You think you know everything!' He brayed back: 'There's nothing to know!' The accent was on the word 'nothing', which was dragged out from the grimace of the 'nu' to the slap of the 'thing' – 'Nuuuuuu – thing!' The tutor was quite upset by this, but he had in fact been hoisted by his own Dadaist petard.

As every art student in the sixties knew, there was indeed 'nothing to know'.

9. I should point out that these mannerisms became gradually toned down from his mid-twenties – and today, in his fifties, they are only infrequently apparent; a sort of doddery archness seems to have taken over.

10. We must have looked even more peculiar when accompanied by Vivienne, who, being a country girl, tripped along at a rare pace, often with her hands behind her back, and was also prone to skipping and turning occasional cartwheels.

11. Oliver Sacks, *The Man Who Mistook His Wife for a Hat*, 1985.

12. Arthur Shapiro, Elaine Shapiro, Ruth Bruun and Richard Sweet, *Gilles de la Tourette Syndrome*, 1978.

13. For example, Simon Frith and Stuart Horne's *Art into Pop*, 1987.

14. Rather different is Bernice Martin's adaptation of Victor Turner's anthropological work in *A Sociology of Contemporary Cultural Change* (1981). Extending Turner's thesis about the socially stabilizing function of the liminal or shamanic figure, Martin suggests that rock music and its associated culture functions partly as a liminal exercise, a way of enacting the collapse of social structure through 'inspired' or shamanic visions and behaviours. This escaping of structure works in concert with structure itself, in a symbiosis which ultimately

underpins and maintains social stability. Martin's thesis overlaps with the position taken here. But one problem with Martin's work is its limited empirical basis. Most of her information on the music scene and about hippies, for example, seems to have come from secondary literary sources, hardly a match for Turner's fieldwork. And it might have enriched her comments on punk to have interviewed a few punks rather than reading about them from the safety of the music press – in fact all of her information about punk seems to come from one *New Society* article by Simon Frith. But the meeting of Johnny and Bernice was always unlikely.

15. Tobin Siebers, *The Romantic Fantastic*, 1984

16. This process. of course, also occurs in other media, notably cinema, but less blatantly. It seems that popular music often tests the water for other media, probing for acceptable limits which are then confirmed by, say, mainstream Hollywood.

PART THREE

Pictures from the Revolution

'Nobody changes. We just go round in wider and wider circles.'

Jean-Paul Sartre

'Fashion is eventually about being naked.'

Vivienne Westwood

Dear Louisa

One Saturday I sat at the table next to you in a buffet in Liverpool Street station. You were with that young man. I would have spoken then, but I get baleful looks from interrupted boyfriends. I realized you must be a model from the way you were scheming through your diary. I've worked with models and know that pattern of times and dates, and that flustered concern you were showing – early mornings and makeup chores.

Later, we met by accident on the 6.30 to Ipswich. You told me it was your twenty-first birthday, that being a model was hard work, but what you wanted to do as long as the work lasted. When we both got off at Ipswich I would have said something more, but your boyfriend was glaring behind your warm smile.

Later I rang round the agencies with a pretext and your description until I found you at Preview. They sent me your model card: 'Louisa Moore. Height, 5.9, bust 34B, waist 23, hips 34, hair dark brown, eyes brown, shoes 7'.

Yours, Fred

1960s

Niall Martin is one of the most ferocious of the Goldsmiths crowd. A spindly youth, explosive with ribald spleen.

One day we are all walking down Piccadilly. As we pass Fortnum and Mason the usual crowd of tourists is gaping and photographing the mechanical figures which emerge on the hour from the ornamental clock.

The tourists are all delighted with this peaceable and innocuous spectacle, secure in their place in a picturesque world, visitors to Her Majesty's very own department store.

As the figures appear, in concert with the chimes of the clock, Niall becomes convulsed. 'PISS OFF!' he screams at the clock. The tourists scatter. They are alarmed, their pleasure suddenly polluted by this horrid young man.

We think Niall is brilliant and that evening we fête him with pints.

I am invited by some Goldsmiths fine art students to help them resist a 'crit'. The tutor is austere and cutting. He struts around the canvases and is especially dubious about Malcolm's effort. Malcolm has gone all Chagall, and added helpings of strawberry jam to his canvas.

'What's that about, Malcolm? Come on, laddie, explain yourself!'

Malcolm looks at me. As the hero of Paris I must intervene.

I interrupt the tutor. Who the fuck is he to tell anyone anything? What the fuck does he know? He's wasted his life, rotting away in Goldsmiths. What a cunt in his corduroy jacket with shop-worn bourgeois notions about art.

Other students join in. The tutor is alarmed. End of crit.

We all storm off to the canteen, pleased with ourselves. As we leave I notice the tutor has begun to sob on the shoulder of a strikingly attractive female student. She pats his head consolingly and glares at me.

*　　*　　*

Henry Adler introduces me to the novelist Alex Trocchi, a large, shambling man with a nose like a hatchet and eyes like a ferret.

There are piles of books and magazines, and folders of notes stacked in tall columns, all over Trocchi's flat. Trocchi is having a row with his junkie girlfriend about who should fetch their prescribed daily dose of heroin from the local chemist.

Henry volunteers and sets off.

Trocchi tells me about his latest project in a slurred Glaswegian growl. This is Sigma, an 'expanding magazine' which will mysteriously connect the underground with the overground.

Henry returns with the drugs and Trocchi disappears.

When I next see Malcolm I say: 'You have to meet this guy!'

We turn up unannounced. Trocchi welcomes us. We might be useful. He is trying to contact the young students who recently occupied the London School of Economics. They seem just the sort to help with Sigma. Do we know any of these students?

Malcolm's eyes sparkle when Trocchi starts to talk about his stint as a pornographer for Maurice Girodias's Olympia Press in fifties Paris. We ask to see some of this work, which at the time is unavailable. Trocchi seems reluctant and lies that he doesn't have any copies. But Malcolm has seen several in Trocchi's study.

Some days later Malcolm returns on his own, and while Trocchi is having a fix steals several of these books.

Extracts from the books later turn up on SEX T-shirts.

Helen Mininberg takes me and Malcolm to a posh party in a high-tech apartment. Helen is a dwarf with a baleful look about her – don't fuck with me! Malcolm is spindly in leathers suggesting reprehensible desires. I am in my powder-blue silk and mohair jacket from Gieves and Hawkes, with mirrored dark glasses.

Helen takes exception to some abstract paintings in the living room. I lend her a felt-tip to improve them. As she is so small no one sees her doing this. I then lock myself in the bathroom and redecorate it with lengthy 'crazed' messages in large and 'bizarre' handwriting. On my return I find Malcolm spraying lighter fuel over a pile of cushions.

Suddenly there is a howl of rage from a woman who has gone into the bathroom. Then the host notices Helen's graffiti scrawled over his paintings. And the settee bursts into flame.

Accusatory fingers point. The host is hysterical. We are bundled towards the front door. Helen and I tumble downstairs. Malcolm is hurled after us. I face the row of enraged party-goers looking down from the door and assure them we'll be back! 'And next time we'll burn your whole fucking place down!'

'Anyway,' screeches Helen, 'your pictures are no – fucking – good!'

I am living in New Cross with my new girlfriend. Malcolm keeps turning up. One Saturday morning I'm immersed in a book when I hear the familiar thumping at the door: 'Freddie, it's me!' I want to finish my book. He can't know I'm in, so fuck it. The hammering subsides. A note is slid under the door. I hear Malcolm depart. I pick up the note: 'I know you're in there! You cunt not letting me in! Malcolm.'

I'm in a pub with members of King Mob. We've been assisting in an occupation of the LSE. Over a lunchtime pint we are devising projects to unsettle the revolutionary consensus. Someone suggests setting fire to some rare maps in the library. Destroying culture, that should break their student hearts.

Suddenly Malcolm turns up. He is breathless, gushing. Ignoring the King Mobbers (this is the first time they meet him), he chatters at me that he's just come from the National Gallery. He went to reassess Van Gogh. It came to him last night . . . The Sunflowers! My God! The power of that picture! . . . the brushwork! . . . He'd never realized what an incredible draughtsman Van Gogh was . . . That yellow!

My revolutionary colleagues gaze at this red-haired aesthete bemusedly. There is a rather prolonged pause while Malcolm notices and takes them all in, looking them up and down. They return the inspection. Could he perhaps be a police informer?

Then someone asks: 'Fancy a pint?' Malcolm settles for an orange juice.

1970s

Vivienne and Malcolm have hired a stall at a rock and roll concert at Wembley stadium. I go along to help. Malcolm wants me to wear a T-shirt, but I decline as that's not my style.

After a while I notice there are other exits around the stadium thronged with Teds who never see our T-shirts. I take Ben and a couple of boxes of clothes and we set up another stall at the opposite end of the stadium. Ben is soon ferrying items from the main stall to this sub-stall.

After the show I point out to Vivienne and Malcolm that by simply creating another sales point I added almost a third to the day's takings. The moral I draw is that they should branch out and license other shops around London and elsewhere.

But they are resistant to the idea. I can see they essentially have a boutique mentality – one shop, one event.

I've been pondering Malcolm and Vivienne's new venture. Does being shopkeepers square with the revolution? I decide they may need advice and criticism. Stylishly presented, enigmatically delivered.

I spend an afternoon in Westminster Reference Library looking up critical definitions and quotations about 'fashion'. Over the next three days I send several postcards of London to the shop, inscribed with mottoes: 'Craft must have clothes, but truth loves to go naked', 'Must passion end in fashion?' and so on.

On the afternoon of the fourth day I visit the shop. Malcolm is inside with an assistant, putting finishing touches to three foam-filled letters covered in fluorescent pink plastic: 'S' 'E' 'X'. This is to be the new shop sign. I am press-ganged into helping erect it. We watch the astonishment of passers-by with satisfaction.

Malcolm confirms having received the postcards. But unfortunately the post office delivered them all together. He says this marred the effect.

Not long after, he spray-paints some of my messages over the shop interior. Several also turn up on SEX T-shirts.

I'm not sure if that's what I meant.

The phone rings. It's Malcolm. He's at a party above the Swanky Modes boutique in Camden Town. He says I must come.

When I arrive I notice several bored louts among the fashion-conscious guests. This is my first exposure to the Sex Pistols. Steve Jones is slumped in an armchair, his arms dangling, a beer bottle in one hand, a fag in the other. The others ostentatiously 'lurk' in corners of the flat.

Malcolm is excited. He explains these yobs are something to do with 'something' he is 'starting'. This 'something' is connected to the fact that, according to Malcolm, the lads have just stolen some jewellery from a bedroom cupboard. Malcolm seems very chuffed about this and proud of his boys, who, he explains, are regular villains. They nick stuff all the time. He boasts they recently broke into Pete Townshend's house and stole some guitars.

Malcolm has recently returned from America. He tells me about his adventures there. He was most struck by the outrageous sexual decadence in New York. 'Man, it's incredible, it's outrageous! People do it right in front of you, anywhere. I was in this café . . . these guys started . . . he was shoving it right up his arse right there in the open!' (This is the height of the sixties' 'permissiveness', a phenomenon which only really got going in the early seventies.)

Malcolm then relates to me the popularization of 'perversions' in America. In particular he keeps talking about 'S&M'. This is the first time I've heard 'sadomasochism' initialized like this. I'm puzzled until I suddenly twig. The term suggests a bizarre commodification. 'S&M' sounds like a trade tag, like 'M&S' for 'Marks & Spencer'. It's a kind of trivialization too, a cute domestication – as if people were trying to make it seem homely, normalizing a previously pathological condition as a lifestyle option.

I file that away as something to theorize about.

*   *   *

I've been out drinking with Malcolm and Vivienne, and now it's closing time. Vivienne says she knows a hotel where we can get an after-hours drink. When we get there a new barman is on the job. He is young and unhelpful. He says: 'No room key, no drink.' I'm prepared to go somewhere else. But Malcolm and Vivienne insist we should stay – it's OK, they will get us a drink.

Then they both go up to the bar and begin a curious routine. It's hard cop Vivienne and soft cop Malcolm. Vivienne expostulates and invokes common sense and fellow-feeling. Malcolm is being charming and guffawing at her occasional excesses while invoking a spirit of laissez-faire. 'What's the big deal, fuck it, man, after all?'

Both of them are trying to probe the barman's weak spots, needling their way into his discomfiture. It's so practised and seemingly rehearsed, with an automatic and silent discipline of purpose, that I wonder if they realize what they're doing, or how eerie it looks.

The barman begins to look as if he is drowning. I can sense he is near tears of frustration.

Then the manager appears. The barman clutches at him as a saviour. He appeals that we don't have keys . . . The manager's eyes narrow, he senses something weird.

Immediately, Malcolm and Vivienne let go. They realize this educated, middle-aged man is not a boy to be seduced or cajoled, but an inexorable square, a bourgeois.

Vivienne sniffs and picks up her coat. Malcolm makes an ingratiating comment to the manager.

We depart.

Finding the Sex Pistols' Glitterbest offices in Shaftesbury Avenue closed, I visit the pub nearby. As I enter I can hear Malcolm's voice, bellowing antagonistically. I stand at the bar and watch. Malcolm is laying into Julian Temple with zeal. He berates and insults Julian at the top of his voice.

'You fucking wanker, you don't know one end of a camera from the other! You're just some fucking student! You should be working in a pizza parlour!' And so on, relentlessly. The whole pub is listening in.

Julian takes all this on the chin, without protest, but with a resigned and bovine expression, his head slightly bowed.

When I finally approach them Julian looks sick. He realizes I've witnessed his humiliation. I wonder what his agenda is.

Tracy, one of Vivienne's shop assistants, has suddenly become ill. Then, in one week, she is dead from a rare disease. Everyone is shocked. Tracy's parents, a respectable couple living in a country town just outside London, claim the body.

Vivienne goes to the funeral in a black bondage suit. When she gets there she finds the family upset.

Malcolm has sent a huge wreath, supposedly from the band, emblazoned with the message: 'Never mind the bollocks, Tracy.' He has also sent a camera crew who are filming the family and relatives, and trampling over flower-beds.

This is one of the many Swindle scenes which ended on the cutting-room floor.

One day Vivienne tells me she and Malcolm have 'decided' about the disc jockey John Peel. She says this with serene finality, as if his fate is sealed, discussion at an end. They'd heard about Peel playing all this punk on his radio show. Vivienne bought a transistor radio, got into bed with Malcolm, and they listened for 'half an hour'. And after that they knew John Peel was not hip. He was, Vivienne said, 'crap'.

It was the effortless candour with which she announced this, a sublime and innocent confidence, that struck me. Two arbiters of taste had retired to bed, made their judgement, and switched off the light.

I've arranged to meet Malcolm in the Coach and Horses in Poland Street. As usual, he arrives late, beaming up with an airy apology. Behind him are three punk girls. These are the Slits.

Malcolm makes introductions. The girls seem sulky and discontented and mutter among themselves. While they are out of earshot Malcolm starts saying that he thinks I should 'do my bit'. Bernard Rhodes has done his 'bit' by managing the Clash. As usual with Malcolm, everything is elliptical.

Suddenly I get the picture. The Slits have asked him to manage them. He doesn't relish it, but was wondering whether I might care? It's the last thing on my agenda. Besides, I don't like the look of them. They seem too full of their punky selves. But I agree to 'check them over'.

We go for dinner. Malcolm will pay! A Soho restaurant – pink tablecloths, elderly couples, yawning waiters. A Slit peers through the window. 'Perfect!' she threatens. Malcolm whinnies with anticipation. Will there be a riot?

But the girls are model diners, sitting up at table, guzzling wine appreciatively, decorously breaking open bread rolls.

I start making caustic remarks about the suburbs, from where I presume they have recently arrived. I've heard there are lots of rats living out there. Also, quite a few cunts.

They look shocked. I ask what is wrong with the word 'cunt'. After all, they call themselves the 'Slits'. They don't understand. Malcolm chimes in: 'Slit – cunt – geddit?'

They don't really.

Over his third glass of wine, Malcolm's eyes cloud over and he begins a reverie about Moonies and Scientologists. If only he knew how they did it! It seems he'd like to start a similar movement.

After the meal we all go to a club where I insult a Slit, who complains to Malcolm. Malcolm explains that if she can't handle me she won't be any good at rock and roll. She leaves. 'That's her fucked,' says Malcolm. 'Portuguese bitch!'

Another Slit says she has run out of money and needs to take a cab. I proffer a fiver, which she grabs and disappears.

Malcolm is incensed by my generosity. 'YOU SHOULD NEVER GIVE THESE PEOPLE ANY MONEY!' he shouts.

1980s

It's Christmas. Malcolm has shown me his script for a film about the 'Mile High Club'. We've met in a pub near Oxford Circus to talk about it. The pub is full of office workers with bags of Christmas shopping.

223

Malcolm has bought himself a flash new overcoat with a fluffy fur collar. He remarks it's a Christmas present to himself, a reward for finishing this script, which had him holed up in the Clapham flat for months.

He comments that joining in the festive buying makes him a bit like 'all those devils' – indicating the office workers. The spiteful way he says this strikes me.

After two Bloody Marys he softens up – two is his usual cue to get tipsy. He now begins a sentimental reverie. So many people in the world are untrustworthy. All these smart-aleck arty types!

But people like that – again he indicates the office workers – they are 'the salt of the earth'. They really are OK. I ought to take his word for it!

Walking down Charing Cross Road I bump into Malcolm and Vivienne. We go to a wine bar, where I show them the book I've just bought on Nazi art.

Vivienne leaves for a musical based on the life of Edith Piaf. Malcolm and I stay. I tell him I'm researching fans, which I say are more interesting than stars. He disagrees and becomes derisive, a sure sign he is impressed.

I wonder how long before he has this idea too.

He now begins to tell me about his new band. I ask him what it's called but he's evasive.

Vivienne turns up unexpectedly, saying the musical was crap and she's going to join us. At this point Malcolm announces that the new band is to be called Bow Wow Wow! Vivienne laughs with appreciation. I wonder whether he made this up on the spot to amaze us. I concede it's a good name, really annoying!

I am directing a photo shoot with Annabella Lwin in the art dealer Robert Fraser's flat. It overlooks Piccadilly and the idea is to get Annabella looking sexy in view of the statue of Eros.

All around the room are clusters of hangers-on and the usual make-up and support people.

Halfway through the session Vivienne turns up. She begins to work her way around the room, muttering to people conspiratorially. I wonder what she's saying. When she gets to me she says, almost apologetically: 'Malcolm thinks Annabella should be in the nude for this session.'

This is the first I've heard of it. I ask Annabella if she wants to strip off. She declines, and I don't press the point. I continue directing the shoot.

All the while Vivienne continues to whisper to onlookers, as if trying to get their support for the idea.

Malcolm has left the Clapham flat to set up on his own in a service flat in Paddington. It's a very Malcolm décor – cold and anonymous. Malcolm is living here with a German girl. This girl seems oddly automotive and vacuous. So I'm not surprised to hear Malcolm telling her she must become a vacuum cleaner!

This is his new idea, for an act called Jimmy the Hoover, based on a sexual fantasy confided to him by one of the Seditionaries staff.

She declines bashfully and I point out loudly to Malcolm that she's an idiot. She goes off in a huff.

Malcolm tells me his great dilemma. Yes, this girl is an idiot but he's besotted. Only he doesn't want to leave Vivienne. And if Vivienne finds out all hell will break loose. Can I suggest something?

I come up with a ludicrously inapposite piece of advice. Vivienne, I bluster, is a woman of the world. She knows about artists. So Malcolm should explain to Vivienne that while this girl is his 'mistress', Vivienne is his 'wife'. Vivienne, I assure him 'will understand'. That kind of arrangement was all the rage in Paris of the belle époque.

Several days later Malcolm comes to me with a rueful look. 'Look here, you cunt. I did what you said. Told Vivienne this girl was just my mistress and all that. But she went fucking mad. She hit me and chased me out the flat! Now she's chucked out all my stuff and told me never to come back!'

The morning after my final row with Malcolm over Bow Wow Wow, I am running a bath when there is a knock. Vivienne and the three

Bow Wow Wow boys are at the door, all dressed in pirate regalia –
Napoleonic hats, floppy boots, etc.

Vivienne has been sent by Malcolm to coax me back into the
operation. I explain at length why I'm finished with it – and with
Malcolm too.

They all go off and when I turn round my bath has overflowed. It
takes half an hour to mop up and fill another bath.

As I lever myself in there is a hammering on the door. It's
Malcolm. He bangs and bangs, shouting: 'Freddie! Freddie! Open
up!' I open the door in the nude, dripping. Malcolm is there, with
Vivienne and the Bow Wow Wow boys looking nervously over his
shoulder. Malcolm raises his shoulders like a small boy squaring for a
fight.

Then he looks curiously at my penis. I suspect he is surprised to
discover I'm circumcised.

I shout: 'I've finished with it, Malcolm. You're just a cunt! A dirty
old man! Fuck off!' Then I slam the door.

A commotion ensues on the doorstep. One of the Bow Wow
Wows peers through the letter-box and then dangles his fingers
inside as if trying to find a key.

While I am looking for a hammer to hit his fingers with, my
neighbour opens her door. She is a doughty East Ender and sees
them off, screaming: 'You fucking punks!' I think, she's got that bit
wrong.

As they walk away Malcolm lets out a shrill, forlorn cry of
defiance: 'Whooooo!'

After my defection from the Bow Wow Wow operation Malcolm lets
it be known he puts it all down to my being 'a Catholic'. He ought to
have known. Catholics apparently plot protracted and implacable
revenges. They are 'weird' and 'frightening'. He has said all this
before when complaining about John Lydon. He too, was 'a
Catholic'.

It's as if Malcolm is saying, from now on I will only trust my own
type. At least with Jews you know where you are.

Summer 1995

I meet Vivienne to discuss this book. I've not seen her since the ruckus on my doorstep. As I arrive at her Battersea workshop she waves from an upstairs window. Andreas, her new husband, lets me in. He is affable and courteous, tall and ruggedly handsome, the antithesis of Malcolm.

Vivienne greets me with an affectionate smile, looking me up and down to see if I've aged and what I'm wearing these days. Her hair is bleached white and curled granny style, but otherwise her face is extraordinarily fresh for a fifty-year-old.

Then I notice her legs have an alarming profusion of varicose veins. I put this down to her constant smoking.

A dog like Milou from Tin-Tin is scampering around the office. Vivienne explains it belongs to Andreas. 'I don't like dogs, but Andreas kept nagging and it really is no trouble after all.'

Andreas sets off home to Clapham with the dog (one of a pair) perched in the basket on the front of his bicycle. Vivienne laughs at this eccentric spectacle and we make our way to a nearby Italian restaurant.

She enters like a grande dame and politely asks for 'that music' to be turned down. The waiters, evidently used to her, comply.

Over dinner I try to explain what I'm writing, about the sixties and so on. She looks puzzled. But she agrees to let me interview her staff and come to her next show as a backstage observer.

She is coughing constantly and almost chain-smoking Gitanes. She orders red wine 'for my throat – that's the only thing that seems to work. Though I do like drinking anyway!'

She jokes about her success. 'I only started all this to help out Malcolm.' And, with an impish grin: 'I feel they want me to climb a pedestal, very slowly.'

I tell her how I've discovered Malcolm has Tourette's syndrome and how this might have influenced his creativity. She listens carefully to my description of the symptomology and confirms my observations with several of her own.

'You're not going to mention that in the book, are you?'

I say I think it's very interesting and pertinent. She then looks pensive and says Malcolm will be hurt to think his artistic output was influenced by any outside factor. 'He likes to think it all comes from him.'

As our conversation turns to Malcolm I realize she is still fond of him, and despite everything, loyal. 'There are things I know about him that would hurt him terribly. But I'll never tell anyone!'

I probe to see if it's anything I don't know. Is it, for instance, about his childhood? She shakes her head.

'Malcolm is impossible. He's done such silly things! He's still doing them.'

I ask if she means about the business. She gives me a noncommittal look, but I suspect that's it.

I mention how jealous he is of her success, taking opportunities to run down her work: 'It's lost the edge I gave it', 'It's all from the same pattern book', etc.

But as we continue to discuss Malcolm, Vivienne, now on her third glass of wine, gets sentimental. I realize with surprise that she's still in love with him.

She makes excuses for his betrayals and chuckles affectionately over his present discomfiture. Then she says earnestly: 'A world without Malcolm would be like a world without Brazil.'

As we leave the restaurant she tells me, apropos of nothing, how important she still thinks 'genius' is. How it must be protected at all costs, and nurtured.

Then she beams at me and clasps my hand.

I first meet Tizer at a fitting of Vivienne's toiles (trial garments cut from calico) for the upcoming show. Tizer seems to have taken over from Susan Stockbridge as Vivienne's keynote model. She is a slight and blonde, in her mid-twenties. Vivienne tells me she's Jimmy Pursey's (Sham 69) girlfriend and has a child by him.

Tizer's hard features are offset by a vulnerable, almost tremulous, smile. I notice her ankles are formed as perfectly as if by a lathe. In between trying on toiles she wears a black lacy bra and skimpy knickers. She appears unabashed by onlookers who drift in and out of the studio.

Vivienne, Andreas and a gathering of pattern-cutters study Tizer for long periods.

Andreas crawls around Tizer, his muscles rippling under his sweater, his azure eyes scanning details of the toiles. Most of the assistants are German and Andreas occasionally converses with them in that language. Vivienne draws suggestions for lapel lines and pockets on to the toiles. Tizer blinks and occasionally giggles. Iris, a German assistant, wears a cushion on her left arm bristling with pins. She darts in and out between Vivienne and Andreas, pinning and adjusting. Tizer is asked to put on a pair of Westwood platform shoes and walk up and down. This she does, swinging her hips and smiling to herself.

All the while, Andreas's two dogs play in the studio, mock-fighting or scurrying under tables or between people's legs.

Vivienne and Andreas spend half an hour arranging buttons on a garment to fit with the flow of the design and accentuate Tizer's hips. Vivienne is concerned this should not look too 'commercial' or too 'sexy', but should remain 'ladylike'. Which word she articulates playfully.

Andreas seems tired and Vivienne complains to me that unusually for him he is bad-tempered. He says he's worried they are late for the October deadline. But then they are always late.

An assistant comes in wearing a Westwood masturbation skirt and comments laughingly that everyone looks glum.

At the end of the fitting Tizer changes out of her bra into a sweater and reveals long, pointed nipples. I notice Vivienne's eyes swivel to where I'm sitting – she wants to see if I have seen this and register my reaction, but she's too cool to turn round and look.

As Tizer leaves she embraces everyone fervently. She shakes my hand, looks me in the eye and gushes: 'Nice to meet you, Fred. And I hope it [the book] works out well for you!'

Vivienne laughs with pleasure at Tizer's enthusiasm. Vivienne always finds such spontaneous incongruities amusing. I can tell she likes Tizer and particularly likes to say the name 'Tizer' – it has a satisfying oddity.

My first interview with Tizer is cancelled when she explains tremulously over the phone that she is having 'trouble' with Jimmy – 'and you wouldn't want to come round and find me in floods of tears, would you, me darlin'?'

As so often with English people, their telephone voice exposes their class and I realize Tizer's background is middle-class.

When eventually I get to Tizer's home in Weybridge I notice that without make-up her skin is spotted and blotchy, the kind of complexion you expect from late nights and chemical substances. She seems sad and resigned and smokes a lot.

Tizer met Jimmy when she was fifteen in Camden Market. 'We both went there to get clothes.' She stresses that he forswore sleeping with her until she was sixteen and therefore not underage. (I think, a likely story!, especially as there is a practised ardour in how she trots this out.)

She moved in with Jimmy, who said she 'ought to be a model'. An agent he knew came round to his country house and named her Tizer Bailey after Jimmy's two cats, Tizer and Bailey.

Tizer never wanted to do this work. 'I hated going out to model, especially trips abroad. Jimmy used to kick me out of bed and make me do it. I just wanted to stay at home and be with him.'

Jimmy buys all Tizer's clothes 'I haven't bought anything in eight years or so, so I don't know anything about fashion any more'.

Tizer is aggressive, 'you have to be dead pushy', but also weepy and frail, 'I cry a hell of a lot'.

Although a tom boy as a child, she always loved to dress up. She says she 'hated how I looked and hated my face in the mirror'. She would spend hours with her thumb pressed against her nose trying to get a turned up button nose.

Tizer is still uneasy about how she looks, and detests her own portfolio 'with a passion – 'cos you've seen it so much and you have to sell those pictures of yourself and they get so old within a week it's unreal. I've never accepted my own face staring back at me all the time.'

She doesn't think she's pretty at all, but then models she suggests rarely are. 'They're more like freaks'.

Tizer learned her trade by watching videos of herself. When she goes on the catwalk she tries to 'imagine a happy walk', to 'fill myself with happiness', and then she walks briskly up and down 'like I'm in a hurry', 'otherwise I would feel completely ridiculous'.

She says being on the catwalk is very exposing, like being an actor but with no character to hide behind, 'so that if you've got a trauma in your life you feel even more bare than you normally would.'

During fittings with all those eyes on her she says she tries to 'catch everyone's eye', and 'smile at every face', ' 'cos you can't speak and I do feel quite strange about that'.

And in those long lonely hours waiting or being made up or dressed, cosseted or pushed about, she daydreams constantly about Jimmy, 'That he is going off with someone while I am at work. I'm quite obsessive about what Jimmy's up to while I'm sitting there.'

She drives me back to the station and says she enjoyed my questions. At the station she jumps out of the car and hugs and kisses me on the cheek. The train is coming in and she tells me to run.

During the journey home I reflect on how she seems trapped. Has she only ever known Jimmy Pursey? I decide she ought to leave him. Perhaps I will save her!

Vivienne Westwood Ltd is a ramshackle organization and extremely hierarchical. Only two people count – Vivienne herself and Carlo D'Amario, her ex-lover and business manager. Everyone else is made to feel like a subordinate. Wages are poor for the industry – £15,000 is average – the idea being you are lucky to work for Vivienne Westwood.

People who complain about money to Vivienne are referred to Carlo, who browbeats and haggles them down. The only way to get a rise is to threaten to leave at a crucial stage.

People tend to move on, but there will always be a fresh supply of enthusiasts – the office is flooded with CVs and enquiries.

Carlo is fat and belligerent, and regarded as macho by many of the staff. He will castigate others in the company for being unbusiness-like or 'hippies'. Carlo despises hippies. His name for Vivienne's former Camden studio was 'Bombay', as it was supposedly overrun by hippies (many of whom were also gay).

Another code for disorganized people is 'Chippenham Mews', a reference to a former habitation of Vivienne and Malcolm's son Joe, a residue of Carlo's irritation with the way the company was run by Joe. This term has caught on and a chaotic show may be referred to by employees as 'Oh, it's Chippenham Mews!'

When Vivienne talks to me about Carlo she makes an effort to say how 'very good' he is, 'and I know I'm very lucky to have him'. But there is a flatness to her tone.

Vivienne refuses to handle the money side and delegates all that to Carlo. She cocoons herself creatively and her brain is given over to the intricacies of design, with little room for business. And when not designing she'd rather read Madame Bovary in the original French (as she currently is) than a balance sheet.

For all Carlo's anti-hippie sentiments the company is hardly structured rationally. The poor wages mean that pilfering is reported to be endemic at every level of the Westwood operation. Pilfering has dogged all of Vivienne's enterprises from King's Road days, but nowadays this pilfering is in the context of multimillion-pound deals, with garments which may cost over £1000 apiece.

Professionals recently drafted in find it a bewildering and frustrating place to work. 'I've never seen anything like it!' laughs one dismissively. Victor Patino, who has come from Dior to manage the upcoming show smirks uncomfortably and raises his eyes silently to heaven when I ask him about the Westwood organization.

The company is on the verge of becoming very big indeed, with major deals, including a Vivienne Westwood perfume in the offing. But several employees suggest privately to me this may all still crash because of what they claim is an arbitrary managerial style and an alleged lack of accountability or standard auditing.

Employees put up with all this because of an intense loyalty to Vivienne, and a belief in her creative genius. However remote or dotty or maddeningly perfectionist or sometimes unreasonable, Vivienne is always described with affection and admiration.

But as I work my way around her organization with my tape recorder I frequently feel that something is being reluctantly left unsaid, hanging in the air. Eventually, as they start to trust me, people, one by one, blurt it out. Vivienne, they allege, is being 'ripped off', and she is the only one who appears not to know.

I recall how I've always found in Vivienne a curious blend of astuteness and credulity. She can cut through most façades to underlying incompetence or stupidity. She once demolished a pretentious artist we knew by calling him 'a Northern fool', as indeed he was.

And yet only Vivienne could fail to see that her friend and mentor Gary Ness is possibly only a 'genius' in the mould of Tony Hancock in *The Rebel*.

Somehow, however, this tension between wisdom and recklessness, sophistication and childishness, is the fragile equilibrium that her work is about – where she is 'coming from'.

Vivienne's PA Mark Palmen is ascetic and nervously poised. He looks like the young Bob Dylan. His work involves everything from booking models to writing up responses and 'interviews' in Vivienne's name – which he does by drawing on a file of old cuttings.

Mark suggests that the relatively small coverage Vivienne gets in fashion magazines is because she never advertises. 'If they have a certain amount of space to illustrate collections they'll choose their advertisers first and then if there's space they'll put Vivienne in.' Editors also worry because Vivienne's designs don't fit on to the usual social stereotypes they envisage as their readers.

Mark confesses that 'Vivienne is a really difficult person to work for', emphasizing this remark with 'she's not the easiest person to work for'. A wry grin follows.

'Because I'm kind of a filter between her and others I have to answer for a lot of things, from the dishes not being washed in the sink to an interview with German Vogue. And Vivienne's character is that she is such a perfectionist that she picks up on a lot of really little things. Like the other day I came home after a fourteen- hour day and I found Vivienne's voice on my answerphone complaining about the tone of my answerphone message! Something on the lines of "if you must have an answerphone then you should at least put on a message which is more appealing and friendly". That's not the kind of thing you want to hear at the end of a day. But it's the kind of perfectionist she is. It can drive you nuts.'

Mark also tells me that when he first began working for Vivienne, Carlo came into his office and menacingly placed a bust of Stalin on his desk.

Although Mark says he couldn't survive on his wages, he is able to supplement them with a private income. 'Otherwise I couldn't afford to work for her.' Nevertheless, he is at pains to stress how much he values the experience, almost making a speech to this effect.

Michaela Callaghan says: 'I'm supposed to be Andreas's assistant but really I follow him and Vivienne about and try to interpret what they want. I find agents who may have the types of fabrics they're looking for and I go with them to appointments and get a feel for what attracts them.'

Michaela wanted to be a fashion designer from the age of six. 'I was the eldest and always on my own just drawing and making clothes and entertaining myself.' She made her first dress out of her mother's quilt pillowcase 'and I got into a lot of trouble for that'.

She also got into trouble for cutting off her four-year-old sister's hair to 'give her a whole new look'.

At the moment, like everyone else in the workshop, she is working till midnight with very little sleep.

'It has an amazing effect on you working seasonally like this. It's the strangest way to work – twice a year you have this mountain.'

She recalls that Carlo has been known to appear late at night with bowls of spaghetti to feed his workers. 'That's probably just to keep you on the job!'

Vivienne also once cooked for them.

'She cooks like she designs, everything thrown into this one big pot. And there were so many herb leaves and twigs it was like someone had gone through a forest! And then we found all these little peppermint tea bags in it. We couldn't work out whether she'd put them in deliberately, or whether they'd fallen in off the shelf!'

Stuart Mackenzie has experienced the transition in the company from being a 'hippie' establishment, to the verge of a more streamlined operation. 'I even used to have long hair in those days.'

He regrets the loss of camaraderie: 'It's become more anonymous', and occasionally snaps at the German contingent: 'Look, can you speak English? This is an English company you know!'

He recalls the days of being closer to Vivienne. How one day, sewing and singing to herself, Vivienne suddenly blurted: 'Whatever happened to Debbie Harry?' Or how she would ask around the workshop if anyone had read the latest biography of Lady Di so they could tell her the juicy bits.

'She does love gossip!'

Approaching showtime, Stuart's dreams become increasingly vivid. 'Stupid dreams like turning up in Paris without any of the clothes and things going wrong and Vivienne going really mad at you. Or a dream where I cooked a load of chilli con carne in Paris and then I realized that nobody had arrived yet to eat it.

'You don't really go into a deep sleep around that time because you work so late and catch up on a couple of hours' sleep, and then it's back to work.

'And you really have to be on the ball in Paris. The fittings are really stressful. You've got one model coming in at a slow pace, then two arrive together, and all of a sudden there are six models looking at their watches and tapping their feet.

'And Vivienne is saying: "Oh, can you get Nina's first outfit, or Kate's third outfit", and you've really got to know where they are. You just have to know because if you don't know then she bites you!'

With a master's degree in tailoring, Iris Steidle is able to interpret Vivienne's ambitious couture ideas. Iris grew up in a small German village, where her parents were hairdressers. 'So perhaps that's where my creative side comes from.'

Coming to England to work for Vivienne Westwood Ltd was a culture shock. 'Especially when I had to go and work with designers of rubber and fetish wear. I had never seen such things!'

For Iris, working in fashion is 'an emotional thing'. She says she 'falls in love' with every piece she's working on. She also enjoys the mania of deadlines as the show approaches – and the climactic last night before departing for Paris.

'The first time was unforgettable. I was nineteen and we had been working through the night and it was the first time I had ever stayed up the whole night. In the morning the weather was beautiful and the sky was bright red and we threw open the windows and played classical music very loud.'

Paris, October 1995

The real work of the Westwood show goes on before and after, in the showrooms at the Cercle Républicaine. This is where the orders are taken, in a sumptuous suite on the Boulevard de l'Opéra.

When I first get there it's late evening and a disco for French deb types is blasting away in the suite below Vivienne's.

Upstairs, the Westwood suite is empty, as if hurriedly abandoned – doors open, clothes on racks, half-empty cups and dog-ends in ashtrays. Files and orders are spilled over tables in the office area.

Anyone could walk up from the party below and help themselves to armfuls of the latest Westwood finery. This is what I like about the Westwood operation, its innocence.

Next morning the suite is bustling with buyers – rich-looking Italians, canny Americans.

The Japanese have their own room and look defensive as I peer in.

It seems the whole Westwood crew is over here doing their bit, some of them looking rather overdressed, as if pleading their allegiance to the Westwood spirit.

They take garments off rails, consult fabric charts, talk sizes. They seem very British and amateurish in this context – but that's their charm.

Some buyers have brought their own models who try on garments and do turns in the crowded rooms. An American snaps about the high-heeled Westwood shoes on offer. 'Yes, but do you have anything more wearable?'

Other people seem to have got the message. The designs are now established and Vivienne's 'quirkiness' is accepted as the focus of a classic range.

The show itself (of which there are two in quick succession) takes place in the Grand Hôtel, one of the swishest in Paris.

A plump South American waddles around the foyer with a look of complacency on his pampered face. Two Sumo wrestlers are being interviewed sitting together in their robes on a long settee.

The collection is shown in a huge, circular domed chamber, encrusted with gilded 'baroque' ornamentation, and hung with an enormous chandelier.

The walls are laden with tall mirrors and statues of draped women which gaze stonily down.

Two engineers, stripped to the waist, negotiate the lighting rig high above, crawling along to adjust the spotlights.

At the end of the catwalk is a large platform for TV crews and photographers.

As the costumes arrive I notice a few students have sneaked in, hiding themselves in corners. Security men in black blazers and red ties mill about aimlessly.

Photographers arrive, hauling formidable cameras with bazooka-like lenses, and set up positions on the platform, or stake them out around the hall with aluminium stepladders. They hail one another as long-lost friends with the cynical bonhomie of all media people.

Two Westwood employees walk up and down the aisles placing tiny boxes of heart-shaped Vivienne Westwood chocolates on each empty seat. The theme for the show is love. The motto: 'Les femmes ne connaissent pas toute leur coquetterie.' (Women do not know all their coquettishness.)

Backstage, fitters are busily ironing garments. Two camp young men sit with their shaven heads together, sewing a corset. Clothes rails, each inscribed with the Christian name of a model, are being hung with garments cocooned in plastic bags.

Stuart tells me how exhausted he is, but I think he loves it.

Downstairs, the make-up room is now packed with models and make-up artists.

Tizer is being plastered with foundation and tells me she's over here for three days: 'Just for Vivienne. I've left Jack [her son] with Jimmy.'

She tells me of her regret that during our interview she didn't say all the nice things she might have about Vivienne. 'But you took me by surprise, asking me about me!'

Here, as everywhere throughout the show, are cameras. Assistants and dressers continually snap away with small tourist flash cameras and video cameras while TV crews pan around and professionals prowl in flak-jackets stuffed with rolls of transparency film.

Two grotesque-looking Japanese girls interview the American model Nina Brosch. They beam and gape as she answers their questions in a monotone under a hand-held light.

'How did you get started in modelling?'

Then, without really listening to the answer: 'What is the meaning of the tattoo on your arm?'

Nina is patient. Presumably she thinks it's good for business. I notice her skin is as bad as Tizer's. Maybe it's all the make-up they have to wear.

Two extremely tall American models are talking as they lounge by a bowl of fruit at the end of the refreshment table.

'Well, I wouldn't mind, but her being that nice – you know what I mean, to use niceness as a weapon – that's not nice is it?'

'I want to have all I can from life, even the shit parts. I mean it's not life without the shit parts. That's what they're for.'

A lanky brunette sweeps in imperiously.

Someone calls out: 'Oh Carla, you're late!' All cameras swivel. Carla pouts by the door, then stalks to her make-up chair.

Vivienne appears, flustered but also radiant with excitement. A model has disappeared! Vivienne wonders whether she might be in the toilet. She sets off to look.

Tizer is now made up. Close up, she looks spectral, with grey-painted eye-sockets intensifying her gauntness.

Upstairs, the auditorium is beginning to get overcrowded and tempers are being lost.

Alex from *Elle* arrives late, cursing.

A fat woman in black furs with Edna Everage spectacles turns up with a tall young man in tow. He fetches a chair and she places a stepladder on the seat and climbs up, swaying precariously. The young man holds her steady and looks embarrassed.

A sweet thing from *i-D* turns up with what looks like her mum's camera. Pressed against the back wall she can see nothing. I advise her to bluff her way to the catwalk. 'Say Zoe [Vivienne's PR] sent you.' She hesitates, then sets off.

When the show starts, three-quarters of an hour late, there is a nicely tuned feeling of near hysteria. Everyone is dying for something to happen, a scandal, or a catastrophe.

A photographer speculates that the camera platform, which is now extremely overcrowded, could collapse, 'and then there will be another tragedy.'

The show is a predictable triumph. No gimmicks or sex this time – just Westwood.

The music is light classical. But played on CD over these massive speakers it sounds incongruous, even pretentious. Better to have a real orchestra?

I'm more interested in the event than the clothes. But I'm taken with a series of sleek black dresses, and the subtle eroticism of diaphanous and see-through layers.

As ever, it's the calculated intricacy of the tailoring which is most remarkable. The ball gowns shown are outrageously belle époque and suit this Grand Hôtel setting.

239

At the end of the first show Vivienne makes her ritual appearance to ritually tumultuous applause. Seeing her up there I wonder, is that the woman I know? But then it's like I'm forcing myself to be surprised. The transition from Clapham to the Grand Hôtel in Paris seems inevitable.

During the interval Vivienne comes up and asks if I'm getting 'enough back stage stuff'. 'I do feel ever so guilty about you,' she confesses. I reassure her, wondering she has time to notice me.

For the second show I secrete myself backstage.

Mark Palmen has a microphone attached to his mouth, and reads the running order, ushering models on and off the catwalk.

There is posturing by models who have been swigging free champagne during the interval and are now tipsy. The champagne has run out.

The models fuss. Are we not the ones doing the work? Why has it run out? A red-faced waiter is sent to fetch more.

Standing among these models, I am struck by how tall they are. At over six feet and in platform shoes they tower like a race of giants.

As the show starts and the girls change in and out of their costumes I get my first view of naked supermodels.

I am shocked by the protruding rib-cages of some girls. It sends a visceral alarm, as if you are seeing a famine victim close up. You want to help! Yet otherwise they don't seem undernourished.

In fact, being such tall people, they also have proportionately large hips and buttocks, and several have ample breasts. Combined with their skinny torsos, this makes them look, in Tizer's term, freakish.

The models constantly preen and primp themselves in front of mirrors.

Once dressed in a costume, they practise a glaciated stare hard into the mirror, past themselves or through themselves – the stare they will have on the catwalk. Some of them seem transfixed with how they look and pull themselves away from the mirror reluctantly to climb the few steps to the outside world of the catwalk.

240

Several dressers mutter about Carla Bruni. One says: 'She's older than I am, but she's acting like a child!'

Everyone agrees that Tizer is 'the best'. She has a nervous poise and practises her 'happy walk' with aplomb. I wonder whether she's still thinking about what Jimmy is up to.

After the show I go to a party at the Hôtel Meurice. The place is awash with Japanese men in dark suits. Model types bustle around. Everyone has that 'Who are you? Who is that?' look of celebrity hunting. Three musicians in evening dress play tasteful, vaguely Schubertian muzak. Tizer greets me drunkenly, swaying on high heels. Perhaps, after all, she doesn't need saving.

Suddenly I see Malcolm. He is exuding a worldly facetiousness, surrounded by simpering girls. I'm surprised at how he's aged. There are gloomy caverns under his eyes and his face is matted with wrinkles.

I suddenly realize that now, in his fifties, Malcolm's face looks set in the mould of weeping, like a child grown used to grief.

I'm reminded of a photo of him at the age of about five in Jon Savage's book. I wonder at that, for crying is the last thing Malcolm would admit to; something he has set his life on avoiding. He was always the hard genius of recalcitrant cynicism, the brutal merchant of the sardonic mot juste.

I realize he's seen me from his sideways look of apprehension. I wonder if I ought to ignore him, but that seems the weaker option.

As I approach he turns and snaps: 'Vampire!' So all is not forgotten. The groupies are startled.

What has caused Malcolm's transformation into a ruffian?

'What's wrong with being a vampire then, Malcolm?' I quip. 'After all, you're one yourself!'

He is momentarily nonplussed. Then, with a swift look at my shaven head, he snarls: 'It's the haircut!'

I gaze at the bags under his eyes and rejoinder: 'Or the wrinkles?'

He looks stung. 'I wish I knew,' he laments. 'I wish I fucking knew.'

Time to leave. As I turn left into the Rue de Rivoli I wonder if this incident would make a suitable ending for the book.

APPENDIX

SHOPS

Let it Rock	1971
Too Fast to Live, Too Young to Die	1972
SEX	1974
Seditionaries	1976
Worlds End	1979–
Nostalgia of Mud	1982–3
Vivienne Westwood (Davies Street)	1990
Vivienne Westwood (Conduit Street)	1992

SHOWS

Pirate, Pillar Hall, Olympia, March 1981, autumn/winter 1981/2

Savage, Pillar Hall, Olympia, October 1981, spring/summer 1982

Buffalo, Pillar Hall, Olympia and Angelino, Paris, March 1982, a/w 1982/3

Punkature, Cour Carrée du Louvre, October 1982, s/s 1983

Witches, Cour Carrée du Louvre, March 1983, a/w 1983/4

Hypnos, Cour Carré du Louvre; Tokyo (Best of 5), October 1983, s/s 1984

Clint Eastwood, Cour Carré du Louvre, March 1984, a/w 1984/5

Mini Crini, Cour Carré du Louvre; Limelight, New York, October 1984, s/s 1985

Harris Tweed, Apex Room, Olympia, March 1987, s/s 1987/8

Pagan 1, BFC tent, Olympia, October 1987, a/w 1988/9

Time Machine, BFC tent, Olympia, March 1988, a/w 1988/9

Civilizade, BFC tent, Olympia, October 1989, s/s 1989

Voyage to Cytherea, Apex Room, Olympia, March 1989, a/w 1989/90

Pagan 5, BFC tent, Olympia, October 1989, s/s 1990

Portrait, Institute of Directors, Pall Mall, March 1990, a/w 1990/91

Cut and Slash (menswear), Villa de Gamberia, July 1990, s/s 1991

Cut, Slash, and Pull, Institute of Directors, October 1990, s/s 1991

Dressing Up, Showroom Azzedine Alaia, Paris, March 1991, a/w 1991/2

Salon, Showroom Azzedine Alaia, Paris,October 1991, a/w 1991/2

Always on Camera, Le Monde de l'Art, Paris, March 1992, a/w 1992/3

Grand Hôtel, Le Grand Hôtel, Paris, October 1992 s/s 1993

Anglomania, Cercle Républicain, Paris, March 1993, a/w 1993/4

Café Society, Le Grand Hôtel, Paris, October 1993, s/s 1994

On Liberty, Carrousel du Louvre, Paris, March 1994

Erotic Zones, Carrousel du Louvre, October 1994

Viva la Coquetterie, Le Grand Hôtel, Paris, March 1995

'Les femmes connaissent pas toute leur coquetterie', Le Grand Hôtel, Paris, October 1995

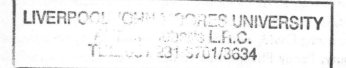

Acknowledgements

First of all thanks to Vivienne Westwood for all those conversations over thirty years and allowing me free access to her staff and present operation. Then my two fashion sleuths, Lucy Rusling and Lucy Williams, who did interviews and other research work. Anne Massey, who allowed me funds and time to do this. For interviews, etc.: Dora Swire, Gordon Swire; Joe Corré; Andreas Kronthaler; Tizer Bailey; Alan Jones; Sarah Stockbridge; Marco Pirroni; Nils Stephenson; Eileen Mellish; Ivan Bell; Marilyn Purcell; Celia Purcell; Jack Holden; Joyce Harris; Miss Leany; Lucy Philips; Spencer Burns; Mark Palmen; Michaela Callaghan; Stuart Mackenzie; Iris Steidle; Ute Emberger; Zoe Brown; Murray; Mark Spye; Victor Patino; Jon Savage; Yvonne Deacon; Catherine McDermott.

The other sources I based this book on represent too many people over too many years to mention adequately. Everyone, for example, cited in this text or in my and Judy Vermorel's *The Sex Pistols: The Inside Story*, 1976. I also especially consulted Jon Savage's *England's Dreaming*, 1991; Craig Bromberg's *The Wicked Ways of Malcolm McLaren*, 1989; and John Lydon's 1994 autobiography. Thanks also to Irving David, who did the deal for me, to my editor at Bloomsbury, Penny Phillips, text editor Richard Dawes, and Rosemary Mason, for help in editing Part One.